Library of
Davidson College

Carnegie Commission on Higher Education
Sponsored Research Studies

THE HOME OF SCIENCE:
THE ROLE OF THE UNIVERSITY
Dael Wolfle

EDUCATION AND EVANGELISM:
A PROFILE OF PROTESTANT COLLEGES
C. Robert Pace

PROFESSIONAL EDUCATION:
SOME NEW DIRECTIONS
Edgar H. Schein

THE NONPROFIT RESEARCH INSTITUTE:
ITS ORIGIN, OPERATION, PROBLEMS, AND
PROSPECTS
Harold Orlans

THE INVISIBLE COLLEGES:
A PROFILE OF SMALL, PRIVATE COLLEGES
WITH LIMITED RESOURCES
Alexander W. Astin and Calvin B. T. Lee

AMERICAN HIGHER EDUCATION:
DIRECTIONS OLD AND NEW
Joseph Ben-David

A DEGREE AND WHAT ELSE?:
CORRELATES AND CONSEQUENCES OF A
COLLEGE EDUCATION
*Stephen B. Withey, Jo Anne Coble, Gerald
Gurin, John P. Robinson, Burkhard Strumpel,
Elizabeth Keogh Taylor, and Arthur C. Wolfe*

THE MULTICAMPUS UNIVERSITY:
A STUDY OF ACADEMIC GOVERNANCE
Eugene C. Lee and Frank M. Bowen

INSTITUTIONS IN TRANSITION:
A PROFILE OF CHANGE IN HIGHER
EDUCATION
(INCORPORATING THE 1970 STATISTICAL
REPORT)
Harold L. Hodgkinson

EFFICIENCY IN LIBERAL EDUCATION:
A STUDY OF COMPARATIVE INSTRUCTIONAL
COSTS FOR DIFFERENT WAYS OF ORGANIZ-
ING ·TEACHING-LEARNING IN A LIBERAL ARTS
COLLEGE
Howard R. Bowen and Gordon K. Douglass

CREDIT FOR COLLEGE:
PUBLIC POLICY FOR STUDENT LOANS
Robert W. Hartman

MODELS AND MAVERICKS:
A PROFILE OF PRIVATE LIBERAL ARTS
COLLEGES
Morris T. Keeton

BETWEEN TWO WORLDS:
A PROFILE OF NEGRO HIGHER EDUCATION
Frank Bowles and Frank A. DeCosta

BREAKING THE ACCESS BARRIERS:
A PROFILE OF TWO-YEAR COLLEGES
Leland L. Medsker and Dale Tillery

ANY PERSON, ANY STUDY:
AN ESSAY ON HIGHER EDUCATION IN THE
UNITED STATES
Eric Ashby

THE NEW DEPRESSION IN HIGHER
EDUCATION:
A STUDY OF FINANCIAL CONDITIONS AT 41
COLLEGES AND UNIVERSITIES
Earl F. Cheit

FINANCING MEDICAL EDUCATION:
AN ANALYSIS OF ALTERNATIVE POLICIES
AND MECHANISMS
Rashi Fein and Gerald I. Weber

HIGHER EDUCATION IN NINE COUNTRIES:
A COMPARATIVE STUDY OF COLLEGES AND UNIVERSITIES ABROAD
Barbara B. Burn, Philip G. Altbach, Clark Kerr, and James A. Perkins

BRIDGES TO UNDERSTANDING:
INTERNATIONAL PROGRAMS OF AMERICAN COLLEGES AND UNIVERSITIES
Irwin T. Sanders and Jennifer C. Ward

GRADUATE AND PROFESSIONAL EDUCATION 1980:
A SURVEY OF INSTITUTIONAL PLANS
Lewis B. Mayhew

THE AMERICAN COLLEGE AND AMERICAN CULTURE:
SOCIALIZATION AS A FUNCTION OF HIGHER EDUCATION
Oscar and Mary F. Handlin

RECENT ALUMNI AND HIGHER EDUCATION:
A SURVEY OF COLLEGE GRADUATES
Joe L. Spaeth and Andrew M. Greeley

CHANGE IN EDUCATIONAL POLICY:
SELF-STUDIES IN SELECTED COLLEGES AND UNIVERSITIES
Dwight R. Ladd

STATE OFFICIALS AND HIGHER EDUCATION:
A SURVEY OF THE OPINIONS AND EXPECTATIONS OF POLICY MAKERS IN NINE STATES
Heinz Eulau and Harold Quinley

ACADEMIC DEGREE STRUCTURES:
INNOVATIVE APPROACHES
PRINCIPLES OF REFORM IN DEGREE STRUCTURES IN THE UNITED STATES
Stephen H. Spurr

COLLEGES OF THE FORGOTTEN AMERICANS:
A PROFILE OF STATE COLLEGES AND REGIONAL UNIVERSITIES
E. Alden Dunham

FROM BACKWATER TO MAINSTREAM:
A PROFILE OF CATHOLIC HIGHER EDUCATION
Andrew M. Greeley

THE ECONOMICS OF THE MAJOR PRIVATE UNIVERSITIES
William G. Bowen
(Out of print, but available from University Microfilms.)

THE FINANCE OF HIGHER EDUCATION
Howard R. Bowen
(Out of print, but available from University Microfilms.)

ALTERNATIVE METHODS OF FEDERAL FUNDING FOR HIGHER EDUCATION
Ron Wolk

INVENTORY OF CURRENT RESEARCH ON HIGHER EDUCATION 1968
Dale M. Heckman and Warren Bryan Martin

The following technical reports are available from the Carnegie Commission on Higher Education, 1947 Center Street, Berkeley, California 94704.

RESOURCE USE IN HIGHER EDUCATION:
TRENDS IN OUTPUT AND INPUTS, 1930–1967
June O'Neill

TRENDS AND PROJECTIONS OF PHYSICIANS IN THE UNITED STATES 1967–2002
Mark S. Blumberg

MENTAL ABILITY AND HIGHER EDUCATIONAL ATTAINMENT IN THE 20TH CENTURY
Paul Taubman and Terence Wales

SOURCES OF FUNDS TO COLLEGES AND UNIVERSITIES
June O'Neill

MAY 1970:
THE CAMPUS AFTERMATH OF CAMBODIA AND KENT STATE
Richard E. Peterson and John A. Bilorusky

The following reprints are available from the Carnegie Commission on Higher Education, 1947 Center Street, Berkeley, California 94704.

ACCELERATED PROGRAMS OF MEDICAL EDUCATION, *by Mark S. Blumberg, reprinted from* JOURNAL OF MEDICAL EDUCATION, *vol. 46, no. 8, August 1971.*

SCIENTIFIC MANPOWER FOR 1970–1985, *by Allan M. Cartter, reprinted from* SCIENCE, *vol. 172, no. 3979, pp. 132–140, April 9, 1971.*

A NEW METHOD OF MEASURING STATES' HIGHER EDUCATION BURDEN, *by Neil Timm, reprinted from* THE JOURNAL OF HIGHER EDUCATION, *vol. 42, no. 1, pp. 27–33, January 1971.*

REGENT WATCHING, *by Earl F. Cheit, reprinted from* AGB REPORTS, *vol. 13, no. 6, pp. 4–13, March 1971.*

COLLEGE GENERATIONS FROM THE 1930s TO THE 1960s, *by Seymour M. Lipset and Everett C. Ladd, Jr., reprinted from* THE PUBLIC INTEREST, *no. 25, Summer 1971.*

AMERICAN SOCIAL SCIENTISTS AND THE GROWTH OF CAMPUS POLITICAL ACTIVISM IN THE 1960s, *by Everett C. Ladd, Jr., and Seymour M. Lipset, reprinted from* SOCIAL SCIENCES INFORMATION, *vol. 10, no. 2, April 1971.*

THE POLITICS OF AMERICAN POLITICAL SCIENTISTS, *by Everett C. Ladd, Jr., and Seymour M. Lipset, reprinted from* PS, *vol. 4, no. 2, Spring 1971.**

THE DIVIDED PROFESSORIATE, *by Seymour M. Lipset and Everett C. Ladd, Jr., reprinted from* CHANGE, *vol. 3, no. 3, pp. 54–60, May 1971.*

JEWISH ACADEMICS IN THE UNITED STATES: THEIR ACHIEVEMENTS, CULTURE AND POLITICS, *by Seymour M. Lipset and Everett C. Ladd, Jr., reprinted from* AMERICAN JEWISH YEAR BOOK, *1971.*

THE UNHOLY ALLIANCE AGAINST THE CAMPUS, *by Kenneth Keniston and Michael Lerner, reprinted from* NEW YORK TIMES MAGAZINE, *November 8, 1970 .*

PRECARIOUS PROFESSORS: NEW PATTERNS OF REPRESENTATION, *by Joseph W. Garbarino, reprinted from* INDUSTRIAL RELATIONS, *vol. 10, no. 1, February 1971.*

. . . AND WHAT PROFESSORS THINK: ABOUT STUDENT PROTEST AND MANNERS, MORALS, POLITICS, AND CHAOS ON THE CAMPUS, *by Seymour Martin Lipset and Everett Carll Ladd, Jr., reprinted from* PSYCHOLOGY TODAY, *November 1970.**

DEMAND AND SUPPLY IN U.S. HIGHER EDUCATION: A PROGRESS REPORT, *by Roy Radner and Leonard S. Miller, reprinted from* AMERICAN ECONOMIC REVIEW, *May 1970.**

RESOURCES FOR HIGHER EDUCATION: AN ECONOMIST'S VIEW, *by Theodore W. Schultz, reprinted from* JOURNAL OF POLITICAL ECONOMY, *vol. 76, no. 3, University of Chicago, May/June 1968.**

INDUSTRIAL RELATIONS AND UNIVERSITY RELATIONS, *by Clark Kerr, reprinted from* PROCEEDINGS OF THE 21ST ANNUAL WINTER MEETING OF THE INDUSTRIAL RELATIONS RESEARCH ASSOCIATION, *pp. 15–25.**

NEW CHALLENGES TO THE COLLEGE AND UNIVERSITY, *by Clark Kerr, reprinted from Kermit Gordon (ed.),* AGENDA FOR THE NATION, *The Brookings Institution, Washington, D.C., 1968.* *

PRESIDENTIAL DISCONTENT, *by Clark Kerr, reprinted from David C. Nichols (ed.),* PERSPECTIVES ON CAMPUS TENSIONS: PAPERS PREPARED FOR THE SPECIAL COMMITTEE ON CAMPUS TENSIONS, *American Council on Education, Washington, D.C., September 1970.**

STUDENT PROTEST—AN INSTITUTIONAL AND NATIONAL PROFILE, *by Harold Hodgkinson, reprinted from* THE RECORD, *vol. 71, no. 4, May 1970.**

WHAT'S BUGGING THE STUDENTS?, *by Kenneth Keniston, reprinted from* EDUCATIONAL RECORD, *American Council on Education, Washington, D.C., Spring 1970.**

THE POLITICS OF ACADEMIA, *by Seymour Martin Lipset, reprinted from David C. Nichols (ed.),* PERSPECTIVES ON CAMPUS TENSIONS: PAPERS PREPARED FOR THE SPECIAL COMMITTEE ON CAMPUS TENSIONS, *American Council on Education, Washington, D.C., September 1970.**

INTERNATIONAL PROGRAMS OF U.S. COLLEGES AND UNIVERSITIES: PRIORITIES FOR THE SEVENTIES, *by James A. Perkins, reprinted by permission of the International Council for Educational Development, Occasional Paper no. 1, July 1971.*

FACULTY UNIONISM: FROM THEORY TO PRACTICE, *by Joseph W. Garbarino, reprinted from* INDUSTRIAL RELATIONS, *vol. 11, no. 1, pp. 1–17, February 1972.*

*The Commission's stock of this reprint has been exhausted.

The Home of Science

The Home of Science
THE ROLE OF THE UNIVERSITY

by *Dael Wolfle*
Professor of Public Affairs,
University of Washington

Twelfth of a Series of Profiles Sponsored by
The Carnegie Commission on Higher Education

MCGRAW-HILL BOOK COMPANY
New York St. Louis San Francisco Düsseldorf
London Sydney Toronto Mexico Panama
Johannesburg Kuala Lumpur Montreal
New Delhi Rio de Janeiro Singapore

The Carnegie Commission on Higher Education,
1947 Center Street, Berkeley, California 94704,
has sponsored preparation of this profile as a
part of a continuing effort to obtain and present
significant information for public discussion.
The views expressed are those of the author.

THE HOME OF SCIENCE
The Role of the University

Copyright © 1972 by The Carnegie Foundation for
the Advancement of Teaching. All rights reserved.
Printed in the United States of America.

Library of Congress Cataloging in Publication Data

Wolfle, Dael Lee, date
    The home of science.

    "Twelfth of a series of profiles sponsored by the
Carnegie Commission on Higher Education."
    Bibliography: p.
    1. Research—U. S. 2. Universities and colleges
—U. S. I. Carnegie Commission on Higher Education.
II. Title.
Q180.U5W6   378.73   78-39642
ISBN 0-07-010044-6

123456789MAMM798765432

Contents

Foreword, xi

1 *Introduction*, 1

2 *The Professionalization of Science*, 5
From amateurs to professionals ▪ What kind of science?

3 *The Search for Sponsors*, 15
Unlikely alternatives ▪ The federal government ▪ From Williams College to Williams Bay

4 *Choosing the University*, 33
First attempts at graduate work ▪ Pioneer graduate universities ▪ Practical education ▪ Planners and schemers ▪ Confirmation

5 *Effects on Science*, 65
Pure science or applied? ▪ A view from abroad

6 *Influences on Higher Education*, 85
Breakup of the college tradition and rationale ▪ Paving the way for other fields ▪ Fragmentation and the dispersal of power ▪ Competition and the multiversity ▪ The prestige hierarchy

7 *1945 and On*, 107
Reconfirmation of the university ▪ Growth of research funds ▪ Geographic distribution ▪ Current scientific capacity ▪ Changing priorities ▪ Military support of university research ▪ Government organization for science ▪ Search for purity

8 *A University's Research Rationale*, 131
University options ▪ Multidisciplinary research

9 *Future Policy,* 149
Constraints and trends ▪ The government-university relationship ▪ Projections of scientific needs and resources ▪ Stable funding ▪ Institutional support ▪ Autonomy and control ▪ Responsibility and accountability

References, 183

Index, 195

Foreword

One of the distinctive features of American higher education is the extent to which national scientific endeavor is regarded as the province of universities. Even in Germany, where research is the characterizing activity of universities, and where the model for modern American research universities was found, scientific enterprise is less concentrated in educational institutions than it is in the United States.

One inevitable consequence of the American dependence on universities for scientific endeavor has been that universities have become central to the nation's technological progress.

Related to this research function are an impressive range of other activities normally considered exclusively those of a university—the granting of Ph.D.'s (as a research degree), the research training of graduate students, operation of organized research units, and the development of university presses for publication and dissemination of research findings.

In this profile, Dael Wolfle traces the introduction of science and research into American higher education and outlines their subsequent development. With great insight, he also indicates where the points of friction are between the idea of a modern university and the traditional college, and how external financing of research divides the loyalties of professors among their disciplines, their sponsors, and their institutions. His analysis of the rationale for continued federal financing of university research and the current policy questions involved in its continuance is particularly welcome.

We concur in his conclusion that universities need to know in advance the levels of support for research that the federal government will provide in years immediately ahead. The Carnegie Commission on Higher Education has consistently recommended that federal support for research not only continue, but that it also increase at a rate equal to the rate of increase in the gross national product averaged over a five-year period.

In his concluding chapter, Professor Wolfle points out the need for universities to clarify their own goals to avoid manipulation by sponsors of research, to become more accountable than they are now for the quality and effectiveness of their research programs, and to consider more interinstitutional coordination and cooperation in large-scale research endeavor as a means of sharing the risk for research that may have only short-term support. Consideration of these needs and other questions presented in this book will be greatly facilitated by his own exposition.

Few men of science have had the experience and involvement in national science policy making that Dael Wolfle brings to this work. Still fewer could write about this important and complex subject with his skill and lucidity.

Clark Kerr
Chairman
The Carnegie Commission
on Higher Education

April 1972

The Home of Science

1. Introduction

Toward the end of the nineteenth century the university became the principal home of science in the United States. It was not chosen for this role by any policy-making body that considered all the alternatives and judged the university best qualified. The second half of the century was a period of great and rapid change in higher education, and there was much discussion about the needs of science. But the discussions about science were often independent of the discussions about higher education. Only rarely were both discussed in the kind of organized, policy-oriented debate that in the middle of the twentieth century preceded the establishment of the National Science Foundation (NSF) and the definition of its responsibilities for supporting scientific research and education. Nevertheless, a binding choice was made — it was made gradually, by a variety of people, at a variety of times and places. Cumulatively, their actions and decisions established a firm national policy that has been of lasting importance for the progress of science in the United States and for the whole character of the American university.

Scientists took the lead in choosing the university, and the story of that choice is the history of their probing and testing of a variety of possible sponsors for the work they wanted to do, and of their tactics, allies, and opponents. They wanted to do research, and to support their ambitions they had a few strong allies: George Washington, Thomas Jefferson, John Adams, John Quincy Adams, and other men in high places. Later, they also had support from agricultural and industrial spokesmen and from other members of the public who wanted help with their own practical affairs, or who were motivated by the spectacular and imagination-stirring discoveries of strange phenomena and ancient animals. The scientists' cause was supported by some staunch friends of science who were presidents of major universities, such as Daniel Coit Gilman of Johns Hopkins, Charles W. Eliot of Harvard, and William Rainey Harper of Chicago. Wealthy men and women also came to the scientists' aid: Elizabeth Thomson, Abbott Lawrence, Joseph Sheffield, Johns Hopkins, Ezra Cornell, and, later, Andrew Carnegie and John D. Rockefeller. And if it was not always evident that God was on their side, the scientists were buoyed up by pious confidence that they were on God's side.

The scientists also had opponents. The faith of early United States presidents in the importance of science was often thwarted by strict constructionists who served in Congress. Public support enjoyed by science was frequently overbalanced by apathy, and even hostility, among other members of the public. Many college presidents and faculty members acknowledged that science was all right in its place but made it abundantly clear that they preferred that place be somewhere else. And the wealth devoted to science was only a small fraction of the wealth being accumulated in America. Despite opposition, in the century between 1802, when the first professor of chemistry was appointed at Yale, and 1902, when the tenth anniversary of the University of Chicago was celebrated, science became firmly established, and research came to be respected and even sometimes endowed.

Throughout that century, four intertwined themes played dominant roles. The first was the professionalization of science. Mostly during the first half of the century, but continuing beyond that period, science was transformed from the entertainment and avocation of a small group of gentlemen amateurs into the vocation of an organized group of professional scientists.

Second was a long, and presently continuing, debate on the nature of science and the kind of scientific work to be pursued. How much of the effort should be devoted to solving practical problems and how much to developing scientific knowledge for its own sake? How much progress could be made by observation and empirical collection and how much required planned experimental work and the development of integrative theories? Debate on these issues was crucial to the nature of the work scientists wanted to do. In fact, the question of where the home of science should be was usually secondary to the question of the kind of work to be done.

The third theme was the search for patrons. Scientists wanted to get on with their work and tried every means of support that would provide that opportunity: scientific societies, wealthy benefactors, popular subscriptions, federal and state governments, independent research institutes, colleges, and the universities. The search for patrons continues today, but recognition that scientific progress is essential to national welfare now means that the scientists' search for patrons is accompanied by a national search for scientific agents to carry forward national interests.

The fourth theme was the development of the university itself. Until fairly late in the nineteenth century, uncertainties over the proper home of science were accompanied by doubts as to whether or not the university idea could be transplanted to American soil. Research was only a minor interest of the British universities, and most of the research being done was conducted in other kinds of institutions. German universities were more hospitable to science, but much of the hospitality was passive tolerance rather than active support; some German professors held concurrent appointments as directors of independently financed research institutes.

The English and German universities were the best known in the United States, and the German universities were the envy of a number of American scientists. The United States had no comparable institutions, and the small denominational colleges that did exist in substantial numbers seemed most unlikely to provide a suitable home for scientific research. Efforts to transform some of the better colleges into universities failed regularly until brand-new institutions—Johns Hopkins, Clark University (despite its almost fatal troubles), and the University of Chicago—came into being and provided successful models for other institutions to follow.

In the evolution of these four themes, scientists were the principal actors. They worked and lobbied on their own campuses and in the halls of government. They took to the platform and sought the support of the public press. They organized themselves for mutual encouragement and support. They used whatever means came to hand to promote scientific studies. And perhaps most important of all, despite lack of time and facilities—and sometimes despite outright opposition—they worked at science and began to make it evident that their work was essential to the achievement of American aims. Their efforts were largely responsible for bringing the American university into being, and in that institution they built a productive home for the work they wanted to do.

2. The Professionalization of Science

In 1802, Benjamin Silliman became the first professor of chemistry at Yale. There were then only 21 other full-time scientific positions in the United States (Daniels, 1968, pp. 13–14) and the professional requirements for most of those few positions were modest. Professors were hired to teach the science that was already known—to add to that knowledge was not expected, as the condition of the Yale appointment indicated. In 1801, Silliman was a 22-year-old law student contemplating accepting a teaching position in Georgia. One warm July morning he met Timothy Dwight, Yale's president and an old family friend, and told him of the Georgia offer. Dwight immediately advised him to decline. Dwight said he should not voluntarily go to a part of the country in which slavery was practiced; the climate was dangerous, and, besides, there was an additional reason. Yale had decided to appoint a professor of chemistry and natural history. No one in the United States was available and qualified; a foreigner, "with his peculiar habits and prejudices . . . [might] not act in harmony with his colleagues" (Reingold, 1964, p. 3). But if Silliman cared to become a chemist, he could have the position. The offer was welcome, even a relief, for Silliman was really not much interested in law. So he became a chemist within a year, going first to Philadelphia—America's scientific capital—and then on to Europe for some quick repairs to his scientific deficiencies.

Such an appointment did not seem as strange then as it would now. In fact, only 42 years earlier a similar appointment had been made at Cambridge University where the first full-time professor of chemistry was Richard Watson, a disappointed aspirant for the chair of theology who "boasted that he knew no chemistry at all" (Bowden, 1967, p. 5). In Silliman's case, Yale wanted a professor "of unimpeachable orthodoxy, and apparently it sincerely believed that any reasonably able person could acquire scientific expertise. The possibility that Silliman might not turn into a creative investigator was not taken into consideration since he was appointed to teach" (Reingold, 1964, p. 1).

Between Silliman's appointment at Yale and the selection of the scientific faculty for the new Johns Hopkins University in 1875, three interrelated tensions concerning the qualifications of university scientists and the nature of their work became reasonably well resolved. One was the question of amateurism versus professionalism in science. The nineteenth century was the period of transition from the gentlemen amateurs who predominated in the eighteenth century to the professional scientists of the twentieth. The second was the distinction between descriptive science of the kind sometimes associated with Francis Bacon and the experimental, theory-based research of a modern laboratory. As scientific interests changed, as new fields were explored, and as different kinds of scientific questions assumed importance, there was a gradual shift from the collecting, classifying, and descriptive activities of the old-fashioned naturalists to the rigorous, theoretical-experimental work of modern times. The third was the question of relative emphasis on science for its practical usefulness and science for its own sake—the question of what motivates a scientist to do scientific work and what motivates society to support that work.

FROM AMATEURS TO PROFESSIONALS

The half-century following Silliman's appointment was a period of steady growth in numbers and developing professionalism. Amateurs continued to be active; there were teachers who were not creative investigators, and there were generalists. But, more and more, there were specialists and professional investigators, men who devoted their lives to the advancement of science. And as the decades passed, the professionals increased and came to have greater control over scientific affairs.

Donald Beaver (1966) has analyzed the contents of scientific journals from 1800 to 1860 and has concluded that there were approximately 1,600 active American scientists within that time span. Of this total, the number who were active at any one time grew steadily from 158 in 1810 to 664 in 1840, and to 1,031 in 1860.

Then, as now, some scientists published much more than others.

The 1,600 scientists published approximately 9,000 papers in American journals between 1800 and 1860. Individual contributions to that total were very uneven. Some published only one or two papers. The prolific Joseph Leidy, a pioneer in vertebrate paleontology, published an amazing 234 papers and notes before 1860, and at that time was only 37 years old. A. A. Gould, who collaborated with Agassiz in writing *Principles of Zoology,* published 138 articles during the period. James Dwight Dana, professor of natural history at Yale and the geologist on the Wilkes expedition to the southern Pacific Ocean, was the author of 105. Altogether, the top 138 producers wrote nearly half of the 9,000 scientific articles, and the 40 most prolific authors averaged over 50 papers each.

At all times between 1800 and 1860, there were active amateurs, but the most productive authors tended to be professionals and also specialists. About 50 percent of the most productive 138 were biologists or geologists; about 15 percent were astronomers or physicists; and the remaining 35 percent specialized in other areas, worked in several fields, or were scientific generalists.

Science was clearly the life work of these 138 men, but there were not enough scientific positions to go around. After finishing college or upon entering employment, 38 of the 138 had academic positions; 41 practiced medicine; 39 went into business; and 11 went into government service. A small number had independent means, practiced law, were theologians, or followed some other career. All 138 men were obviously highly motivated scientists — as their publication records attest — and even if they had to do something else for a while to earn a living, science was still a dominating interest in their lives. And if scientific positions became available later, they were willing to move. Fewer than half remained in one location throughout their careers, and as time went on they shifted away from business and medicine and into academic and government positions. Government posts offered full-time scientific duties, usually in geology or astronomy, and academic positions were more conducive to scientific work than business or the practice of medicine.

Several historians have tried to assign a date to the transition period from amateurism to professionalism, but the change was too gradual for any date to be precise. Historian George Daniels (1968, p. 7) has described the 30 years following the War of 1812 as the period when "American scientists evolved from a disorganized group of amateurs without common goals or direction into the professional body that they had become by mid-century." During that 30-year period, new scientific journals were started; scientists began to publish much more systematically, and they laid a solid basis for professional organization and work. Daniels has described the 56 scientists who published more than half of all the articles that appeared in the leading American journals of science and medicine from 1815 to 1845. Of the 56—all charter members of the group that established the profession of science in America—27 were trained in medicine and 20 in other fields of science; 9 had no college training, and 21 were educated in Europe. Professors of science numbered 41; 5 held other scientific posts; 3 were practicing physicians; and 7 were strictly amateurs. The 7 productive amateurs, 5 of whom wrote only on natural history, included a clergyman, a professor of modern languages, a publisher, the librarian of Yale College, two independently wealthy men, and Charles Bonaparte, a well-to-do political refugee whose uncle, Napolean Bonaparte, founded the French Academy of Sciences.

Among these 56 productive men, 1 in 8 was an amateur. By 1850, amateurs were clearly losing out to the professionals, but some of them were still highly respected members of the scientific fraternity. For example, when the American Association for the Advancement of Science (AAAS) was established in 1848, the first man chosen for the presidency was William C. Redfield, a saddler and harness maker, early steamboat and railroad entrepreneur, self-taught meteorologist, and the man who demonstrated the circular nature of violent wind storms.

Whether science provided a livelihood or was a consuming after-hours activity, in a larger sense all the leaders were professionals. They wanted to advance science, and as the century progressed they saw more and more clearly what they needed:

1 Means of communication—through journals or meetings—so that they could share ideas and knowledge with each other and benefit from the criticisms or confirmation of other workers.

2 Means of collecting data, which became more and more demanding, expensive, and extensive as science advanced.

3 Means of testing interpretations, analyses, and concepts, which called for laboratories, equipment, biological specimens, and other tools of scientific inquiry.

4   Enough duplication of facilities so that there could be independent testing and verification or refutation of new claims—all so that general agreement might result.

5   Freedom to criticize old ideas and try out new ones, and freedom to challenge accepted dogma and to search for truth. Although science is always largely influenced by the problems, concerns, and values of the larger society, in the nineteenth century it needed to break free from the undue restrictions of old dogmas (Burtt, 1957, pp. 99–106).

The first of these requirements—improved communications—scientists developed for themselves. Growth in the number of scientists and their research and aspirations led, naturally enough, to the development of aids and tools of an organized profession. In 1805, there were only 12 journals in the United States that published scientific material. Forty years later, there were 76, including most notably Benjamin Silliman's *American Journal of Science and Arts,* which was established in 1818 (Daniels, 1968, pp. 231–232). Scientific societies also came into being, some lasting only briefly because interest and numbers were not yet great enough.

The AAAS was founded only 16 years after the British association was established and 26 years after Germany had convened the first such public meeting of persons interested in the advancement of science. Membership in the AAAS was open to anyone who cared to join (professional accomplishment has never been required). Of the 461 founding members, only about 15 percent were professors of science. More than twice that many were physicians, and there was a significant sprinkling of Army and Navy officers, ministers, and men of public affairs. The largest group, about 40 percent, were identified simply as "Esquire" or occasionally as "Mr."

Amateurs were welcome in the new association, but the statement of its objectives made it clear that the organization was primarily by and for, even though not wholly of, professionals:

The objects of the Association are, by periodical and migratory meetings, to promote intercourse between those who are cultivating science in different parts of the United States; to give a stronger and more general impulse, and a more systematic direction to scientific research in our country; and to procure for the labours of scientific men, increased facilities and a wider usefulness.

With these objectives, the professionals, mostly professors, were clearly in charge. The original executive committee included William C. Redfield, the distinguished amateur who was elected the first president, and Dr. Alfred L. Elwyn, a physician who served as treasurer. All the other members of the executive committee were professors, and their names made a distinguished list: Joseph Henry, Eban Horsford, Walter R. Johnson, Alexander Dallas Bache, Louis Aggasiz, Benjamin Peirce, Asa Gray, James Hall, and Benjamin Silliman, Jr.

For two members of the committee, "Professor" was a title of respect and honor, but no longer an indication of employment. Joseph Henry had left Princeton in 1846 to become the first secretary of the Smithsonian Institution. Alexander Dallas Bache had left the University of Pennsylvania in 1843 to direct and reorganize the Coast Survey. These two close friends, with the help of other scientists who were stationed in Washington, or who visited there from time to time, became leaders of the scientific community in attempting to secure the resources and opportunities that scientists needed but could not provide for themselves.

It would have been difficult to find two better representatives in Washington, or two more effective leaders of scientific politics. Henry was the country's leading physicist, the rival of Faraday in discovering and understanding the phenomena of electromagnetic induction. His professional training as an actor, attractive presence, strong will, and determined plans to develop the Smithsonian Institution were all assets. He knew exactly what he wanted for science and set out to make the Smithsonian a leader in that effort.

Bache's credentials were every bit as good. He was the great-grandson of Benjamin Franklin. One grandfather was Richard Bache, the president of the Republican Society of Philadelphia at the outbreak of the Revolution, and the other was Alexander James Dallas, Secretary of the Treasury from 1814 to 1816. A brother-in-law, Robert J. Walker, was a senator and later Secretary of the Treasury. An uncle, George M. Dallas, was Vice President of the United States from 1845 to 1849, the years when Bache and Henry were establishing their positions in the political and governmental world of Washington. In the political capital, one could not ask for a better introduction, but Bache had much more than family background in his favor. At the age of 19, he had graduated from West Point at the top of his class and was immediately appointed a teacher there. His Army career was short, however, for at age 22 he was elected professor of natural philosophy and chemistry at the University of Pennsylvania. By the time he arrived in Washington 15 years later to take command of the Coast Survey, Bache had established a solid reputation for research, served as the leader of the Committee of the Franklin Institute on Explosions of Steam Boilers, which had received the first grant of the United States for a research project (Sinclair, 1966), reorganized the school system of Philadelphia, and been president of Girard College.

Later in the century, John Wesley Powell enjoyed somewhat comparable stature, but probably not until World War II had cast Vannevar Bush into a position of dominant and effective leadership did any scientist play as prominent a role in scientific-governmental affairs as did Bache. When he died in 1867, there could have been little objection to his eulogist's characterization: "He, who by common consent, unquestioning and unchallenged, stood forth preeminent as our leader in science, our first counsellor where her welfare was at stake, unflinching in the maintenance of her interests, wise in the guidance of her affairs" (Gould, 1869, p. 1).

WHAT KIND OF SCIENCE?

As scientists became more numerous and better organized there was much scientific work they wanted to do. What was known seemed so little in contrast with what was still to be learned. Any gain in knowledge seemed desirable, and the search for new knowledge was supported by several motives.

American pride in practical achievement and frequent quotations from Alexis de Tocqueville seem to have overemphasized the practical motivation of nineteenth-century scientists. True, scientists often did have useful applications in mind, and practical use was the hope of nearly all their supporters. It was no accident that the earliest scientific activities of the federal government were in exploring, mapping, and surveying the West and new territories, and in devising improved aids to navigation. The potential value of these activities was manifest, and it was clear that real progress would depend upon a better understanding of nature. If the naturalists who accompanied the Western surveys came home with strange plants, the bones of extinct animals, and new ideas about the earth's history, that was quite all right, but the backers of the surveys also hoped for more tangible returns.

Scientists shared the practical interest, but if one can judge correctly from what they wrote, many of the leading scientists of the period were even more interested in pure science and its advancement (Daniels, 1968, p. 21). Pure science and applied science, however, were not mutually exclusive. Many scientists did not distinguish between the two, and in some fields of science, new knowledge served both purposes. Better knowledge of the heavens advanced astronomy and aided navigation. Survey parties returned with new specimens to classify and with information useful in trade and in consolidating an expanding empire. As chemistry developed, science was broadened and agriculture was improved.

Moreover, all science, regardless of its immediate practicality, had two other pillars of support: piety and patriotism. Studies of the heavens and the earth and of past and present forms of life helped man to understand the grand design and the purpose of the Creator of all things. Benjamin Silliman's oratorical defense of geology (1842, p. 243) is a good example:

The records inscribed upon the volumes of the earth's solid strata, and often buried beneath the mountains, are more copious, more legible, and more authentic, than historical medals, than Arundelian marbles, than Egyptian hieroglyphics, or Persepolitan characters. They cannot be falsified, corrupted or suppressed, and will remain, while the earth shall endure, a visible, tangible history, written by the finger of God upon the work of his own hands.

Silliman's pious sentiment was echoed in hundreds of speeches and articles, for the few agnostics and free thinkers among scientists were greatly outnumbered by those who shared the piety of the times.[1] Scientists were helping man to understand God's work. If the new truths could be put to practical use, so much the better, but even if they never proved useful in a commercial sense, new truths were good in themselves.

Moreover, if those new truths were discovered by Americans, that was even better. Daniels (1968, p. 192) writes:

After the close of the War of 1812, it seemed to Americans that no more obstacles stood in the way of the rapid progress of scientific thought,

---

[1] Even as late as the twentieth century, a letter to *Science* began with the reminder, "There is but one truly scientific mind in the universe, whose vision sweeps from Sol to Alcyone, which notes the sparrows as they fall, and numbers the hairs of our heads" (Holland, 1902, p. 601).

with all the material and spiritual advantages it would supposedly bring with it. The real political independence achieved by the war was accompanied by a desire to extend that independence to economics, to literature, and to science. . . . Advance was so rapid that an almost childlike faith in science became the rule among educated Americans.

A substantial amount of public interest also supported scientists in their work. In 1836, Silliman went to Boston to give a series of popular lectures. From there he wrote to Joseph Henry that he was lecturing to a thousand persons, that he had to repeat the lectures in the daytime to 300 or 400 more who could not go out in the evening, that the lectures were received with great enthusiasm, and that as soon as the series was finished he would go to New York to deliver a series of public lectures on geology (Reingold, 1964, p. 76). Louis Agassiz was often on the lecture trail, greeted by thousands of interested listeners. And later when John Tyndall, Faraday's successor at the Royal Institution of London, was brought to the United States for a public lecture tour, over half a million copies of his lectures on light were sold (*Science,* 1883, p. 181).

Supported by piety, patriotism, a satisfying amount of public interest, and considerable evidence of the practical usefulness of their work, scientists did not have to worry much about distinctions between pure and applied science. There were few enough of them, their financial needs were modest by later standards, and, except for a fortunate few, the time available for research was limited by heavy teaching loads or by other duties. Under such circumstances they took advantage of whatever opportunities they could find to advance their work.

Early in the history of scientific investigation, interesting problems and the resources necessary to investigate those problems lay close at hand or could be provided by the scientists themselves. But as knowledge increased, so did the resources necessary to gain new knowledge. Simple questions inevitably led to more complex ones. Work on nearby plants, animals, or geologic formations increased the desire to explore farther afield. Reliance on measurements that could be made with the unaided senses or with common measuring instruments gave way to a need for measurements that could be made only with more precise and specialized equipment. Observation and description of natural phenomena raised questions that could be answered only by experimentation.

Physical scientists were primarily responsible for changes in the concept of fruitful scientific work and the resources necessary to pursue such work. Joseph Henry's work on electricity and magnetism was the high-water mark of American experimental investigation during the first half of the nineteenth century, but American scientists knew that across the Atlantic Faraday's studies paralleled Henry's and that a number of other fundamental advances were being made. It was this period that saw Wöhler's first synthesis of an organic compound, Leibig's pioneering work in agricultural chemistry, development of Avogadro's hypothesis, and in biology the birth of the cell theory of Schleiden and Schwann, and the observations and thinking which led to Charles Darwin's *Origin of Species*.

With such models before their eyes, American scientists also wanted to become experimentalists. The proper course for scientists, Joseph Henry wrote, was "to pour fresh material on the apex of the pyramid of science, and thus to enlarge the base" (Miller, 1970, p. 9). That was what European scientists were doing, and Americans should do no less.

Scientists could supply some of the elements necessary to get ahead on the new basis. They could provide the ideas, the brains, and the willingness to work. They could publish the journals and arrange the meetings that subjected new ideas and new findings to the public test of examination and criticism by one's peers. In their homes, their colleges, or elsewhere, they could still find some of the materials that were required. A very few even had enough wealth to supply more expensive needs.

But all that was not enough. What was also needed were astronomical observatories, field stations, laboratories, and a growing variety of specialized equipment. To fill these needs, scientists had to turn to others for help.

3. The Search for Sponsors

The growing need for better research facilities was a frequent theme of scientists' talk in the latter half of the nineteenth century. The need could be met only with more dependable and continuous financial support than had been available in the past. Much scientific investigation could be pursued without expensive equipment, and the cost of some kinds of investigation could be covered by the money appropriated for other purposes, such as the Western surveys. But laboratories, astronomical observatories, and other expensive equipment cost more than individual scientists could afford and more than Congress was willing to include in occasional appropriations intended primarily for other purposes.

The need for new facilities and opportunities led scientists to woo any sponsor who volunteered or could be persuaded to give assistance. The ways that potential supporters responded helped determine the ultimate selection of the university as the principal center of research in the United States.

Had the choice of the major home for science been made in the eighteenth instead of the nineteenth century, academies of science would have been selected. American scientists were well acquainted with the scientific academies of other countries, and from colonial days onward some of them had belonged to the Royal Society in London. They wished for the United States an organization similar to the Royal Society, which had an annual grant from the Crown and which provided English scientists with a rallying ground, a means of communication, and modest financial aid. Although the American Philosophical Society had existed in Philadelphia since 1743 and the American Academy of Arts and Sciences in Boston since 1780, neither was truly national in scope, and neither had enough money to support extensive research activities. Academies had their uses, but the American academies could not support much research.

UNLIKELY ALTERNATIVES

In the nineteenth century, independent, permanently financed research institutes would have been eagerly greeted as choice places for the advancement of science, and pleas for their establishment were made repeatedly. Frank W. Clarke (1877, pp. 729–736), professor of physics and chemistry at the University of Cincinnati, developed plans for a research institute. Much useful, though often scattered, work could be done by college professors, but physics and chemistry, he explained, required "laboratories especially and liberally endowed for purely scientific research." Henry Rowland (1883, pp. 105–126), first professor of physics at Johns Hopkins University, wanted a "grand laboratory" for physics. William Trelease (1896, pp. 367–382), the first president of the Botanical Society of America, joined in with the statement that botany also needed more research than could be conducted in the spare time of professors and that botanical gardens, herbaria, and specialized libraries were needed. Other scientists, on other platforms, made similar proposals.

Some of the advocates thought it would be desirable to establish independent research institutions close to a college or university. Research might be improved by the necessity to do some teaching, and there would also be budgetary advantages: easy access to a college library would save money on books, and advanced or graduate students would be available as assistants, either on a voluntary basis or, if necessary, at low wages.

Except for James Smithson, however, no wealthy patron stepped forward to finance the institutions these men and others called for. If private wealth was not ready to endow research institutes, perhaps the federal government would do so. Shortly after the Franklin Institute had completed its "General Report on the Explosions of Steam Boilers," demonstrating that excellent and useful work could be accomplished under a federal research grant, Walter R. Johnson, a member of the committee responsible for the report, memorialized Congress to establish a great national institution for experiments in physical science (Rhees, 1879, pp. 172–184). He wanted to make the United States independent of foreign science in the exploitation of its national resources and the development of its military and economic strength. To accomplish that objective he proposed a wide-ranging research institution that would have facilities for work in agriculture, physical sciences, engineering, military problems, mining, commerce, mapping and topography, and architecture. When Johnson's memorial reached Congress, John Quincy Adams, always a friend of science, moved that it be referred to the select committee on the Smithson bequest. There it rested, getting no further than most earlier proposals for federal endowment of science or education.

George Washington's proposal to establish a national university in Washington failed, and failed whenever repeated by later presidents. John Quincy Adams wanted an astronomical observatory—a "lighthouse in the sky"—but Congress did not. Any proposal for congressional support of scientific activity could expect to encounter the charge of being unconstitutional.

Occasionally, however, congressional reluctance was overcome or circumvented. Dupree (1957, p. 26) gives an illuminating account of the scheming Thomas Jefferson found necessary to get the Lewis and Clark expedition approved by Congress:

In the fall of 1802 President Jefferson asked the Spanish minister in Washington in a "frank and confident tone" whether Spain would object to a group of travelers exploring the Missouri River, who would really "have no other view than the advancement of geography." But he would "give it the denomination of mercantile, inasmuch as only in this way would Congress have the power of voting the necessary funds; it not being possible to appropriate funds for a society, or a purely literary expedition, since there does not exist in the constitution any clause which would give it the authority for this effect." When he sent a secret message to Congress in January of 1803, to ask for money for the expedition, the President reversed the emphasis. After urging the wresting of the Indian trade in the upper Missouri regions from the British, he made a glancing reference to the "Western Ocean" and then reassured Congress that Spain and France would consider the expedition a mere "literary pursuit." Thus science as an objective was for foreign ears; commerce as an objective was for Congress; and the real purpose, which had to do with the claims of empire, was carefully screened by silence, secrecy, and an ambiguous title to the act.[1]

---

[1] This was not the first time Jefferson had used science to cover other purposes. In 1791, when he and James Madison sought to establish a new political party to counter the ambitions of Alexander Hamilton, they wanted to consult with a number of influential leaders throughout New York State. To hide their real purpose from Hamilton and his friends, they set out "with studied innocence" on a month-long sight-seeing, botany-studying tour, letting it be known that a special purpose was to study the Hessian fly, which had become a menace to crops (Fleming, 1969).

Once in a while Congress made other exceptions. Congress did approve the Coast Survey, and there were others. And when the long, weary debate over how to use the Smithson bequest finally ended, Congress had established the Smithsonian Institution as a national research center, although not as practically oriented as Johnson had proposed, or as large as Joseph Henry, the first secretary, wanted. Henry managed to get rid of the Institution's library responsibilities by turning them over to the Library of Congress, and in this way he got some additional money for science. He would have liked to get rid of the national museum that some members of Congress wanted, but specimens kept arriving from the surveys and other sources. His assistant and successor, Spencer F. Baird, was a biologist who valued the collections given to the Smithsonian; and thus there was not as much money for research as Henry would have liked. Even so, the Smithsonian was a research agency in which scientists could take pride. It was small, but Henry's plan of selecting men of demonstrated research competence and of giving them time for thought and facilities for experimentation was a good start toward what scientists wanted.

But the Smithsonian Institution was an exception, rather forced, unexpectedly, on a reluctant Congress by the will of an unknown Englishman. Had any congressman introduced a resolution expressing the intent of Congress to support science as a contribution to the general welfare he would have been soundly defeated, for many members of Congress believed that appropriations for scientific purposes would be unconstitutional.

Industry was no more ready than Congress to support science. From mid-century or earlier there was talk of the contributions science might make to industry, but most of the talk was optimism for the future rather than realism of the present. The few exceptional scientists who were involved in industry did not yet see much potential use for research, and it was not until the end of the century that Charles Steinmetz began to serve the General Electric Company as scientist, inventor, and valuable advertising symbol of a progressive, technical industry.

Colleges were a possibility, but a quite unattractive one. Faculty members were hired to teach, not to do research. Clarke, Rowland, and Trelease all based their pleas for independent research institutes partly on the oft-deplored fact that college professors were rarely given opportunities or encouragement to do original work.

Clarke lamented that "nearly all the research accomplished . . . has been done by university or college professors, in the intervals between their regular duties, or as an incidental matter, and usually with meager appliances." Trelease said that most botanical research had to be conducted by professors in what little spare time they could find. Asa Gray's appointment in 1842 as professor of botany at Harvard was the kind of exception that proved the rule. In writing to offer him the position, President Josiah Quincy was careful to point out that although the annual salary of $1,000 was less than the $1,500 usually paid to Harvard professors, the appointment was intended to leave Gray time to carry on the important studies in which he was engaged (Dupree, 1959, p. 110).

William Rainey Harper (1905, p. 107) went so far as to charge, "The American college system has actually murdered hundreds of men who while in its service have felt that something more must be done than the work of the classroom, and who, because of this feeling, have died from overwork. It has actually destroyed the intellectual growth of thousands of strong and able men."[2]

Although the university which grew out of the college did become a great research institution, through most of the nineteenth century the college seemed an unlikely source of support for much scientific work. In fact the search for other sponsors was to a considerable extent motivated by the desire to escape from the inhospitable climate of the college.

THE FEDERAL GOVERNMENT

Despite congressional reluctance to support science in its own right, government agencies needed scientists to help solve practical problems and for most of the nineteenth century employed more scientists and spent more money on research and other scientific activities than any other segment of society. Perhaps government agencies which needed science could be expanded.

Even the states needed scientific help. Before 1840, two-thirds of the states had organized geologic surveys, and those surveys provided employment for enough geologists to make geology the

---

[2] Even as late as the 1950s, some college presidents objected to faculty members engaging in research. In a questionnaire circulated by the president of Kalamazoo College in 1957, presidents of 12 good liberal arts colleges were asked, "Do you consider time devoted to research when planning the teaching loads of individual instructors?" Four replied that they always did, but six said they *never* did (L. Gould, 1959).

best-organized science in the country. Thus when scientists were becoming a professionalized group it was the Association of American Geologists that in 1848 broadened itself to become the American Association for the Advancement of Science, a professional organization for scientists in all fields.

Surveys were also needed at the national level. The Lewis and Clark expedition was authorized. Later, other surveys were sent to the Western Territories. After several years of debate the Wilkes Expedition was sent to explore the West Coast of America and the Central and South Pacific. Congress was often reluctant, yet sometimes there were ways to get around congressional reluctance. Thomas Jefferson was not the only man of ingenuity to serve in the executive branch. Congress, as John Quincy Adams learned, was adamantly opposed to the use of federal funds to build an astronomical observatory. Yet the Navy built one. Hunter Dupree (1957, pp. 62–63) describes its origin as:

... the classic example of the surreptitious creation of a scientific institution by underlings in the executive branch of the government in the very shadow of congressional disapproval. No more hated proposal existed, and nowhere had more pains been taken to prevent the creation of a new agency. Yet despite this vigilance the forces that required an observatory gained their ends. Before 1830 each ship of the Navy obtained charts, chronometers, and instruments individually, with no tests before purchase and no responsibility for what became of them at the end of a cruise. In that year the secretary, on the advice of interested officers and the Board of Navy Commissioners, issued an order setting up the Depot of Charts and Instruments which would take care of all nautical instruments, books, and charts when they were not in actual use.

Lieutenant L. M. Goldsborough, the first to be in charge, at a very early date mounted a transit instrument for the purpose of determining accurate time for the rating of chronometers. ... Thus the practical need for taking care of chronometers opened the way to astronomical observations. ... [A] permanent organization had arisen without benefit of specific legislative blessing.

Lieutenant Goldsborough, the first director, Lieutenant James Gilliss, the chief architect of the Navy coup, and their colleagues succeeded, but an occasional bit of scientific smuggling did not alter deeply entrenched congressional doubts about the constitutionality of government support of science.

Gradually, however, pragmatism, the presence of James Smithson's bequest, and the needs of the executive agencies extended the range of scientific activities Congress was willing to support. The Smithsonian Institution was established. The Navy included a number of officers who were actively interested in scientific investigations and who used Navy problems and Navy resources to further those interests. Under Bache's direction the Coast Survey recovered from its earlier troubles and by the middle of the century was by far the largest scientific enterprise in the nation. It employed more scientists than any other organization, and its budget dwarfed all others, including the Smithsonian's. In its peak year, 1854, the Coast Survey received an appropriation of $489,537.20 (Dupree, 1957, p. 104).

In the 1860s the U.S. Department of Agriculture (USDA) started out on an expanding program that quickly surpassed the Coast Survey and that soon made it the largest research agency in the United States. Shortly afterwards, John Wesley Powell, leader of the Washington scientific corps and director of the Geological Survey, was building the Geological Survey into a research agency second only to the USDA. For an extended period both the USDA and the Geological Survey not only conducted research but also offered temporary appointments to graduate students and served as effective graduate schools in their fields.

By 1901, appropriations for federal scientific agencies totaled over $8 million. Charles D. Walcott, (1901, pp. 1001–1015) director of the U.S. Geological Survey, estimated that more than $2 million of that amount could "be regarded as expendable for scientific and research work and in the interests of higher education." The larger appropriations consisted of almost $4 million for the USDA, over $1 million each for the Interior Department and the Treasury Department (which included the Coast Survey and the Bureau of Standards), and approximately $0.5 million each for the Smithsonian Institution, the Commission on Fish and Fisheries, and the Library of Congress. Altogether, Walcott could boast, "In the city of Washington the Government has assembled the largest body of original investigators to be found in any one place in the world" (ibid., p. 1014).

The federal government conducted enough scientific work that in the 1880s there was the first serious discussion of the possibility of a Cabinet-level Department of Science. Political and congressional interest sometimes wavered, however, and at about the same time that a Department of Science was being considered, the director of the Coast Survey was being forced to resign in a messy political brawl that involved some false affidavits and much wild gossip. *Science* editorialized that scientists in government had become so demoralized that "a year or two more such as the last will leave nothing worth preserving of an organization which was once the pride of American applied science" (Dupree, 1957, p. 222).

No college or university had as much money as the federal agencies, but universities offered greater stability. No university could compete in size, but collectively university scientists outnumbered government scientists. And even more important, many scientists and many political leaders did not believe the federal government should be responsible for the major part of the nation's scientific work. Joseph Henry was skeptical of government support of science, partly because he feared that his scientific colleagues would not accept congressional judgment. "I put little faith in appropriations of Congress," he wrote to Asa Gray. "On the first application for an appropriation the friends of those who have been left out will make war upon the establishment" (Reingold, 1964, p. 209). Henry Rowland (1883, p. 118) mistrusted congressmen and categorically rejected the idea of government appropriations because "no political trickery must be allowed around the ideal institution."

FROM WILLIAMS COLLEGE TO WILLIAMS BAY

To the scientists of the middle of the nineteenth century, the unhappy truth was that there was no ready and willing source of support for the work they wanted to do. Neither business nor private philanthropy was ready to satisfy their wants. The colleges were poor and often unfriendly to research. The government was in fact the largest source of support for science, but support was sometimes unsteady and was for special purposes dictated by practical rather than scientific needs. Moreover, many scientists and politicians agreed that support of science was not the government's business.

Nevertheless, science needed money. Scientists wanted salaries for themselves, of course, but this was only part of the problem. They wanted the facilities that would allow them to do the first-class scientific work that would satisfy their professional ambitions and be of advantage to their country.

Perhaps no bit of American scientific history so well illustrates both the willingness of scientists to accept support from any patron and the variety of efforts they made to cultivate potential patrons as does the rapid development of astronomical observatories in the United States after 1838.[3]

Astronomy is one field of science which regularly enjoys popular interest. Eclipses, comets, and meteors are spectacular, awe-inspiring, or frightening events. The ties between the heavens studied by astronomers and the heavens of religion may be superficial but are none the less appealing. Astronomy is a field for which it is easy to keep score. A new planet or a double star — nowadays a quasar — is a newsworthy event; and it is always easy to tell who has the biggest telescope.

Yet until 1838 the United States had no permanent observatory. During the 1830s, a succession of comets, including Halley's comet, and brilliant meteoric displays aroused much public interest. In 1838, for a cost of only $6,000, Albert Hopkins, professor of mathematics and natural philosophy at Williams College, Williamstown, Massachusetts, and brother of Williams's famous president, Mark Hopkins, built the first permanent observatory in the country. Between then and 1951, when the 200-inch reflector went into regular and continuous operation at Mt. Palomar, a succession of larger and larger telescopes was built. The scientists who planned and promoted them called upon every source of support they could find.

Two years before Hopkins built his telescope at Williams College, Ormsby MacKnight Mitchel, a West Point graduate who was later to die as a brigadier general during the Civil War, became professor of mathematics, civil engineering, mechanics, and machinery at Cincinnati College. In the winter of 1841–1842, at the invitation of Cincinnati's Society for the Diffusion of Useful Knowledge, he gave what must have been an exciting, and surely highly successful, series of public lectures on astronomy. As interest remained high through the whole series of lectures, he gradually conceived the idea of building a great observatory in Cincinnati. To the audience of 3,000 at his concluding lecture, Mitchel announced a novel plan for financing his dream. He proposed selling 300 shares, at $25 each, to raise $7,500 for the best telescope obtainable, promising shareholders membership

---

[3] The following brief account of the development of larger and larger telescopes and astronomical observatories is drawn chiefly from Miller (1970, chaps. 2, 5). Other references are given where necessary.

in the Cincinnati Astronomical Society and the privilege of viewing the stars through the new telescope. Public support was generous and rapid. Within a month all 300 shares were sold—to grocers, physicians, carpenters, lawyers, innkeepers, clergymen, and other interested supporters. The cost turned out to be more than $7,500, but Mitchel raised additional funds and bought a 12-inch objective lens in Munich. A local land speculator provided a hilltop site, and on November 9, 1843, a year and a half after the scheme was first proposed, John Quincy Adams journeyed to Cincinnati to dedicate the observatory atop the hill that had appropriately been renamed Mt. Adams. At last, just before his death, John Quincy Adams achieved his "lighthouse in the sky."

In February 1843, as the Cincinnati observatory was being built, the appearance of a brilliant comet aroused fear, awe, and public interest, and the competition intensified. Harvard scientists welcomed the comet as an opportunity to plead for a new observatory. Benjamin Peirce, who had just become professor of mathematics and astronomy at Harvard, was eager for astronomical equipment that would enable American astronomers to compete with Europeans. Citing the achievement of an upstart Ohio River town, Peirce called upon Boston to do better. The response was immediate, and by May, public men and business leaders had contributed $20,000. By 1847, when the Harvard Observatory was built, contributors had given additional funds to pay astronomers' salaries. And in 1848 Edward Bromfield Phillips, a Harvard graduate, bequeathed an astonishing $l00,000 to employ observers for the new facility.

Albany became the next challenger, trying to outdo both Cincinnati and Harvard. Early in the 1850s, Albany leaders and promoters began to lay plans to develop the nation's greatest university. Some of the leading scientists, who were always willing to endorse any proposal that promised better opportunities for science, rushed to support those plans. Louis Agassiz, Benjamin Peirce, and Joseph Lovering of Harvard and James D. Dana and John P. Norton of Yale even agreed to leave their posts to accept professorships at the new university in Albany. A great observatory was to be a prominent part of the new university, and Ormsby MacKnight Mitchel was persuaded to take enough time away from Cincinnati to design the building, select the instruments, and become astronomer in charge.

Plans for the university fell apart for lack of funds, but a gift of $10,000 from Mrs. Blandina Dudley and promises of $15,000 from other sources ensured completion of the Dudley Observatory. Its character, however, soon changed radically from the original Albany expectations. When Mitchel decided that his duties at Cincinnati did not allow sufficient time to serve also as the Albany astronomer, Dr. James Armsby, one of the principal promoters of the Albany plan, went to an AAAS meeting to confer with Benjamin Peirce. Peirce persuaded Armsby that America needed a heliometer in order to make accurate determinations of longitude and that Benjamin A. Gould, of the Coast Survey, was the man to appoint as astronomer in charge. Armsby's acceptance of this advice meant that Albany was going to get a special-purpose research instrument instead of a telescope through which interested citizens could view the stars. That change, plus Gould's prickly character, quickly led to misunderstanding and heated disagreements. Gould's uncompromising insistence on using the observatory exclusively for research clashed with the wishes of the institution's patrons to view the stars. When Gould barred the doors to the institution's trustees and hired Albany's chief of police to keep visitors away, the whole affair became a national scandal. The observatory's scientific council, which included Joseph Henry, Alexander Dallas Bache, and Benjamin Peirce, made a strategic withdrawal from the fight, leaving Gould to the mercy of the trustees, and leaving the observatory to sink into its useful but unspectacular future—unspectacular, that is, after the newspapers tired of reporting the Albany fight.

Clearly the Albany form of popular patronage, at least when managed by as unbending a purist as Gould, was not the model to follow in seeking a patron for research. In this respect, the Albany experience was not unlike the much less virulent experience at Cincinnati. Support by popular subscription invited clashes between subscribers who wanted to use "their" observatory and astronomers who wanted to make progress in astronomy. The Harvard formula was a happier one for astronomers. There, funds were provided by wealthy patrons who wanted to support science and who were willing to leave planning and management to the scientists.

In 1855, when the Dudley Observatory was dedicated, one of the men in the audience was Frederick A. P. Barnard, who was destined to become president of Columbia College in New York and to give his name to Barnard College (Fulton, 1896). The previous October, Barnard had gone to the young University of Mississippi as professor of mathematics and natural philosophy. His first year at "Ole Miss" turned out to be an exceedingly busy one. Because the professor of chemistry failed to show up, Barnard added chemistry to his list of expected courses in higher mathematics, physics, astronomy, and the elements of civil engineering. On Sundays he served as clergyman for the Episcopal church of the university town of Oxford, Mississippi.

As if that were not enough to keep a man busy, Barnard accomplished a masterly bit of financial sleuthing and persuading. The act of Congress by which Mississippi had been admitted to the Union in 1817 provided that certain lands be granted to the state to provide for a "seminary of learning." The act made the state Legislature the sole trustee of this endowment and specified that the principal acquired from the sale of the lands be kept intact and never diminished. These conditions were repeated in the state constitution. The Legislature sold and leased some of the land and banked the receipts. Severe losses were incurred during the bank failures of the middle 1830s, and when Barnard began his investigations, only $180,000 was supposedly still in the account. Barnard's reading of the constitution, all the subsequent relevant legislation, and the financial records convinced him that the fund should amount to $1,100,000, that the state had expended only $200,000 on buildings for the university, and that the state had a moral and legal obligation to provide the other $900,000. The Governor agreed, and arranged for Barnard to address a joint session of the two chambers of the state Legislature. The Senate also agreed, but the House hesitated and asked for an independent investigation. Pending its completion, both houses passed a bill authorizing appropriations of $25,000 a year, for five years, to be used exclusively for the improvement of the university's library and its scientific equipment and apparatus.

With what must surely rank as one of the busiest years ever spent by a new professor behind him, Barnard went off to Albany to attend the AAAS meeting that had been scheduled to coincide with the dedication of the Dudley Observatory. On the day of the dedication, he received a telegram informing him that the trustees had elected him president of the University of Mississippi. Returning to Oxford, he started a campaign to use the annual grants of $25,000 he had won from the Legislature to increase greatly the university's scientific competence. He wrote a long and carefully constructed letter to the trustees in which he extolled the values of scientific discovery and research, gave many examples of the time lag between earlier discoveries and their practical application, pointed out that at the time of discovery the discoverers themselves usually did not know what practical applications would follow, and emphasized the value of scientific inquiry unfettered by restrictions to what seemed likely to be immediately useful (Fulton, 1896, p. 221).

After this vindication of pure research in general, Barnard went on to apply it to astronomy. The university had quite good collections and equipment in other sciences (Kennon & Gladden, 1938, pp. 1–7) but no observatory, and he wanted one.

Barnard's letter was addressed to the university trustees, but to bring pressure on them to accept his recommendations, he released the letter to the public and the Legislature. The strategy of making his recommendations known to the public and trying to enlist popular support for the university was one he used regularly throughout his tenure as president. He had early evidence of its success. Enrollment increased; popular support for the university increased; and he was granted funds for an astronomical observatory and a companion magnetic observatory.

Barnard's *Memoirs* say that he wanted "a modest astronomical observatory," but clearly his goals were higher. Cincinnati, Harvard, the Navy, and other institutions had their telescopes. Albany had its troublemaking heliometer. At the Pulkova Observatory in St. Petersburg, Freidrich Georg Wilhelm von Struve (great-grandfather of Otto Struve, who was later to have a distinguished career as an astronomer in the United States culminating in appointment as the first director of the United States National Radio Astronomy Observatory at Green Bank, West Virginia) directed the greatest telescope in the world, a 15-inch refractor made by Fraunhofer in Germany. Barnard's "modest astronomical observatory" was to be larger than any of these.

Instead of going to Germany for his lens, Barnard boldly contracted with Alvan Clark of Cambridge to grind a 19-inch lens. Alvan Clark had been an engraver and portrait painter, and an amateur astronomer. In 1846, he established the firm of Alvan Clark and Sons and quickly gained a reputation for making fine small lenses, but he had never undertaken anything nearly as large as Barnard wanted. He succeeded, however, in grinding a lens $18\frac{1}{2}$ inches in diameter—the largest in the world. On the first night of testing the new lens, his son Alvan Graham Clark verified the existence of the postulated companion star of Sirius, an observation for which the French Academy of Science awarded the two men the Lalande gold medal.

In 1861, Clark wrote that the lens was ready and that if Barnard would come to Cambridge about the end of June he could try it out. The trip was never made. The North and the South became locked in a fratricidal war; postal communication came to an end; and travel between the South and the North was impossible without a passport. Barnard's dream of a great observatory at the University of Mississippi was one of the war casualties, and it was impossible for him to pay Clark for his work.

Thus the lens was never installed in the duplicate of the great Pulkova Observatory Barnard had constructed to receive it (Kennon, 1947). Nor, for the same reasons, were the special instruments made for the magnetic observatory ever received and installed in the companion building constructed for their use.

Clark sold the lens to the Astronomical Society of Chicago, which later presented it to Northwestern University where it is still in service at the Dearborn Observatory. Barnard learned of its quality and of the sighting of the companion star of Sirius when he reached Washington, D.C., in 1862. One of the first people he met was Lt. James Gilliss, the man principally responsible for building the Naval Observatory, and who, in 1861, had finally become its superintendent.

The war frustrated Barnard's ambitions, yet the experience added evidence that with proper cultivation the individual states, through their legislatures and with wide popular support, might become generous patrons of science. Moreover, Barnard's confidence in Clark helped launch the firm of Alvan Clark and Sons on a career of grinding larger and larger lenses. Within the next dozen years they produced a 23-inch lens for Princeton, 26-inch lenses for the Naval Observatory and the University of Virginia, and a 30-inch lens for Pulkova. They ground the first achromatic lenses and for decades kept up with the demands of astronomy for larger and larger apertures.[4]

When Clark produced a 30-inch lens for Pulkova, the title

---

[4] A popular history of the work of Alvan Clark and Sons is contained in Pendray (1935). A list of the increasingly larger lenses ground by the company is given in Dimitroff & Baker (1945, pp. 282–291).

"Biggest" was lost by the United States. Urged on by Joseph Henry, Louis Agassiz, and other prominent scientists, California interests set out to regain that title.

George Davidson began his scientific career as a high school student assistant to Alexander Dallas Bache in the Philadelphia High School Observatory. Later he followed Bache to the Coast Survey, and by the 1860s he had become chief of the Survey's Pacific Coast activities, the leading organizer of scientific affairs on the Coast, and president of the California Academy of Sciences. By 1869, he knew that the high Sierras would provide an excellent location for a great new observatory for work in astrophysics.

Early in 1873, a gift from James Lick to the California Academy of Sciences seemed to Davidson to provide a possible opportunity to get his astrophysical observatory in the high Sierras. A promise of support from Lick was quickly secured. But between October 1873, when Davidson announced the telescope gift to the California Academy of Sciences, and 1888, when the observatory went into operation, it frequently seemed unlikely that the observatory would ever get built.

James Lick was a successful businessman who wanted to leave a great monument to himself. And he wanted it right in the heart of downtown San Francisco where people could see it. At first he thought of a huge pyramid, and later considered a million dollars' worth of statuary of himself and his relatives. Davidson and others —for Davidson's patience wore out and he withdrew from the negotiations—first had to persuade Lick that the biggest telescope in the world would be a better monument than a pyramid or a garden of statuary. Then it was necessary to move the planned location out of the fog, city lights, and vibration of downtown San Francisco. Lick refused to accept the high Sierras but did compromise on the 4,200-foot Mt. Hamilton.

Alvan Clark doubted his ability to produce a lens larger than the 30-inch one at Pulkova, but he agreed to try and succeeded in making one with a 36-inch aperture. Lick's original gift of $500,000 was $700,000 short of Davidson's estimate of the total required. But Lick had nearly $4 million, and despite much frustration and several torn-up or changed deeds of trust, within 15 years the observatory was completed and the eccentric patron had his monument. In fact he had several monuments, for included in an odd mixture of bequests were $160,000 for statuary for San

Francisco, money for a public bath, and, in spite of the irritation he must have felt toward those hard-to-deal-with scientists, approximately $1 million for the California Academy of Sciences. Yet the observatory on Mt. Hamilton has been his principal monument. He died before construction was completed, but his remains were sealed in the pier supporting what was then the most powerful telescope in the world, in the observatory still known as the Lick (Miller, 1970, pp. 98–103).

The presence of the world's largest telescope in the San Francisco Bay area was a challenge that southern Californians could not resist. Regional pride called for a bigger one near Los Angeles, and a land boom there promised the wealth necessary to get it. A 40-inch lens atop Mt. Wilson would put Los Angeles ahead, and arrangements were made with Alvan Graham Clark to grind it. The collapse of the southern California land boom and, shortly thereafter, the death of Edward Spence, the principal promoter of the Los Angeles plan, spoiled the dream of outdoing San Francisco. The University of Southern California, like the University of Mississippi in an earlier day, was forced to default on its contract.

Clark dashed off to the AAAS meeting to try to find a buyer for the orphaned Mt. Wilson lens. One of the men who heard Clark's tale was George Ellery Hale, the brilliant 24-year-old professor of astrophysics at the brand-new University of Chicago. Another was Edward C. Pickering, director of the Harvard Observatory. Pickering already knew of the Los Angeles predicament and had started to search for a patron whose generosity would enable Harvard to pick up the new lens and build an observatory in the Southern Hemisphere.

Harvard had a head start, but Chicago moved faster. With help from William Rainey Harper, Chicago's brilliantly persuasive president, Martin Ryerson, chairman of the board of trustees, and Charles Hutchinson, a trustee who was president of the Corn Exchange Bank, Hale persuaded Charles Tyson Yerkes to bring the 40-inch lens to Chicago. Yerkes was a rich, socially ostracized robber baron. In Philadelphia he had served a prison term for misappropriating public funds. After moving to Chicago, he had become the boss of Chicago's transit system; made a fortune by following his enterprising formula, "buy old junk, fix it up a little, and unload it upon other fellows"; and contributed notably to Chicago's reputation as the "Boodle Capital of the World." Hale wrote to Yerkes, explaining what a monumental contribution the great lens would make to Chicago and its new university, and what an enduring monument it would be to the donor. Yerkes, seeing an opportunity to buy respectability, quickly promised funds for the Chicago Observatory, before Pickering at Harvard was able to raise the purchase price.

As was true with other patrons who understood little of science and its needs—Albany and San Francisco had already provided examples—the road from initial promise to successful completion was a rocky one. But when on October 21, 1897, it came time to dedicate the new observatory at Williams Bay, on Lake Geneva, Wisconsin, "anxiety and hatred were lost in a haze of rhetoric and good fellowship." Charles T. Yerkes sat on the platform, heard himself lauded, and responded to the ovations with a speech of presentation of the observatory in which he explained why it was so difficult, and so necessary, to find men of wealth willing to support those branches of science, such as astronomy, that did not lead immediately to salable products (Miller, 1970, pp. 105–111).

The lens that was originally planned for Mt. Wilson in California went to the University of Chicago, but southern California's disappointment was only temporary, for by 1904 Hale was moving to Pasadena where his efforts helped to bring 100-inch and then 200-inch instruments to Mt. Wilson and Mt. Palomar and gave southern California undisputed title to the world's largest telescope.

Astronomy is illustrative of that large portion of science for which the necessary means of study are costly enough to require special funding. The succession of new observatories built after 1838 illustrates the variety of support that scientists tried out in their search for patrons. At some time between 1838 at Williams College and 1897 at Williams Bay, title to the largest telescope in the United States, and for most of that time the largest in the world, was vested in several different kinds of institutions, and possession of that title was made possible, successively, by a private college, the Navy, popular subscription, private wealth, a state legislature, and a new university's ability to get support from a robber baron.

The success of astronomers was both an inspiration and a cause of envy to other scientists. Henry A. Rowland (1883, p. 120) asked, "What would astronomy have done without the endowment of observatories?" He answered his own question. "By their means, that science has become the most perfect of all branches of physics." Other scientists wanted to do as the astronomers had done.[5]

---

[5] Anyone who doubts that the search for sponsors still goes on should consider the note to a recent article on archaeology which states that the investigation "was sponsored by the American Philosophical Society, Bauer Kompressoren, the Catherwood Foundation, The Corning Museum of Glass, Nixon Griffis, the Littauer Foundation, Mr. and Mrs. James P. Magill, the Main Line Diving Club of Philadelphia, the National Geographic Society, the National Science Foundation, and William Van Alen" (*Scientific American,* 1971, p. 13).

4. Choosing the University

The sectarian college of the mid-nineteenth century was surely an unpromising base on which to build a university. A few visionary professors dreamed of converting their colleges into universities, but the typical college lacked the faculty, students, money, or vision to be anything other than a small college, and most of them were small, indeed. The 239 that were open in 1850 employed a total faculty of 1,678 teachers—an average of only 7 per campus! Those colleges that were large enough to become universities faced other difficulties. On no campus did the faculty as a whole want the college to change into a university. Among both faculty members and college presidents there were many who believed the college should remain a strictly undergraduate institution and who resisted all proposals to add graduate work. Not that the colleges were altogether satisfactory. On the contrary, there was much evidence that change was necessary. The rigid classical curriculum and emphasis on drill were being challenged. For several decades, while population had expanded, enrollment had remained static, and the influence and prestige of colleges had declined.

In 1863, G. Stanley Hall, who was to become one of the first professors at the Johns Hopkins University and the first president of Clark University, tried to hide from his friends the fact that he had been admitted to Williams College. Of course the fact leaked out, and in his autobiography he recalls that he was "unmercifully jibed" by his young friends. Hall's reluctance to let it be known that he was going to college was a personal illustration of a state of affairs more seriously marked by the fact that the number of doctors and lawyers who had college degrees actually declined in the latter part of the nineteenth century (Veysey, 1965, pp. 5–6).

The poor reputation of the colleges and the dissatisfaction on the campuses had several roots. Expanding knowledge, especially in the sciences, made it increasingly difficult both to retain the entire classical curriculum and accommodate the new knowledge and new subjects that some faculty members wanted to add. The old curriculum seemed largely irrelevant to the changes going on outside of college walls. Students were often unruly, and the emphasis on drill and recitation must have been particularly irksome to those with quick and inquiring minds. Student rebellion was more frequent than requests for advanced work.

The nature of the reform that was in the wind, however, was not yet clear. As things were to turn out, two more or less independent reforms came together to give the American university its distinguishing characteristics.

One reform started in the colleges. A minority of faculty members —chiefly but not exclusively scientists—wanted to develop a higher level of education, a postgraduate level. Some of those who had studied abroad envied their European colleagues the wealth and more enlightened intellectual climate that supported graduate work in real universities. They wanted comparable institutions in America and took advantage of whatever opportunities they found to work and agitate for the development of real universities.

The other reform started outside the colleges. The rigid classical curriculum that was still being taught, largely by recitation and drill, had little relevance to practical affairs. As a result, there were growing demands for more useful forms of education, especially in agriculture since farming was the principal occupation of the time.

The old sectarian college grew into the contemporary university onto which were grafted graduate education, called for mainly by scientists, and practical education, called for mainly by politicians and agriculturalists. In both reforms, science was in the vanguard. Yet the original aim of scientists was to create not primarily a home for research, but opportunities for advanced education for prospective teachers and scholars. In fact, many scientists did not think of colleges and universities as the proper place for research. Joseph Henry was one who took that view. In a recent summary of prevailing mid-century attitudes, Handlin and Handlin (1970, p. 33) cited with approval the generalization, "Men interested in the advancement of science did not conceive that the college was a likely setting for its pursuit." This attitude persisted for a long time. Samuel Langley, secretary of the Smithsonian Institution from 1887 to 1906, thought of colleges and universities as institutions intended "exclusively for teaching where it would be foolish to believe that research could ever gain a foothold" (Ripley, 1969). And as late as 1915, John Henry Newman (1915, p. xxxvii) argued that "to discover and to teach are distinct functions" and that there should be academies for research and universities for teaching.

Research has become so much a part of the American university that it is difficult for contemporary Americans to think of a university without research. But research was not even the distinguishing characteristic of the German university that many Americans wanted to copy. True, some German professors conducted research in affiliated institutes, and some students gained research experience in those institutes, but more general characteristics distinguished the German university from the American college. The German university started at a higher educational level, and it granted the Ph.D. degree. Instead of getting daily drills on the details of a classical curriculum, students attended lectures, participated in seminars, studied on their own, and were free to pursue a wide range of ideas and topics. These characteristics made the German university the mecca of American students who wanted a higher education.[1]

In the mid-nineteenth century many American colleges were little better than secondary schools, and many of them, in fact, gave work at the secondary level. They conferred the bachelor's degree, and many also awarded the master's degree—but as a freely given honorary degree. At most colleges the master's degree was available for a fee to any graduate who survived for a year or two beyond receipt of the bachelor's degree. Harvard, for example, continued to award its automatic $5 M.A. until President Eliot abolished the practice in the 1870s.

Rebellion against the low standards of American colleges,

---

[1] The German university has not always enjoyed such a reputation or offered such high-level work. Tobias Danzig tells the story (Morton, 1969, p. 4) of a fifteenth-century German merchant who asked a professor for advice on the education of his son. The professor's reply, says Danzig, was: "If the mathematical curriculum of the young man was to be confined to adding and subtracting, he perhaps could obtain the instruction in a German university; but the art of multiplying and dividing, he continued, had been greatly developed in Italy, which in his opinion was the only country where such advanced instruction could be obtained."

the meaninglessness of some of the high-sounding degrees, and envy of the heights to which the German university had risen impelled a number of American educators to try to establish universities here. They wanted to enable interested, able young scholars to go beyond the limits of the American college. Whether research would be carried out in those universities was often not even considered.

FIRST ATTEMPTS AT GRADUATE WORK

Harvard, the oldest college in the country, was the first to offer graduate work.[2] (Thomas Jefferson had hoped to offer graduate work at the University of Virginia, but those hopes were not realized until later.) In 1831, Charles Beck introduced a seminar for the training of teachers of the classics which extended over the senior year and one graduate year. No provision was made for student scholarships, and without such subsidies the demand was small. Only six graduate students enrolled the first year, and the whole program soon withered away. However, Beck's seminar broke a barrier; the first formal graduate instruction had been given.

Meanwhile, in New York City, the University of the City of New York (now New York University) was being founded. Chartered in 1831, it began collegiate instruction the following year and in 1835 announced the opening of a graduate department which would offer work leading to an earned master's degree. As at Cambridge, there were few students. Even if there had been more, success was still uncertain. The university was soon riven by internal dissension. So much of the original endowment was spent on brick and mortar that not enough was left for operating expenses. By 1838, retrenchment was necessary, and on September 28 seven of the eight professors were dismissed. The most significant dismissal was that of Henry P. Tappan. His first attempt at graduate education had failed, but for 25 more years he would continue to try to develop a graduate university in the United

[2] Much of the following account of early efforts to begin graduate programs is based on Storr (1953), which describes the proposals and attempts that preceded the institutionalization of graduate schools of arts and sciences. Other useful volumes in connection with the development of graduate education and the place of science in the universities are: Ryan (1939), which concentrates on Johns Hopkins, Clark, and Chicago Universities; Veysey (1965), which discusses the conflicts among rival conceptions of what university education should be; and Handlin & Handlin (1970), which describes the nature of the colonial college that later gave rise to the university.

States, and he would be fired again for being too zealous in that effort.

The 1840s saw three attempts to establish graduate programs. Least successful was the attempt at Western Reserve University. Beginning in 1847, Western Reserve offered graduate instruction in ancient and modern languages, mathematics, and the sciences. Eleven students were enrolled in 1847–48, six in 1848–49, and after that, none.

Back at Harvard, Benjamin Peirce was proposing the establishment, outside of the regular academic faculty, of a school of science for young men who were not interested in intensive study of the classics but might be attracted by the opportunity to receive a practical education in the sciences. When Edward Everett returned to Harvard in 1846 as president, Peirce found an ally.

Everett, the first American to earn a Ph.D. (at Göttingen), had long been interested in graduate work, and when he became professor of Greek at Harvard in 1822, he immediately began discussions of graduate education with several faculty colleagues. Nothing came of these discussions until Beck's abortive seminar nine years later, and by that time, Everett had left Harvard to become a congressman and later United States Minister to the Court of St. James.

Everett (1856, p. 217) accepted Peirce's idea of a separate school of science, and in his inaugural address he sent up a trial balloon:

It is a question well worthy to be entertained, whether the time has not arrived [to organize] . . . a school of theoretical and practical science, for the purpose especially of teaching its application to the arts of life, and of furnishing a supply of skillful engineers, and of persons well qualified to explore and bring to light the inexhaustible natural treasures of the country, and to guide its vast industrial energies in their rapid development.

This call was obviously for a school of applied science rather than a graduate school, but both Peirce and Everett had something more than an additional undergraduate program in mind.

An offer of $50,000 by the wealthy Abbott Lawrence soon made it possible to found the Lawrence Scientific School. Provision already existed for the education of young men in theology, law, medicine, and surgery. "But where," Lawrence asked, "can we send those who intend to devote themselves to the practical application of science? How educate our engineers, our miners, machinists, and mechanics? Our country abounds in men of action. Hard hands are ready to work upon our hard materials; and whence shall sagacious heads be taught to direct those hands?" (Lawrence, 1856, pp. 217-218).

Peirce, Everett, and Lawrence all agreed that the time had come to educate some practical appliers of science. Theoretical science, however, was not to be excluded from the new school, and Lawrence's insistence that only "first-rate" men be appointed to the faculty pretty well guaranteed that theoretical science would not be forgotten. When Louis Agassiz was appointed as one of the first professors, that direction of development was assured.

Harvard's failure to appoint a professor of engineering, aggravated by the grandiose plans and free spending of the headstrong scientific faculty, soon disillusioned the wealthy sponsor, and he redirected half of his $50,000 gift into the endowment of a chair in engineering. Nevertheless, the scientists outmaneuvered him. As Miller (1970, p. 82) reports:

The Lawrence Scientific School had taken on a life of its own. The first graduating class of four (1851) was a fair sampling of the kind of "intelligent mechanics" who sought its offerings. William L. Jones would become a professor of natural science in his native state of Georgia; Joseph LeConte quickly became an eminent naturalist; David A. Wells, after a brief career in scientific journalism, turned to political economy; John D. Runkle subsequently rose to the presidency of the Massachusetts Institute of Technology.

Lawrence was not permanently dissatisfied, however. He had faith in science even though the school had not taken the direction he intended, and at his death in 1855 he bequeathed another $50,000 to the school.

Ironically, the new school's most direct contribution to commerce came not through the education of young engineers, miners, and chemists, but through the defection of the entrepreneurial Eben Horsford, whose Rumford professorship was "on the Application of Science to the Useful Arts." Horsford apparently took the title seriously, for in 1863 he resigned to manage his successful chemical works making Rumford baking powder and a "reliable tonic for morning sickness, nervous prostration, and the immediate ill effects of tobacco" (Miller, 1970, p. 83).

President Everett had wanted a full university, not a school limited to the sciences, and Charles W. Eliot, the young chemist who was later to become Harvard's president, proposed pulling the scattered scientific interests together into a university organization. But Louis Agassiz and Benjamin Peirce, always strong-willed, liked the private fiefdom of the semiautonomous scientific school. The scientists took charge, and under their guidance the Lawrence gift became a great aid to the development of scientific work at Harvard. Able scientists were appointed to its faculty, and they made substantial advances in their chosen fields. They gave good starts to several hundred young men, some of whom went on to become scientific leaders of the country. In 1906, after six decades of arm's-length coexistence, the Lawrence Scientific School was absorbed into the Harvard structure.

Concurrently, history was taking a similar course at Yale. What started out to be an effort to offer education for agricultural and chemical uses led gradually to the creation of the Sheffield Scientific School. Just as Peirce at Harvard proposed an educational program for practical-minded young men who did not take to the classics, Benjamin Silliman, Jr., at Yale proposed a course of instruction intended to appeal to professional rather than academic students. The Yale authorities were cool to the idea, but accepted it on sufferance. They authorized a new professorship of agricultural chemistry and vegetable and animal physiology, with the stipulation that support of the professorship not be charged to the regular funds of Yale College. They then tried to dilute Silliman's scientific emphasis by adding that the curriculum would also include philosophy, literature, the moral sciences, and other fields. Scientists were in charge of the new program at Yale, however, just as they were at Harvard, and they emphasized science, not the other subjects the Yale Corporation added to the charter.

The Department of Philosophy and the Arts, the name given to the new venture at Yale, was small, but from the beginning it attracted a few able students. The department had some lean days, for Yale Corporation backing was only halfhearted, and external support was precarious. Affairs took a better turn when John A. Porter joined the faculty. Porter was a Yale graduate who had studied at Giessen for three years under Justus von Liebig, the world's leading agricultural chemist. He had also been Horsford's assistant in the Lawrence School at Harvard. Not long after assuming his new title of professor of agricultural chemistry and vegetable and animal physiology, Porter married Josephine Sheffield, daughter of Joseph Sheffield, a wealthy New Haven railroad magnate. Even before the marriage, Sheffield made a gift of $6,000 to his future son-in-law's struggling scientific school. In following years he regularly made substantial contributions to fund-raising campaigns, some of which were managed by young Daniel Coit Gilman, who was later to be the founding president of Johns Hopkins University. By the time of his death, Sheffield had contributed over $400,000 to the school to which he allowed his name to be given (Miller, 1970, pp. 87-96).

Like the Lawrence School at Cambridge, the Sheffield School conferred its degrees on many more future scientists than agricultural workers or practical chemists. Indeed, it went further than Harvard in research training. John P. Norton, Porter's predecessor, had asked the Yale authorities to allow the new department to award the Ph.D. degree. A decade later the authorities agreed, and the first earned Ph.D. in the United States was conferred at Yale in 1861. In the next decade, before any other American college began to offer the doctorate, that degree was conferred on 20 Yale graduate students, 14 of whom were in science. One was the great Josiah Willard Gibbs, who took his doctorate in 1863 and soon became America's leading contributor to theoretical science. Even Gibbs's record, however, indicates that some attention was given to the practical aspects of science. His doctoral dissertation was "On the form of Teeth of Wheels in Spur Gearing," and before he turned his great talents to theoretical physics he invented a railroad braking device and a steam-engine governor (Reingold, 1964, pp. 315-316).

Both the Lawrence Scientific School at Harvard and the Department of Philosophy and the Arts at Yale turned out to be permanent additions to their parent colleges. Both came to be important centers of graduate education in the sciences, although neither was started primarily as a graduate school. And both were looked upon by some of their friends as being only part of what was needed. At Harvard, Charles Beck, whose classics seminar in 1831-32 had pioneered graduate instruction in the United States, objected to the name "Scientific School" as too narrow, and President Everett wanted a full university. At Yale James D. Dana (1856, p. 374), professor of natural history, asked an audience of Yale alumni, "Why not have here, in this land of genial influence, beneath these noble elms, . . . THE AMERICAN UNIVERSITY,—where nature's laws shall be taught in all their fullness, and intellectual culture reach its highest limit!"

The true American university was still in the offing, not to emerge until after several other efforts had foundered. In 1852, Union College announced a plan to offer graduate work, but the plan never materialized. Bishop Alonzo Potter, who earlier had been professor of mathematics and natural theology and also professor of moral philosophy and political economy at Union, was a member of the committee that worked on the unsuccessful plans. Simultaneously, but in another role—as a member of the board of trustees of the University of Pennsylvania—Bishop Potter was trying to get graduate work started at Pennsylvania. Several members of the faculty opposed the idea vigorously, and Potter was no more successful at Pennsylvania than at Union College. The Pennsylvania episode was important, however, as an indication of the growing cohesiveness of leaders of American science. Potter's efforts had active support from Louis Agassiz, Alexander Dallas Bache (a former member of the Pennsylvania faculty), James D. Dana, Benjamin Peirce, and Henry Tappan—all names that appeared again and again in efforts to establish better opportunities for scientific research and education.

In 1855, Alexander Dallas Bache used his position as president of the American Association for the Advancement of Education to introduce a discussion of the need for a true university in New York City. An adequate corps of excellent professors was available, he told his audience; Peirce, Dana, Agassiz, and others were available—just as they had been ready a few years earlier to move to Albany had the dream of a university materialized. All they needed, Bache contended, was financial support and an opportunity.

Henry Tappan, who in his 1851 book, *University Education,* had fired the opening gun in the campaign to establish a real university in New York, followed Bache on the platform—in the chapel of the University of the City of New York, which had dismissed him in 1838 (Storr, 1953, p. 83). He had gone in 1852 to Ann Arbor to become president of the University of Michigan, but his heart was in New York, and now, in 1855, apparently he was ready to take every opportunity to put in a good word for the university he hoped New Yorkers would support. The public discussion of Bache, Tappan, and F. A. P. Barnard, the third speaker on the program, was followed by a period of intensive effort, with Tappan as the leader and Bache and other leading scientists as willing workers. For a while prospects looked hopeful, but that effort also faded into history as a failure.

Back on his own campus at Ann Arbor, Tappan was also trying to establish a real university. By 1858, he had persuaded the regents to start a graduate program and had augmented the faculty for that purpose. The new program attracted a few graduate students, but after the first year the number declined and by 1863 was down to zero. And in that year, Tappan was fired. New members of the board of regents opposed his plans, and he was accused of trying to "Prussianize" the young men of Michigan. Despite Tappan's dismissals, it was of him that Andrew D. White, the first president of Cornell, said, "To him, more than to any other, is due the fact that, about the year 1850, out of the old system of sectarian instruction, mainly in petty colleges obedient to deteriorated traditions of English method, there began to be developed *universities,* drawing their ideals and methods largely from Germany" (Ryan, 1939, p. 10).[3]

The final decade before the outbreak of the Civil War saw three more failures. In 1852, Columbia trustees began to consider the possibility of extending the college's offerings up to the graduate level. There was much discussion and considerable dissension, and there was also clear recognition by some of the participants

[3] Andrew White was very fond of the University of Michigan. In 1857, he was appointed professor of history and English literature at Michigan and was one of two professors President Tappan expected to be the nucleus of the university's graduate faculty. White remained at Michigan for six years, leaving at about the time Tappan was fired, but not for the same reason. Business interests, election to the New York State Senate, and then election to the presidency of Cornell kept him in New York most of the time. Even so, he retained a lectureship at Michigan, "and as long as possible I continued to revisit the old scenes, and to give courses or lectures" (White, 1907, vol. 7, p. 283). In several places in his autobiography White refers to the Michigan period as the most enjoyable, the most educational, and the most rewarding of his life. On Tappan's role in the development of the American university, he wrote (ibid., p. 272) that Tappan "had been greatly impressed by the large and liberal system of German universities, and had devoted himself to urging a similar system in our own country. On the Eastern institutions—save, possibly, Brown—he made no impression. Each of them was as stagnant as a Spanish convent, and as self-satisfied as a Bourbon Duchy; but in the West he attracted supporters, and soon his ideas began to show themselves effective in the state university over which he had been called to preside; "the real beginning of a university in the United States, in the modern sense, was made by Dr. Tappan and his colleagues at Ann Arbor" (ibid., p. 292).

that if graduate work were to succeed it would be necessary to offer stipends to the graduate students. No such stipends were available when graduate work was started in 1858. Only a few students appeared, and in 1861 the program was dropped. Only three years later, however, the Columbia School of Mines began to offer advanced work, which soon covered civil and mining engineering, chemistry, metallurgy, geology, and paleontology. This program fared well, and the School of Mines later became the first unit of Columbia to offer the Ph.D. (ibid., p.11).

In 1858, Frederick A. P. Barnard tried to start graduate work at the University of Mississippi. He did not succeed, but for a time it looked as if he might be offered the best opportunity any American had yet had to create a true university. In 1856, Leonidas Polk, Episcopal Bishop of Louisiana, began promoting among his fellow bishops the idea of a great Southern university. Regional arguments and favorable prospects for financial support moved plans forward rapidly. Professors were to be paid $3,000 a year, provided with houses on the campus, and permitted to collect up to $2,000 a year in fees from students. The cornerstone of the new University of the South was laid on October 9, 1860, at Sewanee, Tennessee. No president was chosen, but Barnard was generally considered to be the leading candidate. He was interested in the post and in graduate education, and graduate education was to be emphasized at Sewanee.

But all these plans soon became casualties of the War Between the States. The university buildings were burned and the endowment disappeared. In 1864 Bishop Polk, then General Polk, was killed in action. And in that same year Barnard went to New York to assume the presidency of Columbia.

Thus, at the time of the Civil War, unless one overemphasizes the Sheffield School at Yale and the Lawrence School at Harvard, there was not a true university in the country. The university as a potential home for research simply did not exist.

Before a true university that would be an effective home for research and advanced education in the sciences could exist and survive, four problems had to be solved.

1 It was necessary to decide what should follow the four undergraduate years. What was the proper content of graduate education, and what was its relation to undergraduate education? Richard J. Storr, the chronicler of the whole pre-Civil War period, points out that the early efforts followed three reasonably distinct lines. One possibility was to create a university

de novo, by bringing together the most eminent scientists and scholars from wherever they might be. This was the intended plan at Albany and at New York City. Another possibility was to extend upward those departments of the university in which four years no longer provided sufficient time for a student to acquire the mastery needed to teach or to do acceptable work in the field. The Sheffield School was an example. The third possibility was to provide to college graduates an opportunity to explore fields they had not had time to sample during their undergraduate years. This was Barnard's theme when he followed Bache and Tappan in the 1855 symposium of the American Association for the Advancement of Education (Barnard, 1856, pp. 174–185, 269–284). He argued that the curriculum was getting too full, that unless some college subjects could be pushed down to the secondary level, an extension upward was necessary. If Latin and Greek had to continue to make up a large part of the undergraduate curriculum, the study of modern languages could be undertaken later. If the classical parts of natural philosophy and natural history were all to be retained in the undergraduate curriculum, newer scientific fields such as chemistry could be studied at the graduate level.

2   Agreement was also necessary on a philosophy of education. What was to be the purpose of graduate education? Laurence R. Veysey (1965, chaps. 1–4) has traced through the entire period from 1865 to 1910 the competition among four underlying philosophies of university education: utility, research, mental discipline and piety, and liberal culture. Scientists came down hard in favor of utility and research, and in many cases did not really distinguish between the two. But from other parts of the campus, and often enough from the office of the president, vigorous support came for mental discipline and piety or for liberal culture. Although the advocates of these two latter educational philosophies could war among themselves, they could also join forces against their mutual enemy, the scientists. Irving Babbitt of Harvard at times was quite willing to oppose the older teaching of the classics, but at other times he urged an alliance "against their common enemies, the pure utilitarians and scientific radicals" (ibid., p. 195), for he and some other advocates of culture and the well-rounded man thought science was intellectually narrow, inhumane, and distasteful.

3   Another problem that had to be solved was how to secure freedom to search for and to teach new truths instead of merely repeating the old truths. The old classroom drillmaster had to give way to the scholar and researcher who could follow the truth wherever it led, who could help students to examine questions and come to their own conclusions, and who could take some of them even farther as apprentices and fellow researchers. Some professors saw this as a problem before the Civil War, but the need came to be more clearly and generally recognized afterward.

4 And finally, of course, there had to be money. Up to the time of the Civil War, no one had yet come forward with an amount large enough to establish a real university.

In 1875, the wealth and foresight of Johns Hopkins, the good judgment of a remarkable board of trustees, and the wisdom and imagination of Daniel Coit Gilman all came together to solve these four problems and to establish the first real university in the United States.

PIONEER GRADUATE UNIVERSITIES

Daniel Coit Gilman is properly given credit for the success of Johns Hopkins University, and he was its first president. But Johns Hopkins himself and the 12 trustees he chose also deserve much credit. When Hopkins, a wealthy Quaker who had no children, decided to leave his fortune of $7 million for the establishment of an institution of higher education in Baltimore, he elected, as Carnegie and Rockefeller were to do later, to delegate full responsibility to a carefully chosen group of trustees. The group of 12 included 7 businessmen, 4 lawyers, and 1 physician. Seven were college graduates, and three others had attended college. None was a professional educator or had been particularly close to educational affairs. But Hopkins knew them all and had confidence in their judgment. Few groups of trustees have worked more constructively in deciding how best to use the funds entrusted to their care.

They bought and studied a score of books on European and American education. They wrote for advice to presidents Angell of Michigan, Eliot of Harvard, McCosh of Princeton, Porter of Yale, and White of Cornell. McCosh ignored the letter and apparently Porter did also, but Angell, Eliot, and White all replied, and Angell and Eliot also accepted invitations to come to Baltimore to talk with the trustees. Although White did not make a similar trip, he was generous in his correspondence with the trustees (Hawkins, 1959, pp. 99–119).

The trustees decided early to aim high. They were thinking of an institution of the quality of Harvard and also thinking of a university in the German sense. To prepare for the visits of Angell and Eliot the trustees wrote out a number of questions they wanted to discuss. Eliot's interview lasted seven hours, all taken down by a stenographer so that the record could be studied later. Angell's interview was shorter, but also probing and detailed. He summarized: "[W]hat few ideas I had . . . were squeezed out of me remorselessly."

As a body, the trustees visited Cambridge, New Haven, Ithaca, Ann Arbor, Philadelphia, and Charlottesville to acquaint themselves with the practices, the problems, and the aspirations of institutions in these locales. They got a great detail of conflicting advice on dormitories, discipline, college newspapers, religious services, the advantages and disadvantages of the elective system, salaries for professors, and many other topics. But on what to them was the main point, they got little encouragement. They did not wish to found a new college; there were enough colleges. Nor did they want to establish a technical school or a group of professional schools. There was to be a medical school, for half of Hopkins's fortune was designated for it, and at one time they considered a law school, but the focus was on a university. Their advisers kept talking of a college.

President Angell recommended emphasis on practical training. President Eliot thought they should start with the freshman year of an undergraduate college and then add sophomore, junior, and senior years one at a time. He expected the work to be at a rather low level to compensate for what he thought were the deficiencies of the preparatory schools from which Baltimore boys would come to the new college. In response to direct questions about graduate work, both Angell and Eliot told of what they were doing at their own institutions to encourage graduate programs. Both lauded graduate work as the highest form of education and thought it much to be encouraged, but not by a new college just starting out in Baltimore. If Harvard with all its advantages could not become a graduate university, Eliot responded, certainly a new school in Baltimore should have no such aspirations.

However, Andrew White of Cornell had just opened a new university, and he knew that starting *de novo* was a time to be innovative. Cornell was placing considerable emphasis on practical education, but that was not the only course to follow. Without the dead hand of old tradition ever present, other kinds of pioneering were possible, and White encouraged the trustees to emphasize graduate work. As one tactic to help ensure success, he recommended providing fellowships for carefully selected graduate students.

Fortunately, the trustees disregarded most of what they heard from their various advisers. From the record of their interviews with Angell and Eliot the trustees "emerge as informed and imaginative figures. It was the penetration of their questions that brought out in such fine detail the ideas of Eliot and Angell, and in what was the most important issue of all, their thinking outran that of the experts they were consulting" (Hawkins, 1959, p. 104).

During their visits to other seats of learning, the trustees asked presidents Angell, Eliot, Porter, and White to nominate a prospective president for the new university. All four men, quite independently, gave the same name: Daniel Coit Gilman. Gilman had already decided he would take the first reasonable opportunity to leave the presidency of the University of California, but what the Johns Hopkins trustees offered was much more than an opportunity to escape the difficulties of dealing with the California Legislature. "The trustees," Gilman wrote, "are responsible neither to ecclesiastical nor legislative supervision, but simply to their own conviction of duty and the enlightened judgment of their fellowmen. . . . Their means are ample; their authority complete; their purpose enlightened. Is not this opportunity without parallel in the history of our country?" (Franklin, 1910, p. 179).

Gilman had been preparing for the presidency of America's first true university for a long time. When he graduated from Yale he went to Cambridge for a year of informal graduate work at Harvard and there lived in the home of Prof. Arnold Henry Guyot (whose name has been given to flat-topped submarine mountains), where he learned some French as well as some geology and geography. Then followed two years of travel in Europe and service as an attaché in the embassy in St. Petersburg (now Leningrad). Returning to New Haven in 1855 as a fund raiser for the Sheffield Scientific School, Gilman also helped Dana write a plan for the organization of the scientific school at Yale, and in the same year he wrote an analysis of "Scientific Schools in Europe" for the *American Journal of Education* (Gilman, 1856, pp. 315–328).

Then followed 16 more years in New Haven, as assistant librarian and later as librarian of Yale College, as acting school visitor (a title that preceded superintendent) of the New Haven school system, as an assistant to Noah Porter in revising *Webster's Dictionary,* and as a member of the staff of the Sheffield Scientific School, where he taught geography, history, and political economy for nine years and served as secretary for six.

In 1862, when the Morrill Land-Grant Act was passed, Gilman was largely responsible for qualifying the Sheffield Scientific

School as the first institution in the country to receive land-grant funds. Nine years later, for the United States Commissioner of Education, he surveyed all the colleges and universities receiving such funds in the Northern states.

His abilities as a leader and organizer were recognized, and offers of presidencies began coming. In 1867, he declined the presidency of the University of Wisconsin and in 1870 the presidency of the University of California. Two years later he accepted a renewed invitation to go to California, and it was from there that he accepted the call to Johns Hopkins.

With repeated urgings from the trustees to find the best men possible, Gilman chose an initial faculty of six professors, three of whom were under 30 at the time of appointment. Obviously afraid neither of youth nor of lack of reputation, he selected for the physics chair Henry A. Rowland, an assistant instructor at Rensselaer Polytechnic Institute. An article on magnetic permeability that Rowland had submitted to the *Americal Journal of Science* had been rejected by the editor, James Dwight Dana, partly on the grounds that the author was too inexperienced to be writing on such topics. Rowland promptly sent the manuscript off to Clark Maxwell in England; Maxwell recognized its high merit, arranged for its publication in the *Philosophical Magazine,* and invited Rowland to prepare a paper for the Royal Society.

Gilman arranged for Rowland to go to Europe for a period of study before assuming his new post at Johns Hopkins. In correspondence concerning possible titles for his chair, and as a forewarning of an attitude he was to express vigorously later on, Rowland rejected the title "professor of experimental and mathematical physics" on the ground that "all physics must be mathematical and experimental" (Reingold, 1964, pp. 262–270).

To supplement the small faculty, and following advice White had given to the trustees, Gilman appointed visiting professors — men of distinction such as Simon Newcomb, William James, Charles S. Peirce, James Russell Lowell, and Sidney Lanier — who spent a few days to a few weeks at the new university broadening the horizons of students, faculty, and townspeople.

Such a faculty should have students of comparable quality. From the beginning, Gilman established 20 scholarships, tenable for from one to three years, for the best students he could find anywhere in the country. Most went to prospective scientists, but not all; men such as Josiah Royce and John Dewey were among the scholars Gilman chose.

Another element in Gilman's success was his insistence on publication. He encouraged the Hopkins professors to establish journals at such a rate that his old Yale friend Dana, editor of the *American Journal of Science,* pleaded with him to stop lest his own journal fail.

When the medical school was established in 1893, again there was insistence on the highest possible quality. Candidates for entrance at Johns Hopkins had to have a bachelor's degree or its equivalent and a real premedical course; they then spent four years instead of the customary two or three studying medicine. As heads of clinical services in the hospital, Gilman selected men who merited, and were given, professorial appointments in the university.

The new university was not exclusively a graduate school. There were undergraduates from the beginning, but graduate work was emphasized. Neither was the university exclusively a school of science, but science was given greatest emphasis. A number of the ideas were not new. They had been proposed or even tried elsewhere, but Gilman brought them together and made them work. Unencumbered by tradition, the need to maintain the status quo, or a faculty reluctant to change, Gilman could pick and choose among the ideas of others, add some of his own, select faculty and students of the highest quality he could find, and use his own personal abilities and organizational skill to lead the whole endeavor to a new level of educational excellence in the United States. He created a great university in Baltimore—a model to which every other university had to pay attention.

After Johns Hopkins came Clark University. G. Stanley Hall, professor of psychology and pedagogics at Johns Hopkins, was the first president. Under Hall's direction, Clark started as a purely graduate institution with work limited to five fields: mathematics, physics, chemistry, biology, and psychology. But Hall was not as fortunate as Gilman. Instead of having the support of a strong board of trustees, Hall had to deal with Jonas Clark, who had wanted to found a college for poor boys of good character and who never really accepted Hall's vision of a graduate university. Clark balked at giving the financial support Hall needed, and in the severe retrenchment that followed, the hard-pressed university dropped most of the fields and concentrated for a number of years on graduate work in psychology and education. Three of the departing faculty members moved to Chicago as heads of departments at that even newer university, and twelve of the sixteen biologists at Clark went to Chicago.

Despite its smallness, Clark exercised a strong influence. The idea of combining graduate instruction with research was staunchly maintained. Hall and his small faculty helped to develop the idea that participation in research is the best method of educating a scholar. And the men so trained went to faculty posts at Harvard, Yale, Johns Hopkins, Stanford, Chicago, Michigan, and many other developing universities, continuing some of the Clark methods and traditions.

After Clark came Chicago. Original scholarship and research were President William Rainey Harper's primary objective for the Chicago faculty. Professors were expected to teach only eight to ten hours a week so that they might give adequate time and primary attention to research. Like Gilman, Harper wanted the best men he could find, and to make it more attractive to move to Chicago he offered salaries above the range available in most other universities. Harper came to the presidency with the support and trust of John D. Rockefeller, whose wealth initially made the university possible, and with the support of the Chicago Baptists who had persuaded Rockefeller that Chicago needed a Baptist college. No university president before him had raised so much money in so little time. Rockefeller's contributions were augmented by gifts from Marshall Field, William B. Ogden, Sydney A. Kent, Charles J. Hull, and Charles T. Yerkes—men who had become wealthy in the growing industry and commerce of the great railroad center of the Midwest.

Chicago, like Johns Hopkins, became a new model, and perhaps an even more influential one. It was larger. It was in the growing Midwest where other universities were emerging, instead of along the more established Eastern seaboard. Harper was a more flamboyant character than Gilman. Chicago educated more graduates who went to faculty positions on other campuses. And in establishing its great national influence, Chicago was helped by coming later, profiting from what Johns Hopkins and Clark had done.

It is not necessary to try to rank the pioneers. Johns Hopkins, Clark, and Chicago all insisted upon high quality. All elevated research and graduate education to new heights. All recognized that a major key to success was in finding the ablest men possible.

And all had another characteristic in common, one that is sometimes forgotten. In the words of their common historian, all three demonstrated "a much more specific sense of responsibility for human welfare and the needs of society than came to be associated with university research activities at a later period" (Ryan, 1939, p. 141). Concern for practical affairs and the immediate needs of society was more persistently and clearly evident, however, in another major landmark in the development of the American university: the Land-Grant Act of 1862, which stimulated the most distinctive contribution the United States has made to higher education.

PRACTICAL EDUCATION

In 1857, Representative Justin Morrill of Maine introduced a bill proposing that several million acres of the public lands of the United States be granted to the states so that they might sell the lands and use the proceeds for colleges to train young men in the agricultural and mechanical arts (Florer, 1968, pp. 459–478). The bill encountered much opposition, and, although it was adopted by narrow majorities in both houses, President Buchanan vetoed it on the grounds that it was unconstitutional.

Four years later Morrill reintroduced the bill under quite different political circumstances. The South, which had been the source of much opposition to the earlier bill, had withdrawn from the Union, and Western opposition had diminished.

Opponents argued that the proposal was unnecessary, an unconstitutional invasion of states' rights, and a bad precedent that would lead to other forms of federal welfare. Besides all that, it was silly; Senator Timothy Howe of Wisconsin implied that his colleagues might as well go totally mad as to toy with the idea of land for colleges.

Supporters argued all these points. Morrill advised, "Pass this measure and we shall have done something to enable the farmer to raise two blades of grass instead of one; something for every owner of land; something for all who desire to own land; something for cheap scientific education; something for every man who loves intelligence and not ignorance . . ." (ibid., p. 467). He then continued with a eulogistic account of the benefits that better agricultural education would bring to farm, family, commerce, railroads, religion, and the nation as a whole. The specter of the

Russian bear was raised, not for the first time, nor for the last. Morrill feared that the emergence of Russia as a dominant power might result from its greater interest in agriculture and education: "Here we find a despotism . . . placing it within the power of her agriculturists and artisans to become educated and skillful, while our people with the government in their own hands, parley on the brink, and do nothing for their own benefit" (ibid., p. 474).

Morrill succeeded. The bill was passed, and Abraham Lincoln, who was already pledged to its support, signed it into law.

When Congressman Morrill proposed the land-grant idea he was seeking a means of responding to a widely expressed need for agricultural improvement. Farmers were raising poorer crops on overused land and knew their soil was becoming depleted. Agricultural societies in many states had called for help. Some states and some colleges had tried to respond, but more help was needed, and Morrill thought the federal government should give financial aid through the gift of land.

Nearly a decade earlier a popular petition in Illinois had led the state Legislature to adopt a resolution calling upon Illinois senators and representatives to work for the passage of a law making public lands available for practical education and research purposes. Horace Greeley, who was impressed by the popular pressure on the Illinois Legislature, wrote a favorable editorial in the February 8, 1853, issue of the *New York Tribune* commending the efforts of a group of Illinois citizens who lacked power and influence but were desirous of learning. Their petition stands as an example of the grass-roots thread in the development of American universities (James, 1910):[4]

To the Honorable Senate and House of Representatives of the State of Illinois:

We would respectfully represent: That we are members of the industrial classes of this state, actively and personally engaged in agricultural and mechanical pursuits. We are daily made to feel our own practical ignorance, and the misapplication of toil and labor, and the enormous waste of

---

[4] Early in this century, President Edmund J. James of the University of Illinois tried unsuccessfully to have Jonathan B. Turner of Illinois recognized as the true originator of the land-grant idea. He recounted Turner's work with farm groups and the state Legislature, the legislative resolution referred to above, and also the petition cited. Turner undoubtedly deserves considerable credit, but Morrill was in Congress where he could take more direct action, and it is his name that is remembered.

products, means, materials, and resources that result from it. We are aware that all this evil to ourselves and our country, results from a want of knowledge of those principles and laws of nature that underlie our various professions, and of the proper means of a practical application of existing knowledge to those pursuits. We rejoice to know that our brethren in the several learned professions have to a good degree availed themselves of these advantages, and have for years enjoyed their benefit. They have universities and colleges, with apparatus, libraries voluminous and vast, able and learned professors and teachers, constantly discovering new facts, and applying all known principles and truths directly to the practical uses of their several professions and pursuits. This is as it should be. But we have neither universities, colleges, books, libraries, apparatus, or teachers, adapted or designed to concentrate and apply even all existing knowledge to our pursuits, much less have we the means of efficiently exploring and examining the vast practical unknown that daily lies all around us. . . . Knowledge alone, here, is power, and our relief is as clearly obvious as our wants. We need the same thorough and practical application of knowledge to our pursuits, that the learned professions enjoy in theirs. . . .

In 1862, the same year that the Morrill Act was passed, agricultural research got another boost in the elevation of the agricultural section of the Patent Office into a new, Cabinet-level Department of Agriculture. The new Department started immediately on analyses of soils, guano, sorghum, sugar beets, wines, and other products. Experiments were conducted on fermentation, the origins of mold, methods of detecting artificial coloring matter in wines, and other useful topics. Systematic research in entomology was undertaken. And in a number of these activities, cooperation between the USDA and the universities began to develop (True, 1937).

Although some of Congressman Morrill's statements had indicated an interest in experimentation, the act itself was not clear in assigning responsibilities for agricultural research to the new land-grant institutions. The Hatch Act of 1887 clarified that point by providing for the establishment of an agricultural experiment station under the direction of each of the land-grant colleges. Farming interests had been pressing for some time for research on agricultural problems, and there were both foreign and domestic models before the Hatch Act was adopted. In England, the Rothamsted Experimental Station had been established in 1843. In Germany, Justus Leibig—teacher of Eben Horsford of the Lawrence Scientific School and John A. Porter of the Sheffield Scientific

School—had started an experimental station in 1852. Experimental farms had already begun to appear in this country also, but widespread development took place only after passage of the Hatch Act.

The Morill Act, the Hatch Act, and help from the new USDA stimulated state universities in Michigan, Illinois, Wisconsin, Minnesota, and other states to develop in ways that helped the economies of their states and also helped determine the nature of American university policies and organization. In working to meet some of the practical needs of their states, the land-grant colleges gave to the American university several functions and characteristics that arose more in response to popular and political demand than to the urging of scientists and scholars.

In a largely agrarian country, interest in improving agriculture developed early, and it was recognized early that science could contribute to that end. The interest, however, was not limited wholly to a populist movement; gentlemen farmers, political leaders, and others who recognized that improvements in agriculture depended partly on improvements in science were prominently involved. In 1819, the New York Legislature adopted a law that provided an annual grant of $10,000 for the support of county societies to promote agriculture and to advance science generally. The state's contribution was to be divided among the counties in proportion to population and was to be matched in each county by local contributions. The law was a popular one, and within a year 26 counties had qualified for their shares of the state's $10,000 (Daniels, 1968, p. 14). Farmers were involved in stimulating such developments as the New York law, Yale's later interest in promoting agriculture, and the petition to the Illinois Legislature, but the press, too, played a leading role,[5] and so did a number of scientists, especially in the new colleges and universities of the Midwest. The leaders all knew, however, that instruction in agriculture and the work of agricultural experiment stations would increase public support for the state colleges and universities, for those institutions would then be working on matters of immediate relevance to the major personal and economic

---

[5] Science news occasionally appeared in the public press at least as far back as Benjamin Franklin's story of his electric kite in his own *Pennsylvania Gazette* of October 19, 1752. But the first regular science feature was a weekly column on scientific agriculture that Horace Greeley started in the *New York Tribune* in 1870 (Hay, 1970).

concerns of the states. Thus grass-roots interest was encouraged and was used to influence legislative decisions.

Actions that were intended specifically to improve agriculture had the broader result of establishing a formal, continuing relationship between the universities and the federal government. Senators and representatives who had opposed the land-grant act on the grounds that Congress would be establishing a precedent that could lead to other requests for the use of federal funds were surely right; the land-grant relationship has always been an example of effective and valuable cooperation between the federal government and the nation's universities.

The actions taken to improve agriculture are also due much of the credit, or blame, depending on one's biases, for the concept of the threefold function of the university: teaching, research, and public service. The University of Wisconsin, which established its experiment station in 1883, provides a good example (Curti & Carstensen, 1949). It was at Wisconsin that Stephen M. Babcock succeeded in developing a simple means of measuring the fat content of milk. Many others had tried unsuccessfully to develop such a measure, for the problem of determining the quality of milk was of widespread interest. Babcock declined to patent his method; it spread rapidly throughout the United States and abroad, and the Wisconsin Experiment Station became famous. From the standpoint of dairymen, storekeepers, and consumers, the method provided a control over quality and price, eliminated many deceptive practices, and encouraged the improvement of dairy herds. In 1900, the USDA estimated that each year the Babcock test saved the state of Wisconsin twice the amount of money spent on its whole university (ibid., p. 389).

It was also from Wisconsin that the world got the Steenbock process of irradiating foods to increase their vitamin D content. In this case the process was patented and arrangements made for 85 percent of the royalties to go to the Wisconsin Research Fund to support university research, lectures, scholarships, and fellowships. Professor Steenbock got the other 15 percent. This approach to ownership rights to commercially useful results of publicly financed research has been followed by a large number of universities.

Babcock and Steenbock were responsible for highlights in a long series of useful studies at Wisconsin, and along with the studies themselves there was an evolution of university policy and practice. Wisconsin and other land-grant institutions made efforts to meet local needs—practical, immediate, and commercial needs of the states. These efforts had much to do with establishing the good reputations of the universities with many state legislators and voters. The institutions rendered valuable services to the states and also provided undergraduate and graduate education and, increasingly as time went by, offered extension programs and short courses for farmers, businessmen, police officers, engineers, and other groups that wanted to take advantage of some of the special kinds of knowledge to be found in a university.

There was also pure research in these same land-grant institutions. Their faculties were not content merely to confer bachelor's degrees on prospective engineers and farmers and to study practical agricultural problems. The scientists on their staffs wanted to investigate theoretical problems as well as practical ones. Thus undergraduate and graduate education in engineering, agriculture, and a wide variety of other fields; experimental farms, extension work, and agricultural research; and fundamental research in genetics, physiology, and other life sciences have all flourished side by side on the same campus.

That the land-grant colleges were to some extent captured by experimental and theoretical scientists has not interfered with their original purpose. Nor would this intellectual upgrading and increased versatility have displeased the author of the Morrill Act. In 1867, Morrill visited New Haven to inspect the work going on at the first institution to have qualified for land-grant funds. He stayed at the home of Daniel Coit Gilman and there spent an evening with several members of the governing board of the Sheffield Scientific School. He answered a question about his reasons for proposing the land-grant act by saying that he had not intended the schools to be merely schools of agriculture, that in fact the title was not his but had been used by the clerk who engrossed the bill. Morrill himself wanted to encourage a new kind of college, one that would emphasize science for agriculture, yes, but also for industry, which in his own New England was beginning to find science important and useful (Franklin, 1910, p. 73).

PLANNERS AND SCHEMERS

"While science is without organization, it is without power." Alexander Dallas Bache (1851, pp. xli–lx), who made this statement to the three-year-old AAAS in 1851, believed the way to get power was to organize for collective action. He was then the leading organizer of science and the chief wielder of power on its behalf. He used the AAAS, his political connections, and his position as director of the Coast Survey, the largest scientific agency in the country. As much as any one man he played an important role in the creation of the National Academy of Sciences. And he was the moving spirit of the Scientific Lazzaroni—an informal club of scientific leaders who worked both behind the scenes and in the spotlight to advance science and to promote the development of universities. "The Scientific Lazzaroni considered themselves the choicest spirits and the best brains of American science. This was the 'Young America' movement among the scientists. They were determined to put down old-fogeyism and to build noble scientific institutions for themselves and the nation" (Dupree, 1959, p. 225).

Included in the Lazzaroni—the name came from the Italian and meant "beggar"—along with Bache, were:

- *Louis Agassiz,* dominant spirit in the Lawrence Scientific School at Harvard, the most lionized scientist of his day, and the most successful money raiser. To start the Museum of Comparative Zoology at Harvard, he raised $71,000 from private gifts, used $50,000 bequeathed by Francis C. Gray, added $12,000 derived from the sale of his private zoological collections to Harvard, and persuaded the Massachusetts Legislature to appropriate an astonishing $100,000 (ibid., p. 256). Little wonder that he became the first director of the Museum of Comparative Zoology.
- *James Dwight Dana,* professor of geology at Yale, member of the Wilkes expedition, and editor of the *American Journal of Science.*
- *Wolcott Gibbs,* associate editor of the *American Journal of Science* and successor to Eben Horsford as Rumford Professor in the Lawrence Scientific School.
- *Benjamin Apthorp Gould,* director of the Dudley Observatory in Albany, founder of the *Astronomical Journal,* and familiar with Washington because of his work on the Coast Survey.
- *Joseph Henry,* the country's preeminent physicist and first secretary of the Smithsonian Institution.
- *Benjamin Peirce,* a leading mathematician of the country, professor of mathematics and astronomy at Harvard, and first planner of the Lawrence Scientific School.

There was no fixed membership, and from time to time other scientists met with the Lazzaroni for the serious business of planning for science or the conviviality of a good dinner: the members enjoyed good food and wine and stated that their purpose was "to eat an outrageously good dinner together" (Dupree, 1957, p. 118).

The Lazzaroni had a large hand in forming the AAAS. Of the men named above, four served on the original standing committee, and all were sooner or later elected to the presidency. They created the National Academy of Sciences (over the opposition of Henry who nevertheless was selected as presiding officer at the organizing meeting), and all the original general officers and sections heads, save the aged Benjamin Silliman, were regulars of the Lazzaroni or close adherents (ibid., p. 142).

Their prominence, their service in various capacities, the popularity of some as public lecturers, and their own eagerness to support science meant that the Lazzaroni got around a good bit. They used these opportunities to work for science, and sometimes for each other. They helped the Albany enthusiasts plan the hoped-for university at Albany, for their desire for a national university meshed well with the aspirations of the Albany promoters. When plans for the university collapsed and only the prospective Dudley Observatory remained, it was Peirce who recommended the special-purpose heliometer that was installed and who proposed Gould for the directorship. It was also Peirce who had first proposed to President Everett of Harvard the idea that led to the Lawrence Scientific School, and it was Agassiz who largely took command of its early development.

When Bishop Potter tried to persuade the University of Pennsylvania to offer graduate work, members of the Lazzaroni rallied round to help. And when Henry Tappan took the lead in trying to arouse support for a national university in New York City, they willingly served as his lieutenants.

The founding of the American Association for the Advancement of Education (AAAE) in 1849 gave the Lazzaroni an additional platform from which to operate. Henry was on the first board of officers, and he and Bache were shortly elected to the presidency.

When Congress finally got around to starting the Smithsonian Institution, Bache and Peirce were selected as regents, and Henry became the first secretary. Later, Agassiz also became a regent. On the Pacific Coast, when it began to seem possible that some part of James Lick's fortune might be secured for science, Joseph Henry and Louis Agassiz visited Lick and talked with him of the good that would come of a handsome gift to the California Academy of Sciences.

As an informal private club, the Lazzaroni included some of the ablest scientists of the period. They also excluded some of equal stature. But from approximately 1850 to 1865, they were the scientific community's board of strategists, planners, and promoters.

The Lazzaroni were the most colorful group of scientific politicians in nineteenth-century America, but they were not alone in working together or campaigning to advance the cause of science. In 1838, Asa Gray gave up the opportunity to serve as botanist on the Wilkes expedition in order to accept appointment at the University of Michigan to the first professorship solely of botany in the United States. As soon as he was appointed, even before taking up his new duties, Gray tried to persuade the board of regents to add to the Michigan faculty John Torrey from New York, Joseph Henry from Princeton, and even Benjamin Silliman, who had been professor of chemistry at Yale for 36 years. He was trying to collect at Ann Arbor what might now be called a critical mass of scientists, not only to make his position more stimulating and attractive but for the same reasons that the Lazzaroni tried later, in Albany and New York, to bring a number of leading scientists together in a national university.

Nothing came of the effort. In fact, Gray never taught at Michigan. After he had spent a year in Europe as Michigan's emissary to buy books and equipment, and also to get acquainted with European scientists and botanical research, financial difficulties forced the regents to suspend his salary and ask him not to report for duty (Dupree, 1959, pp. 72, 93).

Undiscouraged by failure to get his friends appointed at Michigan, Gray tried, in 1842, when he became professor of botany at Harvard, to get Jeffries Wyman, Joseph Henry, and James Dwight Dana invited to join the Harvard faculty. He succeeded with Wyman, failed with Henry, and helped Dana get an attractive counter offer that kept him at Yale (ibid., p. 149).

The most productive scientists from 1800 to 1860—the 138 identified by Donald Beaver (1966) as authors of nearly half of the scientific articles written during those years—were a highly interconnected group. Ninety percent of them were born in Northeast and Middle Atlantic states. Of the 138, 85 were linked by teacher-pupil relationships, chiefly at Yale, Harvard, and the

University of Pennsylvania. In their work they were concentrated in Philadelphia, Boston, and, after 1845, also in Washington. They held similar and often closely related positions. Some collaborated on joint papers. They were members and officers of the same scientific societies. Of the 124 who could have joined the AAAS between 1848, its founding date, and 1860, the end of the period Beaver considered, 106 did so. At all times during the 1850s, 60 percent or more of the AAAS officers and committee members came from the group of 138 most active scientific producers. These same men worked together in the American Academy of Arts and Sciences, the American Philosophical Society, the Academy of Natural Sciences, the Boston Society of Natural History, the Coast Survey, and elsewhere.

Interconnected by location, work, interest, education, society membership, and in some cases also by blood or marriage, they had many opportunities to talk and work together to advance their common interests. Of course there was nothing unusual in this cooperation; men who share common interests and have the opportunity to work together are always likely to do so. Nevertheless, it was significant for the development of scientific work and organization that the scientific leaders were able to work together in so many crosscutting relationships.

In the latter half of the nineteenth century, scientists continued to work together, for science and the university. The long and cordial cooperation of two of the most influential university presidents provides a useful example. Daniel Coit Gilman and Andrew D. White met at Yale, where they belonged to the same debating society. After college, they went to Europe together and each served as an attacheé in the American Legation in St. Petersburg. Later, their professional paths diverged. Gilman returned to New Haven and then went to Berkeley and Baltimore. White served as one of the two graduate professors Henry Tappan was able to appoint at Michigan and then came back to New York where he and Ezra Cornell got acquainted while both were serving in the state Legislature — and where he became the first president of the university that bore Ezra Cornell's name.

Professional separation did not break the bonds of mutual respect and friendship. White was a consultant to the trustees in planning the Johns Hopkins University and recommended Gilman for the presidency. The two men served together on the commission appointed by President Cleveland to determine the boundary between Venezuela and British Guiana. Half a century after they met at Yale and went to Europe together, they were still collaborating. Both advised Andrew Carnegie on the organization and program of the Carnegie Institution of Washington. White was then United States Ambassador to Germany, and when Gilman arrived to study German models to get ideas for the new institution to be established in Washington, the two traveled together to a number of scientific centers. White (1907, vol. 2, p. 206) wrote of these travels: "Of all public duties I have had to discharge, I recall none with more profit and pleasure." When the Carnegie Institution was established, White became a trustee and Gilman the president.

Answers to the questions of how the American university came into being or why the university became the principal home of science in America are largely found in such examples as given above: the cooperation of a small and closely knit group of scientists in the Jacksonian era, the scheming of the Scientific Lazzaroni, and the long friendship of Gilman and White. At no time, except in connection with the land-grant act and related legislation, did Congress, the AAAE, the AAAS, the National Academy of Sciences (NAS), or any other body take stock of needs and conditions, weigh all the alternatives, and decide "this is the way it is going to be." Instead, that determination was made by the energy, persuasiveness, and planning and scheming of a group of dedicated men who wanted to develop universities and improve opportunities for research, and who tried every possible sponsor, before settling on the university as the principal site of scientific work.

Of the two ideas of the university—the university which offered graduate education and the university as the primary home of science—it was the former idea that was more clearly formulated. The German model was known, and many American scientists and educators wanted to copy that model. At the 1855 meeting of the AAAE, Henry Tappan (1856, pp. 247–268) called upon New Yorkers to found a great national university in their city, traced the history of education from pre-Christian times, and concluded that "the wisest philosophers, and the greatest educators have united in commending" the German system as the "highest and most perfect" form.

Not everyone agreed with this appraisal of the German university, as Tappan was to learn in Michigan. Not even all college presidents agreed. For example, a few years later at Yale, President Noah Porter denounced the idea of changing the school's name to Yale University (Veysey, 1965, chap. 4). But gradually opponents of change capitulated, became worn out, or died, and the supporters prevailed. And occasionally, as in the founding of Johns Hopkins, the university idea made a great leap forward.

However, the university as the principal home of research was a reluctant choice for many scientists. Their first dreams were of special research institutions. But until the turn of the century when the Rockefeller Institute for Medical Research and the Carnegie Institution in Washington were founded, and except for some astronomical observatories and government laboratories, special research institutions were generally not available.

CONFIRMATION As a final date of confirmation of the university as the home of science, 1892—the date of the founding of the University of Chicago—serves as well as any. William Rainey Harper, who was president, had no training in science; Hebrew scholarship was his specialty, and his experience had been in theological seminaries. Yet when he organized the University of Chicago, he placed much emphasis upon research laboratories and opportunities. Harper sought the most highly qualified research men available, offered them light teaching loads as encouragement, and assured them of freedom to pursue the search for truth wherever their findings and ideas might lead. If this was the proper course for a Hebrew scholar given responsibility for a great new university, surely it had become the course for American science.

As a single landmark date, the year 1892 serves well enough, but the entire period centering on the founding of the University of Chicago was a time of rapid change and broadening responsibility in American higher education. The land-grant colleges had been in existence long enough to get past their sluggish start. Cornell and Stanford, as well as Johns Hopkins and Clark, had started out on lines very different from the older colleges. Endowment funds were becoming available from new sources quite unlike the pioneering Quaker philanthropists Ezra Cornell and Johns Hopkins. And scientific and professional aspirations were reaching new heights.

Drawing a conclusion from the whole history of the rival concepts of the higher learning that had been in ferment since the Civil War, Laurence Veysey (1965, pp. 174–176) points to the two decades between 1880 and 1900 as the decisive period in determining the course of university development and the place of science in the university:

Looking back, it is clear enough that in the 1870's research played no important role in American higher education. Indeed, at that time the idea of a formal academic career was still in its infancy. Even after the founding of the Hopkins in 1876, several years were required before the influence of the scientific approach became readily apparent in the American academic world at large. Around 1880 a definite change occurred. It then began to be believed—whether rightly or not—that most of the "bright young men" were going into science. At just this time Harvard undergraduates began using the college library in significant numbers for research purposes, and it was also in 1880 that Harvard first granted sabbaticals on half-pay to its faculty members. The next year a chorus of articles demanded that professors be allowed to specialize and make original investigations. The turn of the tide was rapid. Now midwestern high school teachers could suddenly be found encouraging their most promising students to go to the Hopkins. Even Yale and Princeton began responding to these new pressures; it was in 1880 that Willard Gibbs first was paid a salary by Yale. Ten years later research had become one of the dominant concerns of American higher education.

The decade of the nineties saw the impetus harnessed into major academic organizations, as the Harvard Graduate School fully blossomed and similar enterprises came into being at Chicago and Columbia. Lesser colleges now encouraged their faculty members to take leaves and study for advanced degrees at places like Chicago. The year 1900 brought a superorganization, albeit a rather clubbish one: the Association of American Universities. The AAU encompassed presidents and deans who wished to discuss policy-making specifically in the area of higher degrees; its title thus suggested that research was the intrinsic function of "the" university in the United States. At the same time, the AAU limited its membership to a baker's dozen of institutions which, on the basis of their graduate schools, could claim to be of the "first rank"; as a result, officials of excluded universities sometimes complained resentfully. For their part, the heads of the state universities, meeting in their own convention in 1905, came to general agreement that research should be a major concern of their institutions, thus officiating at a semiofficial wedding of investigation to the older purpose of useful vocational training.

5. Effects on Science

To assert that the modern university has taken its nature from the activities of academic scientists would be to give the scientists too much credit, or—if one prefers—too much blame. To claim that the nature of contemporary scientific activities is a result of university sponsorship would assign too much responsibility to the university. Yet there have been strong reciprocal influences. Universities have been greatly influenced by the ways in which scientific teaching and research have been conducted and financed. And all science has been influenced by the fact that so much scientific work has been carried out in universities.

The most fundamental and pervasive factor in the universities' growth into the nation's principal research agencies was decentralization. Decentralizing research in many universities instead of centralizing it in a few national research centers guaranteed a dispersed, competitive scientific community. The existence of many universities, all independent of each other and of the federal government, meant that no governmental or other centralized agency could control science, set limits, determine national priorities, or establish orthodoxies. Instead, scientists were free to follow their own system of values, to choose the problems they wanted to investigate, and to reward those among them whose work they regarded most highly.

What scientists wanted to do and how they evaluated scientific work have long been influenced by the tendency of scientists to think of themselves as an international community. Because the persons whose judgments count most are likely to live in many places, communication is as rapid and extensive as scientists can make it. Thus American scientists of the past century were reading European as well as American scientific journals and books and were communicating by letter with their colleagues abroad and at home. Darwin's *Origin of Species* was published in London on November 24, 1859. By Christmas, readers in America had copies, and by the following May 1, Appleton's in New York had sold 1,750 copies of an American edition, which included a number of minor corrections and the first version of Darwin's historical introduction (Dupree, 1959, pp. 267-272).

Decentralization, independence of external control, extensive international communication, and a reward system that depended upon the esteem of one's scientific peers throughout the world meant that scientists both competed with and copied each other. They competed for priority, for being the first to announce a new finding or a new analysis, for taking the next significant step in the advancement of knowledge. They copied each other in working on similar problems that seemed of greatest interest, or for which a new theory, a new discovery, or a new means of investigation created an opportunity that had not been apparent before.

Competition was sometimes deliberately stimulated. Joseph Henry (1848, p. 83) announced that the Smithsonian Institution would offer prizes to stimulate research. International competition was an oratorical theme that was frequently employed to urge Americans to catch up with Europe. Benjamin Peirce (1853, p. xviii) exhorted the AAAS: "Gentlemen, we have come to study our duty as scientific men, and especially as American scientific men. We are to learn the apparent, and not very pleasant paradox, that America cannot keep pace with Europe in Science except by going ahead of her."

Benjamin Gould's AAAS presidential address 16 years later echoed Peirce's theme. Gould (1869, p. 6) paid tribute to the United States' achievements in developing the steamboat, cotton gin, sewing machine, telegraph, steam engine and steam boiler, the telescopes built by Alvan Clark, and other technical products of American ingenuity. He referred to American contributions to political thought and organizational theory. But, alas, he had to point out that American scientific contributions had not kept pace with her achievements in these other areas, or with the scientific contributions of several European nations.

But not all the oratory was devoted to European superiority. There were some American successes to celebrate. Bache (1851, p. lx) exulted: "What a triumph for American science when the 'American method' of observing is adopted at Greenwich!" And he thanked "the illustrious astronomer of Greenwich" for using the name that recognized American priority.

Science (1885) was pleased to quote Sir Lyon Playfair—chemist, member of Parliament, and member of the British Cabinet—in a favorable comparison of American methods of promoting fisheries: "In England there are expensive commissions to visit the coast and question the fishermen; and the fishermen, having only a knowledge of a small area, give the most contradictory and unsatisfactory evidence. 'In America, the questions are put to nature and not to fishermen,'—and the results of the inquiry are therefore far more fruitful."

There were, in truth, some very substantial and internationally recognized American contributions to fundamental science. Joseph Henry's work on electromagnetic induction ranked with Faraday's. Asa Gray's contributions to plant geography and the detailed information he supplied Charles Darwin in their extended correspondence gave major support to Darwin's theory of evolution (Dupree, 1959, p. 262). When Herbert Spencer said the British considered Gray the greatest botanist in the world, even greater than their own Joseph Hooker, that indeed was an accolade (ibid., p. 339).

Americans were making some solid contributions to the world's scientific literature, and they could boast from time to time, but Europe was still number one, and the fact was repeatedly used to spur America to greater efforts. If the record was not as good as the aspiration, it appears that the record could sometimes be doctored to create a better impression in Europe. When the AAAS met in Cleveland in 1853, the city followed the established custom of agreeing to print the proceedings. The result was not at all to the liking of the association's leaders, who bought up and suppressed the Cleveland edition and then published their own. The later, "official" proceedings included many of the papers of the Cleveland version, but left out some and added others. The official selection, Holmfeld (1970, pp. 22–36) concluded, contained those papers which the association's officers thought would make the best impression abroad.

Copying other scientists, unlike competition, was not a topic for speechmaking, but it was perfectly clear that any scientist who wished to make real contributions could learn from his fellow scientists and that if he wished to establish a reputation he must follow the work of others closely enough so that they would appreciate the importance of what he did. The "others" who counted most were the leading scientists throughout the world. As one advised his colleagues, "Let us look to the other physicists, not in our own town, not in our own country, but in the whole world, for the words of praise that are to encourage us, or the words of blame which are to stimulate us to renewed effort" (Rowland, 1883, p. 122).

Competition with one's fellow scientists while seeking their approval was encouraged by the fact that scientists were scattered, not under any central control, and free to work as they chose.

It seems reasonable to speculate that science advanced more broadly than it would have if, in the 1850s or 1860s, scientists had had more power or more wealth at their disposal. They would then probably have created a few major national research institutes or a great national university. Had one or a few national scientific centers towered over the country, research in selected areas would probably have progressed more rapidly than it did under decentralization. The few prestigious centers would have monopolized the ablest scientists and attracted the most promising young men. What they chose to work on would have progressed rapidly. But what they chose not to work on would have been pretty much neglected. Thus it seems probable that under a centralized system progress would have been on a narrower front, but perhaps more rapid along that front. Moreover, concentration in a small number of dominant centers would have raised the danger of greater rigidity, of more scientific orthodoxy and less opportunity for a free market of ideas, and more elation over early "success" and less long-term vitality.

Thus if the objective was to progress as rapidly as possible in selected areas of scientific research, many independent universities probably did not do as well as a few large research institutes would have done. If the proper first objective was to lay a wider base and to build for the future, the universities probably outpaced their hypothetical alternative.

In retrospect, it was probably fortunate for the long-range advancement of science that the national university was always a dream and never a reality.[1] George Washington failed to endow a national university in Washington; the Lazzaroni failed in Albany in the 1850s; and Henry Tappan and the Lazzaroni failed again in New York. Half a century later, some scientists still thought a national university was the best way to use the money Andrew

---

[1] The history of the national university idea from George Washington to 1961 is recounted in Madsen (1966).

Carnegie gave to found the Carnegie Institution of Washington. But by that time a number of people knew better. At the first meeting of the board of trustees, Carnegie demonstrated his wisdom as a philanthropist. "My first idea...," he explained, "was that it might be reserved for me to fulfill one of [George] Washington's dearest wishes—to establish a university in Washington. I gave it careful study... and was forced to the conclusion that if he were with us here today his finely balanced judgment would decide that such, under present conditions, would not be the best use of wealth." The objection Carnegie could not overcome in his own mind was that a national university would tend to weaken existing institutions; his desire "was to cooperate with all kindred institutions, and to establish what would be a source of strength to all of them and not of weakness" (Haskins, 1967, pp. ix–x).

Gilman explained that the objectives of the new Carnegie Institution would be to seek and find men of exceptional talent and aid them in their work; to encourage research by awarding grants to support particularly meritorious proposals; and to provide for the publication of scientific memoirs so that new findings could be widely disseminated. Although Gilman could not "imagine anything like rivalry existing between this institution and any other," the objectives he described were designed to stimulate scientists wherever they might be, to foster intellectual competition, and to raise standards widely. They were not intended to concentrate effort in a powerful institution that might stifle competition (Franklin, 1910, pp. 396–397).

Competition among more or less equal universities is considered by Ben-David (1960, pp. 828–843) to have been the key factor in giving Germany, and later the United States, leadership in medical research. The same processes were at work, and effective, in all scientific fields. In England and France the universities were under tight central control. In Germany and the United States there was no central control. Competition determined the crucial decisions; and these countries "were quicker than France and Britain in the recognition of new disciplines, the creation of specialized scientific jobs and facilities for research. They were also quicker to abandon traditional notions that had lost their usefulness." A centrally controlled system, as in a group of government laboratories, could have been conducive to good scientific work, but there would not have been the constant spur of competition with other laboratories under other auspices, and there would not have been as many independent sources of financial support.²

PURE SCIENCE OR APPLIED? In the early part of the nineteenth century there was an easy partnership between pure and applied science. The distinction was recognized, but most scientists were not overly concerned with it. Some of their work contributed directly to both ends: a larger telescope brought new astronomical knowledge and provided more precise aids to navigation. When their work was primarily directed toward practical ends, often enough they were also adding to pure knowledge, as discoveries made in the course of the geologic surveys amply demonstrated. When their primary motivation was to advance science, it was generally expected that new knowledge would lead to practical use.

The attitudes of the time were nicely exemplified by the first issue of the *American Journal of Science*. The full, florid title was *The American Journal of Science, More Especially of Mineralogy, Geology, and Other Branches of Natural History, Including Also Agriculture and the Ornamental as Well as Useful Arts.* In an editorial explanation of the plan of the new journal, Benjamin Silliman (1819, p. 8), the founder and editor, combined science, the practical arts, and piety in a single harmonious whole: "The whole circle of physics is directly applicable to human wants, and constantly holds out a light to the practical arts; it thus polishes and benefits society, and everywhere demonstrates supreme intelligence, and harmony and beneficence of design in The Creator." Even Silliman's identification of himself was indicative of cultivated nonspecialization; he was "Professor of Chemistry, Mineralogy, etc." and author of a book on travel in the British Isles.

By mid-century such catholicity was going out of style. Scientists were becoming specialists, and the distinction between pure science and its applications had to be sharpened. Some of the leading scientists began consciously trying to enhance the status of pure science and to secure for it both greater resources and greater recognition. This emphasis was partly a reaction against the fear of being overshadowed by the engineers and inventors whose telegraph, railroads, and other new machines were of great

---

² The correspondence in *Science* (1902) concerning the use of the Carnegie money included a warning from Hugo Munsterberg: "Every cent from Washington which disburdens the local officials is an opiate for this feeling of responsibility."

popular interest and commercial significance. The emphasis was also an expression of the sincere conviction that a more thorough understanding of physical principles was, in the long run, the most effective road to developments of practical use. And, finally, the emphasis on pure science was an effort to secure better opportunities for the kind of work that scientists found most interesting.

Joseph Henry's statement that the proper course for scientists was to pour fresh material on the apex of the pyramid of science, and thus broaden the base, represented both a desire to raise the scientific edifice to new heights and the expectation that society as a whole would profit more from such an endeavor than from work aimed directly at some of the practical problems lying around the base (Miller, 1970, p. 9). Similar ideas were expressed by Benjamin A. Gould in his AAAS presidential address in 1869 and by other scientists from a variety of other platforms.

As part of the campaign to enhance the status of pure science, Joseph Henry and a committee of scientists brought John Tyndall to the United States in 1872 for a lecture tour. Tyndall was Faraday's long-time associate and successor as director of the Royal Institution, the oldest research laboratory in England. He was famed as a scientist and even more as a highly skillful lecturer and popularizer of science. For his American tour, Tyndall decided to speak on the physics and optics of light, a topic he knew would interest popular audiences and one that he could illustrate with some of the spectacular demonstrations for which Royal Institution lectures had always been famous. After thus arousing the interests of his audiences, Tyndall devoted part of the final lecture in each city to arguing the case for pure research. "Keep your eye upon the originator of knowledge," he told his listeners. "Give him the freedom necessary for his researches, not overloading him either with the duties of tuition or of administration, not demanding from him so-called practical results—above all things, avoid that question which ignorance so often addresses to genius, 'What is the use of your work?'" (ibid., p. 121). The plea was sincere, and as a further aid to American science, Tyndall left the $13,000 of proceeds from lectures as a fellowship fund for American students who wished to go to Europe for graduate work in physics.

Tyndall's choice of words in the passage, "the question which ignorance so often addresses to genius," was revealing evidence of the tendency of some of the champions of pure research to think of themselves as on a higher plane than those lesser men who worked on the applications of science. Henry Rowland, professor of physics at Johns Hopkins, made it unmistakably clear that he belonged in this camp in an address entitled "A Plea for Pure Science" which he gave at the 1883 meeting of the AAAS. With unabashed arrogance, Rowland (1883, p. 106) told his audience:

American science is a thing of the future, and not of the present or past, and the proper course of one in my position is to consider what must be done to create a science of physics in this country, rather than to call telegraphs, electric lights, and such conveniences by the name of science. I do not wish to underrate the value of all these things; the progress of the world depends on them, and he is to be honored who cultivates them successfully. So also the cook who invents a new and palatable dish for the table benefits the world to a certain degree; yet we do not dignify him by the name of a chemist. And yet it is not an uncommon thing, especially in American newspapers, to have the *applications* of science confounded with pure science; and some obscure American who steals the ideas of some great mind of the past, and enriches himself by the application of the same idea to domestic uses, is often lauded above the great originator of the idea, who might have worked out hundreds of such applications, had his mind possessed the necessary element of vulgarity.

Later in the same address, Rowland hammered home the point:

For a man to occupy the professor's chair in a prominent college, and, by his energy and ability in the commercial application of science, stand before the local community as a newspaper exponent of his science, is a disgrace both to him and his college. . . .
  I do not wish to be misunderstood in this matter. It is no disgrace to make money by invention, or otherwise, or to do commercial scientific work under some circumstances; but let pure science be the aim of those in the chairs of professors.

Such a charge could be given only to university professors, and not even to all of them. Professors in the agricultural and mechanical departments of the land-grant institutions had neither the right nor, in many cases, the wish to separate themselves from applied science, nor did the scientists in such agencies as the Coast Survey. But scientists in the old colleges and in the graduate divisions of universities could, and often did, adopt the position Rowland advocated.

Their ability to take this position was made easier by the fact that on their own or on other campuses there were other scientists who were concerned with agriculture, engineering, and other applied fields. Their presence gave students an option. Those who preferred could go to the professional schools. Those whose interests were in pure science could enroll in the graduate school.

This option, on the same campuses, was one of the ways in which the developing American university differed from universities in Germany. As a consequence of this difference, as Ben-David (1968–69, p. 8) has summarized, "The idea that research and teaching at the graduate university must not be determined by anything except the state of science and the creativity of the professor was put into effect much more radically than in Germany."

Professors and students who were single-mindedly committed to pure science supported and reinforced each other as their numbers increased.[3] As Rowland's students went out from Johns Hopkins, and as the students of like-minded professors at Chicago and elsewhere went out from their universities, many of them carried to their new posts the distinction between the higher pure science in which they were interested and the less praiseworthy applications which they gladly left to anyone else who cared to bother with such mundane matters. The invidious distinction they created is still causing trouble.

It seems altogether unlikely that the "prestige gap" between pure and applied science would be so sharp, or perhaps even exist, if the Coast Survey—to take the best example of a mid-nineteenth century government agency—instead of Johns Hopkins had been the model to follow. The Coast Survey was a practical agency; its purpose was to determine latitude and longitude precisely, to make accurate maps, and to develop improved aids for land and sea travel. It was also a research agency; to do its job well it had to learn more of astronomy, geophysics, and the physical environment generally. Alexander Dallas Bache and his colleagues understood fully the difference between pure science and its applications, but

---

[3] Fifty years ago, in the years just prior to 1921, 12 leading universities in the United States had combined totals of 1,893 scholarships and fellowships for graduate students in the humanities and arts, 1,299 in pure sciences, and 196 in applied science. Chicago, Harvard, Johns Hopkins, Pennsylvania, and Stanford (despite early emphasis on practical matters) offered a total of only three fellowships in applied science. Columbia offered six, and California, Cornell, Illinois, Michigan, Wisconsin, and Yale offered more than twenty each, but every one of these universities had substantially more fellowships for students of pure science than for students of applied science (Hall & West, 1922, pp. 424–428).

they took it for granted that in their work the two should go forward together. They knew that careful scientific work was required if one was to learn anything significant about the physical environment. Consequently, even

> routine technical work had to have an accompanying research component. . . . [Moreover,] both the routine work and the research were ideally related to a theory in mathematical form — the theory giving direction to the research and the routine work, while the resulting data confirmed, extended, or refuted the theory. Mapping the lands and the oceans, applications to civil works, and the various uses of astronomy and terrestrial magnetism as aids to travelers conformed to this position on the relations of theory and practice. . . . In the world of the Coast Survey, applications were preceded, accompanied, and followed by basic research (Reingold, 1970, p. 174).

As a consequence of this attitude, the Coast Survey made both practical and theoretical contributions and in the middle of the last century had an international reputation as an excellent scientific agency. It was a government agency, responsible to Congress and the public, but it was also responsible to the scientific community, for both politicians and scientists kept watch over what it did.

Even when pure research and applied research are conducted in the same organization there is likely to be tension between practical interests and pure-science interests. Bache, a respected scientist and an astute administrator, kept these competing interests in good balance. Lacking such direction, a government research agency can get into serious difficulties with political leaders, the scientific community, or both. The California State Geological Survey will serve as an example (Nash, 1963, pp. 217–223).

In 1860, the 10-year-old state of California organized a survey to map the state; to study its geology, paleontology, and geologic resources (gold worth $0.5 billion had already been recovered, and oil deposits were hoped for); and to study the state's botany and zoology. Selected to head the survey was Josiah Whitney, for whom Mt. Whitney was named. Whitney had worked on the surveys of Michigan and Illinois and had also been state chemist for Iowa and an industrial consultant on mining. Despite his governmental and practical experience, Whitney's interests were in pure science; he belonged in a university, and when he left California, he joined the Harvard faculty.

Whitney's first task for the California survey, as he defined his own job, was to conduct a detailed exploration of the geologic structure of the state, a task he expected would require 10 years. That completed, he would then examine promising looking areas for commercial resources and information of practical value. He made good progress for five years before legislative impatience caught up with him. The legislators wanted practical results, and Whitney's first publication, which came in 1864 and was on fossils, gave them no encouragement. Other irritations accumulated; miners and farmers became increasingly dissatisfied; and after a few more years the Legislature cut off funds for the survey.

The survey resulted in many significant scientific contributions. Yet it was a failure. It provided neither the practical information the state wanted nor a continuing base for obtaining the scientific information that was Whitney's primary interest.

Benjamin Silliman (1842, pp. 217–250) had warned against such fiascoes. A quarter of a century earlier he had advised geologists to make frequent reports to their legislators and to the public in order to sustain public interest in what was of necessity "a long continued labor." If they lost public confidence, "there might be danger that the necessary annual appropriations of money would be withheld, and that thus an important enterprise might be defeated."

Bache so managed the Coast Survey that it contributed to both pure and applied science. Whitney so managed the California survey that after a brief period it contributed to neither. After Bache's death, under a different director and in a different political climate, the Coast Survey almost met the fate of the California survey. Bache succeeded, and there have been other excellently managed and productive scientific agencies within the government, but for most of the past century—until recently—it has been easier to maintain a university laboratory at a high scientific level than to maintain a government laboratory at such a level. The manager of a government laboratory had to satisfy both politicians and scientists. The manager of a university laboratory was fairly well insulated from politicians and could concentrate on gaining and keeping the respect of scientists.

It is perhaps idle to speculate on the possibility that government agencies rather than universities might now be the nation's major scientific resources. Neither in the past century nor in this one have most scientists or politicians thought they should be. Yet the contrast between the Coast Survey and Johns Hopkins University as models for later developments helps to indicate some of the consequences of the fact that it was the university that was chosen.

Emphasis on pure science, naturally enough, has been advantageous for pure science. The university system, with scientists in control of scientific work, aided by large amounts of federal money in the past 25 years, has brought the United States acknowledged scientific leadership among the nations of the world. It is highly doubtful that the status would be as high had most of the scientific activity of the past 25 to 50 years been carried out in government laboratories. At the same time, the schism between pure science and applied science is probably greater than it would be had the Coast Survey been the model that was followed.

Moreover, under university auspices, science has lost some of the public understanding and public support it might otherwise have had. Legislators and the public have become less well informed and more skeptical of the esoteric studies carried out by pure scientists than of the more immediately useful research of medical centers, industry, and other agencies that have worked on problems of obvious relevance to public concerns.

When on occasion scientists rally to the nation's needs in a large and obvious fashion as they did during World War II, or when individual scientists solve some problem of great public concern as Jonas Salk did in developing a vaccine for poliomyelitis, they became public heroes. On the other hand, when the nation becomes aroused over pollution or other environmental dangers, scientists are often made the scapegoats.

The fact that the university has been the location of so much of the nation's basic research has made it less necessary for scientists to explain and justify their work to the public, has enabled them to concentrate on science, and has encouraged the rapid advancement of abstract science. Had the Coast Survey instead of Johns Hopkins been the national model, pure science would probably not have advanced as rapidly, but public understanding of science and public support for scientific work would probably be more widespread and more dependable.

The heavy emphasis (overemphasis?) on pure science was not the desire of any of the major sponsors of scientific work in the nineteenth century. It was not a characteristic of government laboratories. Walter R. Johnson's memorial to Congress and some of the other proposals for special research institutes called for work on practical matters. The Dudley Observatory in Albany and, to a lesser extent, the Cincinnati Observatory ran afoul of their public sponsors for not paying sufficient attention to public interests. The Lawrence Scientific School at Harvard and the Sheffield Scientific School at Yale were originally intended to aid industry and agriculture. The land-grant colleges and their associated research stations had a practical orientation by design. Two of the outstanding new universities, Cornell and Stanford, started off with considerable emphasis on practical subjects, and when G. Stanley Hall tried to make Clark University a purely graduate institution he lost the confidence and financial support of the founder. Even at Johns Hopkins and Chicago, presidents Gilman and Harper expected that considerable attention would be paid to problems of current public concern.

In setting the goals for Johns Hopkins, Gilman had both pure and applied science in mind, but at that stage in university development, he believed it was pure science that required special defense: "Remote utility is quite as worthy to be thought of as immediate advantage. These ventures are not always most sagacious that expect a return on the morrow. It sometimes pays to send our argosies across the seas; to make investments with an eye to slow but sure returns. So it is always in the promotion of science" (Cordasco, 1960, p. 81).

Pure science was important, but should not overwhelm other scientific concerns. Although the medical school was not opened until 17 years later, in 1893, Gilman was planning for it from the beginning and devoted part of his inaugural address to an account of those plans (Franklin, 1910, pp. 245–247). Engineering, too, was important, for Gilman "believed in the direct application of university teaching and research to the needs of everyday community life (Ryan, 1939, p. 30). Even more broadly, and idealistically, in his inaugural address he mentioned some of the general social benefits to be expected: "less misery among the poor, less ignorance in schools, less bigotry in the temple, less suffering in the hospital, less fraud in business, less folly in politics" (ibid.). Gilman's faith in the widely ramifying utility of the work that would be done at Johns Hopkins may have been unduly idealistic, but the intent was clear.

These views, however, were personal views, not commands to the faculty. Gilman would issue no commands, for he feared rigidity, encouraged spontaneity and initiative, and expected the faculty members to be responsible men who would guide and direct their own work.

At the University of Chicago, William Rainey Harper expressed similar views and followed a similar course. At the outset, there were no engineering or other technological departments at Chicago. They could come later, for in the beginning, Harper explained, "It seemed upon the whole wise to devote the entire energy of the institution in scientific lines to departments of pure science, with the purpose of establishing these upon a strong foundation. This work being finished, there would be ample opportunity for the other work, and the other work would be all the stronger when it came, because of the earlier and more stable foundation of pure science" (ibid., p. 123). More generally, Harper proclaimed, the university should be "an agency recognized by the people for resolving the problems of civilization . . . [one which helps] to guide the people in the decision of questions which from time to time confront them" (ibid., p. 123).

These were Harper's views, and Harper was a strong president, but not even strong presidents can both control professors and give them complete freedom, and Harper was even more insistent than Gilman on the principle of academic freedom. His highest purpose for the University of Chicago was to discover truth; to discover truth required, along with great men and good equipment, "absolute freedom from interference of any kind" (ibid., p. 123).

Giving the professors freedom really meant putting them in charge. Giving them able students, excellent equipment, scholarly colleagues, and freedom to seek the truth as they saw fit was exactly the right prescription to encourage them to concentrate on pure science. Given the nature of scientific values and the basis for scientific reputations, no other outcome could be expected.

Emphasis on pure science and the prestige accorded such work by many scientists have influenced nonacademic as well as academic values and attitudes. Applied science is usually the primary objective of governmental and industrial laboratories, but if these laboratories also make contributions to pure science—as the Naval Research Laboratory, the Bell Telephone Laboratories, and others have done—their reputations are greatly enhanced. Receipt of a Nobel prize is as much a cause for jubilation at the Bell Telephone Laboratories as it is at the University of Chicago. The directors of some industrial laboratories have reported that they can recruit abler staff members by offering permission to use laboratory facilities and to devote some working time to individually chosen problems. With such permission, the recruit knows he will have an opportunity to make individual contributions to the body of scientific knowledge. Interestingly, many industrial scientists do not take full advantage of these privileges; they quickly become too interested in the applied problems on which they are working. Nevertheless, the fact that the promise is effective in recruitment indicates the extent to which the value system of the pure scientists has pervaded the whole scientific community.

The emphasis of university graduate schools on pure science has also had the effect of requiring the establishment of a number of separate research institutes. Graduate schools have sometimes been inhospitable to applied research, and academic specialization often makes it difficult to work on problems that require the close cooperation of scientists from several different disciplines. As a consequence of these academic barriers, special institutes have been established for research on military, social, medical, or environmental problems. Some of these institutes, like the prototypical agricultural experiment stations, have been attached to universities. Others have been organized under other auspices or as independent entities.

The need to create these institutes indicates how fully Rowland and other purists succeeded in persuading "those in the chairs of professors" to concentrate on pure science. A hundred years ago, their problem was to secure better opportunities for men interested in pure science. They succeeded so well that now a major organizational problem for universities is to arrange for better opportunities for scientists who want to work on practical problems of great social concern, or for representatives of several different disciplines who want to pool their talents in an integrated study of a large complex problem.

A VIEW FROM ABROAD Was primary location in the university rather than in government laboratories or other separate institutions a good choice? Of course there is no simple answer. It was good for science. It was good for the development of great scientific competence not only at Johns Hopkins and Chicago but at other universities that gave their faculty members comparable freedom and opportunity. In the judgment of most scientists—including many in engineering, medicine, and other applied areas—in the long run it has also resulted in more effective applications of science than would have resulted from narrow frontal attacks by separate institutions on the practical problems that seemed important at any particular time.

Foreign observers of scientific and educational affairs may be able to see the faults and virtues of the American system more clearly than can Americans. To get a clear view of any system it is often necessary to go outside that system. In the middle 1960s, when Europeans were becoming increasingly worried about the "technology gap" that separated their countries from North America, the Organization for Economic Cooperation and Development asked Joseph Ben-David, professor of sociology at the Hebrew University of Jerusalem and an internationally recognized authority on the evolution and development of universities, to give advice on how European universities and European management of research might be improved. Ben-David's (1968) recommendations will be summarized later, but here it is relevant to give his analysis of the reason for the scientific and technological gap between the United States and Western Europe. In addition to obvious differences in the numbers of people involved and the amounts of money spent, and the fact that the United States is a unified country with a common language while Western Europe is crisscrossed by political boundaries and linguistic differences, Ben-David concluded that technological superiority was based on scientific superiority, American scientific progress was in no small measure due to the intimate association of basic research with higher education, and the difference between American and European scientific achievement was of much longer standing than had been generally recognized.

A listing of the major inventions and discoveries of modern times shows that the United States was responsible for 37 percent of those that appeared between 1880 and 1899; 54 percent between 1930 and 1939; and 88 percent between 1940 and 1949. There is no surprise in these figures; American industrial and technological achievements were, after all, the cause of European concern over the technology gap. Ben-David went on to analyze the sources of original ideas as well as the countries in which those ideas received effective commercial development. For this purpose he used the 50 major industrial inventions of the twentieth century as judged by three British authors in 1958 (Jewkes, Sawes, & Stillerman). In 32 of these 50 cases, industrial development took place in one country, and in 22 of the 32 cases the United States was the country. In the remaining 18 cases, two or more countries shared responsibility for the development, and the United States was involved in 16 of these cases. Thus in terms of industrial development, the United States was a partner in 16 and the sole exploiter in 22 of the 50 major inventions of the period.

As for the original ideas which lay behind these industrial developments, the United States was wholly responsible in 22 of the 33 cases in which the idea was initiated in a single country and was a partner in 13 of the 17 situations in which two or more countries participated. Thus United States scientists and engineers were wholly or partly responsible for the basic ideas which lay behind 35 of the 50 major industrial inventions of the first half of the twentieth century.

But all this, one can object, concerns applied science and industry, where everyone recognizes that American achievement has been high. The basic policies of support for applied research and development in the United States have been essentially the same as those used to support basic research: decentralization and competition. In industry, as in the universities, these policies have had a stimulating effect in helping to produce rapid progress across a broad front. In 1967, the House of Representatives Committee on Science and Astronautics brought together a group of American and European leaders of science policy for a discussion of government, science, and international policy.[4] Two of the participants who had long been involved in the planning and directing of research and had frequently served as advisers on science policy to their own governments and to international organizations specifically compared the decentralized American system with the more centralized system of European countries. H. W. Julius, director of the Central Organization for Applied Scientific Research in the Netherlands, called the American system the diametric opposite of the Dutch system and gave the American system of government contracting for research with industry the credit for raising the research capacity of industry and helping to create "the unprecedented scientific leadership of your nation." Robert Major, director and principal founder of the Royal Norwegian Institute

---

[4] See U.S. House of Representatives, Committee on Science and Astronautics (1967). Danhof (1968, chap. 10) cites this publication and Walsh (1967, p. 1655) gives a somewhat more extended appraisal of the system of contracting for research and development.

for Scientific and Industrial Research, said that that institute had operated primarily through its own research laboratories and that he had recommended to the Norwegian government that the institute and the technical agencies of the Norwegian government be authorized to write research and development contracts with Norwegian industrial firms in order to strengthen their competitiveness in fields in which national production should be encouraged.

Also in 1967, P. M. S. Blackett, then president of the Royal Society, told the Parliamentary and Scientific Committee of the British House of Commons that he had gradually come to the conclusion that Great Britain had made a mistake in the years following World War II in retaining within government so much of its military and atomic energy research. The United States had followed the more productive course of contracting much of its research and development with industry. As one result of this difference, he concluded, "Few would now doubt that the U. S. A. has gained greatly from the resulting strengthening and building up of very strong firms, and that Britain has lost relatively" (Walsh, 1967, p. 1655).

In the United States, since World War II, the policy of contracting has been followed as extensively for basic research as for applied research and development. In fact basic and applied research have often been pursued together. In basic research as in applied research and development, decentralization and contracting out have stimulated and built up national scientific capacity to the point that led Ben-David to conclude, "It is impossible to say whether the gap is greater, smaller, or the same in fundamental as in applied research. But it is certainly true that it . . . exists over the whole field of science and at all levels and types of research" (Ben-David, 1968, p. 27).

Reputations always follow along after the fact, and the current American reputation began to be earned while Europe was still generally considered the world's leading center of scientific progress. Again, Ben-David (ibid., p. 26) summarizes:

The broad outlines of the situation are clear: in the 1940's, with a delay of 3–4 decades, there emerged similar differences in fundamental science between the United States and the major Western European countries as had existed in applied research and development even before World War I. This gap did not occur as the result of the cataclysmic events of Nazism and war, since the trend had been unmistakable even early in the century. By 1910, and certainly by 1920, the United States system of scientific research had been growing at a more even and rapid rate than that of the European countries. Europe, especially Germany, still had most of the excellence, as evidenced by the Nobel prizes and by the general consensus of the scientific community, until the early 1920's. But much of this had been living on capital accumulated in the pre-World War I period. The majority of the great European scientists between the wars had been mature people by 1910 or 1920, and the fields where European scientific production surpassed the American were the more mature parts of fundamental science.

These European views agree with the prevailing American view: decentralization and competition have a positive, stimulating effect on scientific research and development. For industrial research these policies are part of a free enterprise system. For basic research, they were not adopted because they were expected to have a stimulating effect; rather, they resulted from the nature of the American system of higher education and the fact that the university turned out to be the principal home of science. The university gave scientists freedom to explore ideas to their limits in order to find their flaws or their new implications. It provided mutual stimulation of teachers and inquiring students, with the resulting need to clarify ideas, explain reasons and objectives, and improve methods. It offered a kind of benign anarchy in which merit could be quickly recognized. And always, after about 1880, there were scientists in a number of universities, and scientists in other institutions as well, competing with and challenging each other, sometimes verifying another's new findings and sometimes demonstrating error. These are conditions that are conducive to broad and rapid progress and to intellectual creativity. These conditions sometimes exist in other institutions, but it is in the university that they are most often found, and it is the university that has been the home of most of the creative scientists and the scene of most of the progress in basic science of the past hundred years.

6. Influences on Higher Education

While the university was influencing the development of science, science was also influencing the development of the university. The major changes in higher education were part of the comprehensive social, political, scientific, technological, and educational movements that turned the nineteenth century into the twentieth. But science played a major role in transforming the old college into the modern university and is still a prime force in determining its current characteristics. The effects of rapid developments in science on higher education can be considered under four headings:

1. Breakup of the old college tradition and its integrative rationale, and the development of graduate programs, including responsibility for public service and work on a variety of practical problems

2. Paving of the way for similar changes in the humanities, the social sciences, and other fields of specialization

3. Institutional fragmentation and the dispersal of power

4. Interinstitutional competition which, combined with items 2 and 3 above, created the complex, multipurpose university which dominates the whole of higher education in the United States

BREAKUP OF THE COLLEGE TRADITION AND RATIONALE

The classical college curriculum could not withstand the impact of growing knowledge and increased interest in science. Publication of Darwin's *Origin of Species* was a landmark in the process, for that book was both the scientific high point of the nineteenth century and in the minds of many of its readers, the most direct challenge science had presented to some of the tenets of organized religion.[1] Neither skeptic nor supporter could disregard *Origin of*

---

[1] Dupree (1959) includes a good discussion of the impact of *Origin of Species* on the religious thinking of scientists.

Species. James McCosh, Princeton's conservative president, admitted that the faculty simply could not prevent students from reading Darwin, Huxley, Spencer, or Tyndall—the new scientific interpreters of man's place in the world (Veysey, 1965, p. 50).

Darwin's book was the most inescapable single example of the growing pressure of science on established thought, yet at the same time it was but an example of the fact that the curriculum had fallen behind advancing knowledge and widening interests. More and more professors and students wanted to explore beyond the restricting boundaries of the standard classical curriculum.

The Lawrence Scientific School at Harvard and the Sheffield Scientific School at Yale were early, but grudging, responses to this demand. Although both colleges kept their new scientific schools at arm's length, the fact that they were authorized at all was an admission that the old, simple, coherent rationale, based largely on religion, emphasizing mental discipline, and intended primarily to prepare young men for the ministry, law, or cultivated leadership of government and society, was no longer sufficient. The development of graduate programs at Johns Hopkins and elsewhere, the Morrill Land-Grant Act, the new agricultural experiment stations, the influence of Cornell with its insistence that one field of study was as worthy as any other, adoption of the elective system at Harvard—all these were also evidence that the old college curriculum was doomed.

Changes in the curriculum required changes in faculty hiring practices. Science moves ineluctably toward specialization. As knowledge advances, further progress can be made only by narrowing one's focus to work on a part of the whole advancing front. True, the greatest advances are made by such giants as Darwin and Einstein who develop a grand new synthesis and who provide a new understanding of a large range of scientific facts and problems. But giants are few. Most scientists who want to make progress must specialize. Therefore, during the nineteenth century, natural scientists were giving way to geologists, botanists, and zoologists, while natural philosophy was breaking up into physics, chemistry, and other specialties.

Silliman's appointment as professor of chemistry at Yale in 1802 was an appointment of the old style. His credentials were religious orthodoxy, an education at Yale College, and the confidence of the college authorities that he would fit well into the Yale milieu. The fact that he had been educated in law instead of science was a deficiency that could be quickly repaired by a few months of study in Philadelphia and Europe.

A century later, no university would have offered the professorship of chemistry to a 22-year-old lawyer. Long before the century ended, professors in science were being selected because of their particular competence in botany, physics, agricultural chemistry, or some other specialty.

The intellectual challenges to the old curriculum, the development of new programs, expansion upward to the graduate level, insistence on specialized qualifications for appointment—scientists were in the vanguard of all these changes. The changes were partly results of scientists' direct efforts, but not entirely, for they had strong supporters in high places. Henry Tappan at the University of Michigan, Daniel Coit Gilman at Johns Hopkins, G. Stanley Hall at Clark, and William Rainey Harper at Chicago have all been cited. There were others whose influence was wide, notably Charles W. Eliot, who started Harvard's graduate department in 1872, three years after he assumed the presidency and before Johns Hopkins opened. Although Eliot later credited Johns Hopkins with forcing Harvard to improve its graduate program (Franklin, 1910, pp. 389–390), Harvard itself became an inspiration to other universities, the institution that Richard Hofstadter called the "bellwether of the university movement" (Hofstadter & Hardy, 1952, p. 30).

Trustees also helped. The farsighted men to whom Johns Hopkins entrusted his fortune were active leaders in planning the university that bore his name. A decade earlier, a conservative majority of the trustees of Columbia refused to appoint Wolcott Gibbs as professor of chemistry, primarily because Gibbs was a Unitarian. The board was made up mostly of Episcopalians and included six ministers, several of whom declared that under no circumstances would they vote for the appointment of any Unitarian—all this despite a New York (state) law which forbade any religious test in the selection of a college president or professor.[2]

---

[2] Gibbs came out of the Columbia affair without loss. Despite his Unitarianism, and with much help from the Lazzaroni, he was shortly appointed to the Rumford professorship in the Lawrence Scientific School at Harvard to succeed Eben Horsford, who had left to manage his chemical works. Gibbs's unsuccessful competitor for the Rumford professorship was the young Charles W. Eliot, who was already at Harvard and hoped to be promoted. In the long run Eliot did not lose either. He left to go to the Massachusetts Institute of Technology but returned to Harvard as president six years later. See Hofstadter & Smith (1961, pp. 440–464).

The liberal members of the Columbia board lost on the Gibbs appointment, but the loss intensified their resolution to overthrow what they considered old-fogyism. When Frederick A. P. Barnard became president a few months later they had a progressive ally to help bring reform. Barnard had not been able to start graduate work at the University of Mississippi. and the University of the South had fallen casualty to the Civil War, but at Columbia he succeeded. The School of Mines began its graduate program in 1864 and soon thereafter offered the Ph.D. In 1880, John W. Burgess organized the School of Political Science that became the model for the later development of other graduate programs at Columbia.

The Barnards, Eliots, Gilmans, and other presidents could help lead the way. The trustees could influence matters by their selection of professors and by their use of funds. But mostly it was, and had to be, the professors who developed graduate programs and emphasized the importance of original research as the highest duty of the university scholar.

Even reluctant presidents could not permanently resist such pressure. Graduate work was not one of Andrew White's highest priorities at Cornell, and he was ambivalent about science, but Cornell became one of the leading research and graduate universities. At Princeton, the conservative James McCosh accepted the necessity of establishing a scientific school to keep up with Harvard and Yale. All he could do was to insist that the students be required to take enough philosophy to neutralize their contamination by science (Veysey, 1965, pp. 49–50). Other presidents, far from trying to stem the tide, left their presidencies in order to devote all their time to science. John M. Coulter, who had left the presidency of Indiana University to become president of Lake Forest University, resigned in 1896 to become professor and head of the department of botany at the University of Chicago. One of his colleagues was Thomas C. Chamberlin, who had resigned the presidency of the University of Wisconsin four years earlier to accept the professorship of geology at Chicago.

The growing army of men such as Henry Rowland and his colleagues at Johns Hopkins; Coulter, Chamberlin, and others at Chicago; and still others in other places were forceful, able, respected men, University presidents and trustees had to do as well as they could in providing them with opportunities, facilities, and support, both because the scientists could make a good case for the work they wanted to do and because in the competition of educational expansion other universities were always looking for established scientific leaders and promising beginners.

PAVING THE WAY FOR OTHER FIELDS

Science led the way in most of the changes that formed the modern university. As changes were made in the scientific departments, corresponding changes followed in other areas. The granting of the Ph.D. degree is an early example. The first American doctorates were awarded by the Sheffield Scientific School at Yale in 1861. Fourteen of the twenty awarded in the next decade were in science. At Johns Hopkins, nearly 60 percent of the doctorates awarded in the first nine years were in the physical and biological sciences and mathematics. The rest were spread over a range of social science, history, philology, and philosophy, and dissertations were written by such notables as John Dewey ("The Psychology of Kant") and Woodrow Wilson ("Congressional Government").[3]

As graduate work expanded, other fields began to award the Ph.D. The percentage of the total that went to young scientists necessarily declined, even though the actual number was increasing. From 1911 through 1945 the physical and biological sciences accounted for a fairly steady 45 percent of the total (Wolfle, 1954, p. 298). By 1970, the proportion was down to 30 percent.[4]

The sciences also led the way in gaining financial support from the federal government. The partnership that started in agriculture in the latter half of the nineteenth century spread through the rest of the sciences, both pure and applied, and then to all other parts of the university.

In recent years this trend has accelerated. The NSF began early in the 1950s to award grants in support of research in the natural sciences. Later social science was added to the list of eligible areas, first rather gingerly, with careful definition of what kind of work in social science could be considered "scientific," and then more boldly, even into the initially disbarred field of political science. After the NSF had been in operation for a dozen years, Congress created a companion organization, the National Foundation on the Arts and Humanities, to support research and creative work in these fields.

[3] Cordasco (1960) lists all Johns Hopkins Ph.D.'s and their dissertation titles for the first nine years.

[4] The U.S. Office of Education and the Office of Scientific Personnel of the National Research Council publish annual totals, by field, of Ph.D. degrees conferred.

Science was also first in receiving federal support for graduate students. At the end of World War II the Atomic Energy Commission (AEC) and later the NSF instituted national, competitive fellowships for students who wished to work for the doctorate in one of the sciences. The National Institutes of Health (NIH) developed traineeship programs in health fields. Both agencies broadened their programs to include candidates in psychology and some of the social sciences. Still later, following the shock of seeing the first Russian satellite in orbit, Congress adopted the National Defense Education Act of 1958, which provided fellowships for graduate students in essentially all fields in which college and university teachers were needed.

After the argument that federal support of education would be unconstitutional had been broken down by the need to improve agricultural education, that argument had little strength to withstand the needs of other fields, except religion. After the principle was established that the federal government could use private institutions to help meet national needs in scientific areas, the principle could be extended to other areas.[5]

Science did not merely set patterns for other fields; scientists often actively helped make sure those patterns were copied. Several were leading participants in developing plans for the National Foundation on the Arts and Humanities. Earlier, the President's Science Advisory Committee had declared it essential to support artistic, literary, and other scholarly activities.

During the congressional debates over the proposal to establish the NSF there was much discussion about including or excluding the social sciences. Most scientists favored including them (Wolfle, 1947, p. 531), but some of the politically shrewd scientific leaders cautioned against including the social sciences at the start. The debate was resolved by an agreement that the foundation would not be instructed to include the social sciences, but might do so later when such a broadening of scope became desirable. Within a few years the social sciences gained an established place in NSF programs, and Congress later urged the NSF to devote greater attention to social sciences and social problems.

In general, the working strategy has usually been to start a new line of development with the most solidly established areas of sci-

---

[5] Babbidge & Rosenzweig (1962) gives a good account of the development of relationships between higher education and the federal government.

ence and those which have obviously led to developments of great practical benefit. Having thus started a new program, the limits can later be extended to include psychology, the social sciences, the humanities, and sometimes even the fine arts. From the first successful efforts to develop graduate education in the United States to the appropriation of massive federal support for university work, science has been the pacemaker for the other areas.

FRAGMENTA-TION AND THE DISPERSAL OF POWER

At the same time that science was helping to build up the university, four forces, all wholly or largely related to science, tended to fragment the university and to decrease its power to control its own development.

1 The first was scientific specialization. As scientists specialized and leading scientists emphasized pure science, the men to whom they looked for inspiration and approval or for criticism and correction were other scientists in the same specialties. In this respect, what was true of scientists became true of other specialists. The judgments that counted most were the judgments of fellow specialists. When professors from all disciplines came together in 1915 to organize the American Association of University Professors (AAUP), it was their intent to increase faculty power and to weaken institutional authority. They made it crystal clear that their primary allegiance was to their professional groups and not to their individual institutions. The original AAUP Committee on Academic Freedom and Academic Tenure (1915, pp. 17–43) proclaimed that "the responsibility of the university teacher is primarily to the public itself, and to the judgment of his own profession." Later on—in fine print, as it were—the committee acknowledged the existence of some responsibility to the university on whose staff a professor served, but this responsibility was clearly meant to be secondary. If one's first loyalty is to fellow experts, obviously first loyalty cannot go to the college or university at which one is employed, or to higher education as a whole.

2 Closely allied to specialization was a second factor in the devolution of power and the fragmentation of the university: the winning of academic freedom. Progress in science is restricted if any authority other than the internal logic of the science itself decides which facts are "true," which theories are to be accepted, or which hypotheses explored. Here again what is true of the natural sciences is true also of the social sciences, of history, of Biblical exegesis, and of every other area of scholarship. The principle of academic freedom is one on which all scholars agree.

Scientists were by no means alone in the campaign for academic freedom, but they were prominently involved. Seventeen of the twenty-eight members of the original council of the AAUP were natural or social scientists. James

McKeen Cattell, editor of *Science,* was one of the leaders in establishing that new buttress of academic freedom and tenure. John Dewey, a philosopher rather than a scientist, but one of Daniel Coit Gilman's early graduate fellows at Johns Hopkins, was the first president, and John Coulter, who had resigned a university presidency to become professor of botany at Chicago, was the fourth.

The winning of academic freedom established an important principle but, at the same time, the establishment of that principle lessened university unity, for a direct corollary of academic freedom is a weakening of the powers of the administrative officers. One cannot honor the principle of academic freedom and at the same time expect a faculty to march in harmony toward the institutional goals of the university. "When a self-governing society grows large," as Eric Ashby (1967*b,* p. 50) has put it, "it either becomes hierarchical, as the Roman Catholic Church has, or it becomes anarchical. Universities have taken the second course."

Freedom meant that the professors were going to act as individualists, that there was little anyone could do to make them agree, and that part of the power that had earlier been centered in the president was spread thinly over the faculty. Faculties have used this power to defend the right of any member to act as an individualist, but rarely to discipline a member whose individualism has gone so far as to infringe on the rights of others or damage the institution as a whole.

Academicians—scientists as well as others—have been reasonably content with this state of affairs. The AAUP general secretary has defended the association's "relative inaction" on matters of professorial ethics and said that ethical problems should be handled by individual universities (Davis, 1970, p. 357). The association, understandably, has been much more zealous in enforcing the freedom clauses than the responsibility clauses contained in its 1940 *Statement of Principles on Academic Freedom and Tenure.*

3 The third force that was fragmenting the university and shifting power away from its central administration was the development of programs of practical utility. This movement started with science. The Lawrence and Sheffield Scientific Schools and the land-grant colleges were early examples. And when Ezra Cornell and Andrew White started Cornell University, they extended the movement to all areas; any subject was to be the equal of any other.[6] Soon one could find instruction in nearly any subject, not only at Cornell but at most universities. Up to the time of the

---

[6] So literally was this intention interpreted in some quarters that a teamster from a Western state came to Cornell to learn to read. President White (1907, vol. 1, p. 345) ruefully reported that "on being told that the public school in his own district was the place for that, he [the teamster] was very indignant, and quoted Mr. Cornell's words, 'I would found an institution where any person can find instruction in any study.'"

Civil War, only the West Point Military Academy and Rensselaer Polytechnic Institute trained engineers, but soon engineering departments became common. Agriculture was added; departments of pedagogy proliferated. Then followed schools of business and departments of domestic science, physical education, oral hygiene, urban planning, and others. And in most cases the tendency was to look to the appropriate professional guild for the setting of standards, the approval of curricula, and the accreditation that indicated that a particular program was officially blessed by leaders in its field. Each department or school might have unity and coherence, but the university was becoming a collection of largely independent and sometimes only loosely related parts.

4   The fourth force aiding fragmentation and diminution of central power was an increase in external funding for particular kinds of work. Ezra Cornell, Johns Hopkins, and John D. Rockefeller founded whole universities, and other philanthropists either founded new institutions or made substantial endowments to existing ones—Stanford, Peabody, Vanderbilt, Duke, and others. During the twentieth century, philanthropy took a different turn. There was relatively less money for endowment and much more for specific purposes determined primarily by the donor rather than by the university as an institution. The private foundations picked their own targets and sought out individuals and institutions that already had or were willing to adopt matching interests.

It was, for example, the Rockefeller Foundation, not any university, that did the planning, selected the men, and provided the financial support for research in molecular biology. In 1932, the Rockefeller Foundation decided that this area was ripe for development and that some of the concepts, techniques, and experimental equipment of the physical scientists could be helpful to the advancement of biology. The foundation began awarding grants for work in experimental biology to selected scientists at the California Institute of Technology, the Biological Laboratory at Cold Spring Harbor, the Pasteur Institute in France, the Medical Research Unit attached to the Cavendish Laboratory of Cambridge University, and other places of high scientific quality. So successfully were promising researchers identified and so keen was the foundation's foresight that, from 1954 through 1965, 18 men who had worked in the field of molecular biology received Nobel prizes. Fifteen of those men had been identified and assisted by the Rockefeller Foundation an average 19 years before their Nobel prizes were received.[7]

This success story and others are to the credit of the imaginative foundation officers who helped make possible important new advances in

---

[7] Warren Weaver (1970, pp. 59–75), who was chiefly responsible for initiating and carrying out the Rockefeller Foundation plan to give special support to experimental biology, tells the story briefly in his autobiography.

science. At the same time, the foundations were becoming another center of power in determining the course of university development. It would not be correct to say that decision-making responsibility was always shifted to foundation offices and away from campus offices, for without the private foundations many of the decisions would not have been made anywhere. Nevertheless, the addition of a new center of decision making further fragmented the whole process and gave faculty scientists a new object of loyalty—the foundation.

The advent of massive federal support for research following World War II gave government offices in Washington a role similar to that of the foundations, but on a vastly larger scale. Moreover, in order to avoid the deep-seated American objection to federal control of education, scientists were given responsibility for deciding which research grants would be made, for what purpose, and to whom. Thus it was geologists, chemists, molecular biologists, and other specialists—some serving on advisory panels and committees—rather than "the government" that determined research directions, priorities, and projects.

Institutional unity has some positive value, but how much is debatable. In the old classical college there was so much unity that innovation was difficult. In the modern university there is so little unity that the institution can go in all directions at once. It is still sometimes called a "community of scholars," but Charles W. Eliot (1907, p. 11) gave a more accurate description over 60 years ago. He described the university as "a voluntary cooperative association of highly individualistic persons for teaching and for advancing knowledge."

It is not disunity that now exists on the campus so much as an absence of unity. The individualists who make up the faculty are not aligned against each other; they tolerate or ignore each other. Each is free to move in his own self-chosen direction.

In this atmosphere, loyalty to the institution is often superficial and temporary. In 1964—a time of high mobility—only 58 percent of physical scientists who went to new academic positions expected to remain for more than three years. Social scientists were even more restless; only 37 percent expected to remain for three years or more. The percentage of faculty members on a typical campus spending their first year was higher than the percentage of new students (Brown & Tontz, 1966).

Scientists in particular have been charged with flitting from one position to another, from academia to government to industry, or from one university to another, depending upon where research opportunities are best and project grants largest. The accusation is an old one, however. In 1924, Harry Woodburn Chase (p. 68) commented on the keen competition among universities for faculty members and the "enormously increased" bidding by government, industry, and others who wished to employ them: "On the whole it seems to me that individual faculty members today are less deeply rooted in the soil of the institutions they serve, less complete in the identification of their interest with its development, less concerned about it as an institution, than were the men who came into university faculties a generation ago."

The method of support of a university determines the location of power over the university's course of development. With much help from presidents and trustees, most colleges and universities have largely escaped from external ecclesiastical and political control, and teachers have gained academic freedom. Major responsibility for appointments and promotions has been transferred to the faculty. Individual scientists have substantial control over research funds. Faculty members generally consider all these changes to be improvements.

From a larger perspective, it is easier to see some disadvantages. Planning for a university as a whole has been weakened. With power so widely dispersed, changes within a department are easy, but larger and more comprehensive changes are difficult. With so much of the power centered in the traditional academic departments, accommodation of new interests and new needs is delayed or prevented. Cooperation across departmental boundaries is often difficult. Ralph Gerard (1957, p. 140) has gone so far as to propose —subject to rebuttal—that "those universities controlled strongly by the faculty have not held up as well as the best of those with a strong administrative leadership. In fact, the generalization has been made that non-faculty controlled universities are commonly more progressive than faculty controlled ones." George Pake (1971, p. 915) has added: "How does it happen that universities, which once could manage, now cannot? There is no simple answer, but I keep coming back to the faculty."

The fragmentation that is evident on most individual campuses is found, on a larger scale, in higher education as a whole. There never was a well-coordinated university system in the United States. Independence and competition, rather than integration and control, guided developments. Increases in federal funding have been eagerly received, but competition for federal funds has added a divisive note, and the uncoordinated colleges and universities have had much difficulty in analyzing policy problems and agreeing upon the means of federal support that would be most beneficial.

Private foundations and government agencies with money for research look for the ablest men and the most promising research projects they can find. Their goal is to find men, not particular institutions or locations. Their major objective is good research, not the permanent good health of the institution in which the research is conducted.

The primary criterion of selection has been merit. This emphasis has been deliberate, and proper—given the government's short-range purpose in supporting research. That purpose is to advance science in general or in particular areas, not to control, restructure, or plan a national system of higher education. And the basic mechanism has been a contract for the purchase of services. The contract was often called a grant, and the nature of the work to be done was often defined by the grantee rather than the grantor. But from the standpoint of fundamental policy, these are minor differences. The basic policy of the government has been to advance science by buying research.

To enhance this effort, it was long ago tacitly agreed that competition within government was desirable. The idea of collecting all scientific activities together in a single large department of science was rejected back in the 1880s, and subsequent revivals of the proposal have never gotten far. With several government agencies each trying to build up the best possible record, each eager to use the universities that ranked highest in scientific qualifications, and with the universities themselves in competition with one another, it was inevitable that federal support would be concentrated in the universities which had the best scientific facilities and the ablest scientists. As a direct consequence, the universities that were already well qualified in science got the most grants and gained additional leverage in attracting able young men.

While the best got better, there was also a more or less constant political counterpressure to achieve a more "equitable" geographic distribution of federal funds. Special large grants from the NSF were designed to finance improvements in universities that were already good and seemed ready to become better. Moreover, from the early 1950s until after the middle 1960s, the total amount of federal money available expanded so rapidly that much could be granted to universities of ordinary quality. Thus while federal funds helped the best universities become still better qualified in research, other universities and some colleges were also helped to improve their research capabilities.

Even so, the system of allotting funds on a selective basis contributed to a divisiveness among the different institutions of higher education. The Association of American Universities (AAU), the National Association of State Universities and Land-Grant Colleges (NASULGC), the Association of American Colleges (AAC), and other groups of colleges and universities each had its constituency to represent in the planning that goes on in connection with federal legislation. As would be expected, organizations have not always agreed. The American Council on Education (ACE), which represents all higher education, has sometimes seemed able to recommend to Congress only the lowest common denominators upon which its entire diverse constituency could agree. The lack of unity has been obvious to Congress and has lessened the collective power of American colleges and universities to influence the ways in which federal funds for higher education are made available for use. Several congressmen who have wanted more federal assistance to higher education have delivered verbal spankings to some of the educational bodies, admonishing them to get together and agree on the priorities among the needs of higher education. Like much good advice, these recommendations have been hard to follow.

COMPETITION AND THE MULTIVERSITY

As new universities were founded and as old colleges were transformed, the men responsible adopted several features of the universities they knew in Germany: the seminar and the lecture largely replaced drill and recitation; more advanced work and the Ph.D. were added; both teachers and students gained greater freedom in teaching and learning.

Other characteristics were American-born: the land-grant movement, hospitality to practical programs, the large number of both private and public universities, and a departmental organization which could include several full professors in the same field. One American innovation is thought by Joseph Ben-David (1968–69, pp. 1–35) to be the unintended result of a misunderstanding. Many Americans apparently thought they were copying the German system when they combined research with teaching and the training of graduate students, all in the university. What most of them did not realize was that the German professors held two distinct positions, professorships in the university and directorships of separately financed research institutes which were almost their personal fiefdoms. The separately financed research institute did not come into the American university until much later, and not on a large scale until after World War II. When it did come, it was quite different from the personal research institute of Germany.

In one very important respect the American university system resembled the German system. In both countries education was a state rather than a federal responsibility, and in both countries the universities were independent and free to compete with each other. This was unlike France, where decisions, customs, and priorities radiated from Paris, and unlike England, where control was not as concentrated as in France, but where Oxford, Cambridge, and London shared a Paris-like influence.

The competition fostered by decentralization started early. The parochialism of American colleges was a precursor to the competition that later marked the universities. Colleges were established so young men would not have to go to Europe to be educated; the raw Midwest was jealous of the effete East; the University of the South was proposed by Bishop Polk so young Southern gentlemen need not leave the South to secure an education.

Colleges and universities competed for faculty. When Thomas Jefferson founded the University of Virginia, he brought some professors from Europe because, as he explained, qualified men could be obtained in America only by robbing other colleges. Not all the founders were so considerate. The abortive university at Albany obtained tentative commitments from several Harvard and Yale luminaries for its initial faculty. The same method and essentially the same cast of characters were involved in the proposed new university in New York. When Harper established the University of Chicago, his initial faculty included distinguished scholars from many seats of learning, drawn to the Midway by academic freedom, the excitement of a brand-new university, and lighter teaching loads and higher salaries than other universities were offering.

The influence of Chicago, Harvard, Johns Hopkins, Cornell, and other private universities and of such rapidly improving state universities as Michigan and Wisconsin forced lesser universities all over the country to seek better-qualified faculty members. Even institutions as remote and undistinguished as the University of Washington had to raise their sights. At the turn of the century, President Frank Pierpont Graves, knowing that "the eastern institutions ... determined the standards of excellence," hired young Ph.D.'s from Johns Hopkins and Yale. He wrote to Harvard, Princeton, Columbia, and Chicago seeking doctors of philosophy with research training, men who were scholars in their special fields. Then he added, as an indication of the mores of a pioneer community, that the men must also be married (Gates, 1961, p. 77).

President Graves's request illustrates one of the principal ways in which the best universities helped spread research and graduate education throughout the land: by exporting their graduates. Of the 1,500 Ph.D.'s of the first 30 years of the University of Chicago, 1,000 were at the end of that period holding positions in colleges and universities from one end of America to the other (Ryan, 1939, p. 131). Wherever the young Ph.D.'s from leading universities went to teach, they carried the aspirations and styles of these universities with them.

Sometimes the universities competed for students. Some of the private institutions claimed quality, while state universities offered lower tuition, and even the most prestigious at times resorted to advertising. Long after its founding, Harvard's Lawrence Scientific School was buying space in *Science* to advertise for candidates for its bachelor of science and civil engineer degrees and to inform nondegree students that they might enter at any time without examination and could pursue any courses for which they were qualified (*Science*, 1885).

Universities also competed for presidents. For example, Daniel Coit Gilman declined the presidencies of the Universities of Wisconsin and California, accepted a second invitation from California, moved to the new Johns Hopkins, declined the presidency of M.I.T., and refused to allow his name to be considered at Yale. In 1896, after he had been at Johns Hopkins for 21 years, New York City offered him the position of superintendent of schools and the opportunity to reorganize and improve the whole public education system of the city. The offer touched an old interest. The New York mayor, the president of Columbia University, and others tried to persuade him to accept. Baltimorians were afraid that this time they might lose him. To make staying more attractive they decided to raise a fund of $250,000 to ease the financial difficulties into which Johns Hopkins had fallen. At a quickly arranged public meeting, $150,000 was collected on the spot, and the remaining $100,000 was raised within a few days.

Gilman continued on at Johns Hopkins (Franklin, 1910, pp. 309–319).

Competition, which Ben-David (1960, pp. 828–843) considers important in raising the quality of scientific work in the United States, affected all parts of the universities and universities in all parts of the land. Some of the keenest competition was within quality groups—the established and prestigious older institutions, the Midwestern state universities—or others. Many universities have identified lists of "reference" institutions with which they compare themselves in terms of salary scales, research productivity, teaching, and other variables. The universities on a reference list must be at approximately the same level as the institution using them for reference purposes, but competition is enhanced and, in the case of state universities, leverage on the Legislature may be greater if the reference universities are a bit ahead.

Competition helped most universities among the early leaders remain in the front ranks and helped others to attain high quality. In one sense the universities have been too successful. They dominate higher education so greatly that alternative models and institutions have been unduly weakened. Their pattern of bigness, excellence in research, emphasis on graduate work, and receptivity to a wide diversity of fields, levels, functions, services, and activities has led them to acquire such great prestige among faculty members as to overshadow all other kinds of institutions of higher education. The most prestigious universities have achieved their status by all competing in the same race, the race leading to the kind of institution Clark Kerr has called a multiversity.

There are exceptions. Some excellent institutes of science and technology have not attempted to become complete universities. Some of the best liberal arts colleges have not tried to be anything else. The junior colleges have developed their own very different pattern. But all over the country, teachers colleges, state colleges, and some private undergraduate colleges have attempted to become multiversities. While each such institution includes a diversity of programs within itself, the diversity among institutions of higher education has diminished. The state that two or three decades ago had a state university, an agricultural and mechanical college, two or three teachers colleges, and perhaps a college for women may now have the same number of institutions (probably plus some new junior colleges), but all are trying to be multipurpose universities with graduate as well as undergraduate programs, one or more professional schools, and research and service institutes.

Science is not wholly responsible for this state of affairs, but the academic values primarily responsible resulted from specialization, emphasis on research and graduate work, and the guild structure of professional scholars—to all of which science was a major contributor. The grip of professional scholars on the whole of higher education forced universities and would-be universities to run in the same race and toward the same goal. The rules of the competition were set by the faculty members who obtained their values along with their specialized training in the country's graduate schools (Jencks & Riesman, 1968).

In a study of institutional plans to 1980, Lewis B. Mayhew has presented some disturbing information (Mayhew, 1970). He finds that an estimated 150 institutions that did not offer the Ph.D. degree in 1968 would try to do so by 1980. (In 1968, 220 institutions offered doctor's degrees.) The number of doctorates awarded annually will increase from 30,000 in 1970 to between 60,000 and 70,000 in 1980 if institutional plans are fulfilled, and the largest percentage increase will be from institutions that have not awarded many in the past or are just beginning. The already highly developed universities—Harvard, Yale, Chicago, Stanford, the Universities of Michigan, Wisconsin, California, and similar institutions—expect to award 55 to 60 percent more doctorates in 1980 than they did in 1968. "Developing" institutions such as the University of South Florida, the University of Missouri at Kansas City, or the Chicago Circle Branch of the University of Illinois hope to award 200 percent more. If these plans are fulfilled, the percentage of all the new Ph.D.'s of 1980 who received their doctorates from distinguished or strong graduate departments will be smaller than in 1968, and the percentage coming from new or weaker departments will be substantially larger. Some of these plans will surely be thwarted by financial limitations, but the fact that they were being made just when the number of Ph.D.'s was catching up with demand and a number of newly graduated Ph.D.'s were having difficulties finding suitable jobs demonstrates the hold that the big graduate university has on the thinking of faculty members in institutions that have not reached that status.

The wide-ranging, multipurpose university is an American institution. The German university idea was brought to this country and grafted onto the American version of the English college. The combination was expected to perform the functions of both college and university and was asked to take on a number of additional functions, some of which in Europe were assigned to courts, hospitals, research institutes, and specialized educational institutions outside of universities. The result was a new kind of institution—sprawling, fragmented, and untidy, but also dynamic, accommodating to shifting student and public needs, and attempting to provide a variety of options for students of widely different abilities and aspirations. The major characteristics were all evident by 1910 or 1920.

The most pressing current problems—finances, relations with the federal government, student and faculty dissent and confusion, determining the appropriate nature and scale of research, maintaining reasonable control over future development and evolution—come largely out of the more recent past. But the structure of the university, its resources, and its difficulties in trying to cope with its current problems are direct outgrowths of the form the university took at the end of the nineteenth and the beginning of the twentieth century.

THE PRESTIGE HIERARCHY

As the university assumed its present form, universities fell into a prestige hierarchy that has remained quite stable over the past 50 years. In 1969 the American Council on Education asked national panels of faculty members in each of 36 scientific, scholarly, and professional fields to rate the quality of graduate faculty in their fields in each of 130 universities (Roose & Anderson, 1970). Those departments in each field which were rated high enough by these knowledgeable judges were then placed in rank order. For example, of the numerous departments of chemistry, 35 were judged by chemists to be "distinguished" or "strong," while of the fewer departments of astronomy, 15 were judged "distinguished" or "strong." Thus 35 chemistry departments and 15 astronomy departments were put in rank order. Similarly, ratings were secured and rankings made of graduate departments in 10 fields of the humanities, 7 of the social sciences, 10 of the biological sciences, 5 of the physical sciences, and 4 of engineering. In each field, a second group of departments which were judged adequate or good but not up to the "strong" or "distinguished" levels were named, but not put in rank order. The remaining departments, of still lower quality, were left unnamed.

Table 1 lists two dozen universities that now rank high among the 220 that award at least an occasional Ph.D. degree. Whether or not these 24 are the "best" universities in the country and whether or not they are listed in their true order of merit are matters of judgment or argument. If one wants to play the game of ranking

TABLE 1   Selected characteristics of 24 excellent American universities

Name	(1) Total number of strong or excellent departments	(2) Ranked science fields	(3) Ph.D. degrees, 1967–68 Percent	Rank	(4) Federal funds for science, 1969 Percent	Rank	(5) Budget in 1907 (thousands)
California (Berkeley)*	35	14	3.64	1	1.93	6	$ 844
Michigan*	34	13	2.48	4	2.33	3	1,078
Harvard*	33	14	2.00	10	2.50	2	1,828
Chicago*	30	13	1.47	16	1.64	12	1,304
Columbia*	30	11	1.87	11	1.91	7	1,675
Stanford*	30	12	2.27	7	2.07	4	850
Wisconsin*	30	13	3.24	2	1.78	9	999
Yale*	30	14	1.03	27	1.35	17	1,089
California (Los Angeles)	29	13	1.83	13	1.98	5	
Cornell*	28	12	2.13	8	1.60	14	1,083
Illinois	28	13	3.00	3	1.78	10	1,200
Princeton*	28	12	1.08	26	0.77	37	442
Minnesota	25	13	2.11	9	1.80	8	515
Johns Hopkins*	24	10	1.08	25	1.51	15	312
Pennsylvania*	23	9	1.27	20	1.49	16	589
Texas	23	10	1.65	15	0.52	56	
Washington (Seattle)	22	12	1.37	18	1.74	11	
Indiana	21	10	1.14	24	0.42	71	
Massachusetts Institute of Technology	19	10	2.36	5	4.10	1	505
Brown	17	6			0.19	100+	
Northwestern	17	4	1.29	19	0.63	44	491
California Institute of Technology	14	10	0.78	37	0.85	33	
Purdue	14	10	2.32	6	0.92	29	
Duke	13	8	0.81	35	1.21	18	

*Founding members of the Association of American Universities.

whole universities, the departmental rankings can be weighted and combined in whatever way one prefers. Here, they were simply counted. Thus the University of California at Berkeley, which heads the list in Table 1, includes more departments judged strong or excellent than in any other university, but some of these departments were ranked below similar departments at Harvard, Wisconsin, M.I.T., or other universities. This method selects a group of excellent universities, but one should not make too much of the number 24. The list could be shorter and more selective, or it could be longer and still include only very good universities. Nor should one make too much of small differences in position on the list. The California Institute of Technology, for example, concentrates in the natural sciences and some fields of engineering. It has no departments in the humanities or the social sciences that were considered good enough to be ranked. Consequently, CalTech is farther down on this list than it would be if the listing were based solely on work in the sciences. The purpose of Table 1 is not to proclaim these the 24 best universities arranged in their order of overall merit. Rather the intention was to pick out a group of excellent universities that could be compared in terms of several variables.

Column 2 of Table 1 indicates the number of biological and physical science departments ranked at each institution. In general, the universities that are best overall are best in the sciences. But there are exceptions. California Institute of Technology has been mentioned. Brown and Northwestern are weaker in the sciences than in other areas.

Column 3 shows the percentage of all Ph.D. degrees awarded in 1967-68 that were conferred by each of the 24 institutions; it also gives the rank among all Ph.D.-granting institutions (the 24 listed here plus all others).[8] There is a substantial correlation between relative overall quality and number of Ph.D.'s conferred, even among this highly selected group of institutions. The correlation would be higher if all doctorate-granting institutions were included. However, the relationship is far from perfect. Yale, Princeton, and Johns Hopkins are excellent, but have remained comparatively small. Public universities tend to be high in the number of Ph.D.'s awarded. Ten of the twenty-four institutions are public, and six of them are among the ten highest producers of Ph.D.'s.

Column 4 shows the standing of these institutions in terms of amounts of money received from the federal government in 1969 for research and other scientific activities. (Funds for nonscience activities, which in some cases were very substantial, are not included in this table.) The two figures indicate the percentage of all federal funds for scientific activities that went to each of the named

---

[8] The figures for Ph.D. degrees are U.S. Office of Education figures, but they are cited—along with the figures for federal funds for scientific activities in column 4—from National Science Foundation (1970*b*, pp. 26-27).

institutions and the rank order of each institution among all such recipients of federal funds for science.

There is a positive and understandable relationship between quality and the amounts of money received. It is the presence of highly competent scientists and scholars that give the universities their high rankings, and the federal agencies tend to make grants to the best scientists. There is also a positive relationship between the number of Ph.D. degrees awarded and the amount of federal money received for scientific activities. The larger universities tend to get more grants than the smaller ones.

The table also permits a significant historical comparison. The universities indicated by asterisks formed, in 1900, the AAU. The founders of the AAU were a self-selected group of universities which thought of themselves as leaders in graduate education and research. The charter members included the 12 universities marked in Table 1 plus the Catholic University of America and Clark University, neither of which is now in competition for high rankings. All the other founders are still well up among the leaders. The AAU has gradually expanded over the years and now includes all the universities named in the table and as many more.

Column 5 shows the total budgets in 1907 for most of the universities (Marx, 1909, pp. 759–787). These amounts seem small now, but at the time they were the largest university budgets in the country. Taken with the fact of charter membership in the AAU, the budgets provide a quality index for the beginning of the century. In general, those universities that had the most money and the greatest prestige at that time are still high among the leaders.

The turnover in quality or prestige has been relatively small. However, it is good that there are exceptions to this generalization. The California Institute of Technology was the unknown little Throop College when the AAU was established. Now it has an international reputation. Clark University was a small but seminal institution in creating the American university. It is still small, ranked relatively high in one department, but no longer among the leaders.

As the number of excellent universities has grown during the twentieth century, those that were outstanding at the beginning of the century have remained close to the top. Not only was the basic nature of the American university established by the early part of this century, but most of the leading institutions were already identified. There has been change, growth, and improvement since then, but in fundamental respects there has also been continuity.

7. 1945 and On

On November 17, 1944, as World War II was drawing to an end, President Roosevelt asked Vannevar Bush, director of the Office of Scientific Research and Development, how the nation's scientific resources which had been mobilized for war might most effectively be returned to peacetime contribution. In a letter to Bush the President wrote:[1]

The information, the techniques, and the research experience developed by the Office of Scientific Research and Development and by the thousands of scientists in the universities and in private industry, should be used in the days of peace ahead for the improvement of the national health, the creation of new enterprises bringing new jobs, and the betterment of the national standard of living. . . .
New frontiers of the mind are before us, and if they are pioneered with the same vision, boldness, and drive with which we have waged this war we can create a fuller and more fruitful employment and a fuller and more fruitful life.

Several committee reports, a Presidential commission, and five congressional sessions later, the National Science Foundation came into being. It was part of Bush's reply to President Roosevelt's request and was created specifically to support research and other scientific activities, primarily in universities and other nonprofit institutions. However, the NSF was more than a new government agency; its creation was also an expression of a policy decision by the federal government to assume responsibility for the advancement of science and technology on a broad front and to the highest level of excellence that could be achieved.

---

[1] The reply prepared by Bush and his colleagues was *Science, The Endless Frontier: A Report to the President* (1945).

This national commitment was based partly on faith that the scientists and engineers whose work had contributed greatly and perhaps decisively to the outcome of the war could make equally great contributions to the nation's peacetime welfare if they were provided with the assistance and the equipment their research ideas called for. The national commitment was also in part a recognition of the disrupted state of European scientific institutions and of the fact that the United States would be more dependent on its own resources for adding to basic scientific knowledge than it had been when European laboratories were world leaders. Joseph Ben-David's analysis (1968) cited in Chapter 6 later summarized evidence that the United States had already earned a higher reputation among the leading contributors to science than most Americans realized, but at the time it was still generally held that although the United States was very good at applied science, of course one turned to Europe for leadership in basic science.

About applied science there was no doubt. A long list of earlier industrial and civilian developments had recently been extended by spectacular contributions to radar, atomic energy, the new wonder drugs, and other products of the scientists and engineers who had mobilized for a wartime effort. It was also clear that the country possessed a large and flexible group of scientific and technical laboratories and institutions. In a wartime emergency it had made sense to expand existing centers of competence instead of creating new ones. For most of the engineering development, testing, and construction, the required competence was found in industry. For most of the research and some of the prototype engineering development, universities that had already demonstrated high scientific competence were chosen. Thus, Columbia University, the University of Chicago, and the University of California were responsible for research on atomic energy; radar research was centered in the Radiation Laboratory of Harvard and M.I.T.; and other major research activities were concentrated at Johns Hopkins, the California Institute of Technology, and other universities.

To maintain the scientific momentum of the universities and other institutions, and to finance peacetime scientific work on a larger scale than had ever before been imagined, a new governmental organization was clearly needed. The NSF was to be a central part of the new structure but was not meant to stand alone, and before it got started, the National Institutes of Health and the military services, led by the Office of Naval Research, took over wartime projects that seemed useful to continue in peace and soon began adding new projects of their own selection.

The new national commitment was a broad one that ranged from basic research and education in the physical, biological, and other sciences to engineering and technological development in all fields of applied science. Aspirations expressed in presidential statements, congressional documents, and agency plans all added up to a stated national policy to advance science and technology on a broad front and to a high level.

RECONFIRMA-TION OF THE UNIVERSITY

To carry out this program, political and scientific leaders agreed that the federal government would provide the necessary funds and that most of the work would be performed in universities and other nongovernmental institutions. This policy for science was part of a broader policy of using the private sector of the economy to supply many kinds of goods and services for the government.[2] The decision to use the private sector as fully as possible was altogether consistent with the American ideology that always talks of keeping government small no matter how large it has in fact become. But it also signified recognition that many of the needed goods and services were so highly technical that the government would have to rely largely on the scientific and engineering talent that existed outside of government.

The decision to use universities and other nongovernmental agencies as the nation's chief scientific arm was, thus, in accord with national procurement policy. But the policy was also explicit for research and was manifested in a number of executive and congressional actions. Conceivably, a different decision could have been made. The decision could have been to build large new scientific programs on the base that already existed within the government, as England and some of the other European countries chose to do. There were well-established scientific resources in the U.S. Geological Survey, the National Bureau of Standards, and a substantial range of laboratories and other facilities for work on agricultural, medical, and military problems. All these could have been expanded, but to have made them the nation's primary scientific institutions would have run counter to the decision to use the private

---

[2] For many of the relevant congressional acts, committee reports, and policy statements, see Danhof (1968).

sector for procurement of other kinds of services, and counter to the wishes of most scientists. In 1945 and 1946, scientists were eager to go home and get back to their chosen work. The policy that was adopted recognized that wish.

The decision to rely heavily on universities and other nongovernmental institutions was made more or less independently at several governmental levels. In 1944, the Committee on Postwar Research recommended this policy to the Secretary of War and the Secretary of the Navy, and it was followed by the Office of Naval Research when that agency began its postwar development. Before the National Science Foundation Act was passed by Congress, the Office of Naval Research had already contracted with over 200 universities to conduct some 1,200 research projects—a volume of work involving 3,000 scientists and 2,500 graduate students (Danhof, 1968, p. 56). When the Atomic Energy Commission (AEC) was established, that agency decided to continue the kind of contractual arrangements that had been adopted during the war years instead of operating its own laboratories. Later, the National Aeronautics and Space Administration (NASA) decided to follow a similar course.

Congressional votes and actions reinforced these decisions. The division of congressional responsibility for executive agencies meant that a number of committees of Congress considered research and development programs and budgets. In authorization and appropriations hearings, these committees repeatedly expressed their approval of the extensive use of universities and other nongovernmental institutions to help achieve the nation's scientific and technological goals. In creating the NSF, Congress went beyond expressing general approval of the use of outside institutions; the NSF was specifically enjoined from developing and operating its own laboratories. In addition to many positive actions, Congress encouraged the executive agencies to comply with the general principle of using the private sector as widely as possibly by expanding budgets more rapidly than personnel ceilings and by increasing civil service salaries more slowly than salaries for comparable work in the private sector.

The Bureau of the Budget gave an additional stamp of approval during President Eisenhower's administration by issuing general instructions that research and development, as well as other services, that could be secured from the private sector should not be started or conducted by government agencies themselves. When

President Kennedy entered office, he asked David E. Bell, the new director of the Bureau of the Budget, to serve as chairman of a task force to review the effectiveness of the government's research and development practices and to recommend criteria for use in deciding whether a particular research or development function should be carried out under grant or contract or conducted internally. The task force concluded that the government should "continue to rely on the private sector for the major share of the scientific and technical work it requires" (Danhof, 1968, p. 119).

The decision to rely on the private sector for most research and development was never intended to be an absolute one. Most government laboratories continued in existence. Many expanded, and some new ones were started. In a very few cases research and development facilities started under private auspices were later converted to full government control—for example, the Naval Ordnance Testing Station at China Lake, California, which was started under contract with the University of California, later came under direct Navy management.

However, emphasis remained on the private sector, and in financial terms the emphasis has increased over time. In 1945, federal research and development expenditures were about evenly divided between internal laboratories and external contracts. But the external portion grew more rapidly and accounted for 63 percent of the total in 1955, 81 percent in 1964, and about 74 percent in 1971.

Of the federal funds for basic research, 74 percent is now awarded in grants and contracts. The research supported by these funds is conducted in universities, independent nonprofit organizations, industrial laboratories, and research centers that are entirely or largely supported by a single government agency but managed by a nongovernmental organization. So strong is the "private sector" policy that when a new national research need is identified which does not fit into any existing organization, a new private, rather than government, organization is created. Thus, for example, the NSF arranged with consortia of universities to manage the national astronomical observatories at Green Bank, West Virginia, and Kitt Peak, Arizona, and the National Center for Atmospheric Research at Boulder, Colorado. In short, the policy of using private institutions as the nation's principal research agencies, a practice that developed gradually during the latter part of the nineteenth and early part of the twentieth centuries, was made explicit in the years following 1945 by a large number of administrative actions, committee recommendations, congressional and executive policy statements, and statutes. During the past quarter century, the policy has occasionally been questioned, but each time it has been sustained, and sometimes extended. It can be expected that this policy will be followed if existing research programs are expanded or new ones started.

GROWTH OF RESEARCH FUNDS

Since the end of World War II, the federal government has spent $200 billion on research and development, and $150 billion more has been provided by industry, the states, universities, and other nonfederal supporters. Annual expenditures multiplied from $5 billion in 1953 to $28 billion in 1971, more than a fivefold increase. Even when the figures are converted to constant dollars to indicate their real purchasing power, the 1971 total was more than three times the 1953 figure.

At the beginning of this period, the federal government provided slightly more than half of the annual total, and for a time it increased its portion more rapidly than did industry and other nonfederal supporters. From 1953 to 1961, federal funds for research and development grew at an average rate of 13.9 percent a year, while the nonfederal portion grew 7.8 percent a year in constant dollars, which provide a better basis for comparisons than do current dollars. From 1961 to 1966 the two growth rates were more nearly the same, 6.8 and 7.5 percent, respectively. Since 1966, the federal government has lagged behind; its rate dropped to the negative side, −3.0 percent a year from 1966 to 1971, while the nonfederal investment in research and development grew at an average rate of 5.2 percent a year. As a result of these differences in growth rates, the federal portion provided a steadily rising fraction until the early 1960s when federal funds accounted for two-thirds of the total. Since then the federal portion has declined, and it is now back down to slightly above 50 percent.[3]

Much of the change in the federal growth rate has been associated with changes in national priorities. When the nation began

---

[3] The National Science Foundation is the recognized and valuable source of information about federal funds for research and development, including amounts; distribution by agency, user, function, geography, and other variables; and historical trends. See the list of references at the end of this volume for several NSF publications that are especially valuable for information about relations between government agencies and the universities.

after World War II to achieve high scientific and technological competence, much of the motivation was military. Thus missiles, atomic energy, and other items to enhance military strength were emphasized. The defense proportion of the national total remained fairly close to half until early in the 1960s, when a decline started that brought funds for military research and development down to 28 percent of the total in 1971.

When the space program began to be emphasized in 1959, research and development in this area grew rapidly until funds reached a peak of 21.5 percent of the national research and development total in 1965. Then it, too, began to decline, relative to other interests, and funds were down to 11.1 percent of the total in 1971. Nondefense and nonspace research and development funds started at about half of the national total in the early 1950s, dropped to 45 percent during the first half of the 1960s, and have since been rising, reaching 61 percent of the total in 1971 (Lederman & Windus, 1969; NSF, 1970*d*, p. 38).

The high costs of development account for two-thirds of the nation's total research and development budget, but only one half of 1 percent, more or less, of developmental expenditures are spent by universities. And those funds have accounted for only 5 percent or less of the scientific activities of colleges and universities. Universities concentrate on research, especially basic research. Tables 2 and 3, respectively, provide data on total research (basic and applied) and on basic research expenditures. In successive columns, each table shows total national expenditures for each year from 1953 to 1971; the percentage of the total provided by federal agencies; the amount and percentage of the total used by universities and colleges; and then in the four final columns the sources from which universities and colleges received their research funds.

Whether one considers both basic and applied research (Table 2) or only basic research (Table 3), many of the generalizations are much the same. Total research funds have grown relatively less rapidly than basic research funds because funds for applied research (not shown separately) have grown less rapidly than basic research funds. The fractions of the total supplied by federal agencies have been approximately the same, with the federal portion for total research ranging from 51 to 60 percent and the federal portion of basic research funds ranging from 46 to 65 percent. The greatest difference between the two tables lies in the fact that universities play a much more prominent role in the conduct of

TABLE 2 Annual expenditures for all research, basic and applied, and sources of research funds used by colleges and universities (millions of dollars)

Year	U.S. total	Percent U.S. gov't.	University and college		University and college sources			
			Total	Percent	Gov't.	Industry	Own	Nonprofit
1953	$1,806	56	$ 319	18	$ 130	$18	$146	$ 25
1954	1,978	55	360	18	151	21	161	27
1955	2,133	53	392	18	161	24	178	29
1956	2,685	51	455	17	198	27	197	33
1957	3,286	52	506	15	217	32	221	36
1958	3,730	52	565	15	242	36	247	40
1959	4,120	54	654	16	293	36	280	45
1960	4,419	55	791	18	387	37	317	50
1961	4,699	56	934	20	480	38	360	56
1962	5,661	57	1,103	20	590	38	411	64
1963	6,077	58	1,319	22	738	39	471	71
1964	6,859	60	1,555	23	894	39	541	81
1965	7,390	60	1,765	24	1,036	39	600	90
1966	7,944	60	2,001	25	1,203	40	655	103
1967	8,404	60	2,239	27	1,346	46	733	114
1968	9,064	59	2,503	28	1,509	52	819	123
1969	9,390	57	2,555	27	1,500	55	873	127
1970	9,650	56	2,585	27	1,485	64	905	131
1971	9,950	56	2,625	26	1,480	74	935	136

SOURCE: National Science Foundation, 1970d. Data for 1970 and 1971 are NSF estimates.

basic research than they do in total research. In 1953, universities spent about 35 percent of all basic research funds and about 18 percent of total research funds. In 1971, they spent 54 percent of basic research funds and 26 percent of total research funds.

The sources from which universities have derived funds for research have varied in much the same fashion whether one considers all research or only basic research. The federal government provided a little more than 40 percent in the early 1950s and increased its portion to 60 percent or more by the mid-1960s. Correspondingly, the portion derived from the internal funds of universities—state taxes, endowment, fees, gifts, etc.—declined from 40 to 45 percent in the 1950s to 30 to 35 percent in the late 1960s. Industrial contributions became less significant during the

TABLE 3 Annual expenditures for basic research and sources of research funds used by colleges and universities (millions of dollars)

Year	U.S. total	Percent U.S. gov't.	University and college		University and college sources			
			Total	Percent	Gov't.	Industry	Own	Nonprofit
1953	$ 489	48	$ 173	35	$ 73	$12	$ 73	$15
1954	548	48	206	37	90	14	85	17
1955	608	47	237	39	103	16	99	19
1956	747	46	286	38	130	18	116	22
1957	857	48	337	39	155	21	136	25
1958	973	48	390	40	178	24	159	29
1959	1,155	53	468	40	226	24	185	33
1960	1,326	52	576	43	299	24	215	38
1961	1,543	55	701	47	382	25	250	44
1962	1,886	58	850	45	481	25	293	51
1963	2,196	60	1,036	47	610	25	343	58
1964	2,559	62	1,261	49	767	25	402	67
1965	2,853	64	1,419	50	879	26	445	69
1966	3,127	64	1,601	51	1,009	27	494	71
1967	3,363	65	1,785	53	1,124	31	551	79
1968	3,638	64	2,011	55	1,268	36	621	86
1969	3,735	64	2,050	55	1,260	39	661	90
1970	3,800	64	2,070	55	1,245	44	690	91
1971	3,900	63	2,110	54	1,245	54	715	96

SOURCE: National Science Foundation, 1970d. Data for 1970 and 1971 are NSF estimates.

period and have remained at a steady 2 percent of the total for nearly a decade. Funds from foundations and other nonprofit institutions have also dropped, relatively, to a recent steady level of 4 or 5 percent of the total.

All these comparisons, it should be noted, are in relative terms. The actual amounts involved have been rising, as shown in the dollar columns of Tables 2 and 3.

When federal appropriations for research and development leveled off in 1968, expenses of the government's own laboratories continued to go up. As a result, there has recently been a reversal of the long-time trend of having an increasing proportion of federally supported research conducted outside of government. In the last few years, there has been a slight decrease in the percentage of federal appropriations for research and development used externally through grants and contracts.

As priorities among federal agencies have gradually changed, and as their congressional appropriations have grown, or sometimes declined, at different rates, the agencies' relative contributions to university research funds have also changed. In the 1950s, universities received more than half of their federal research funds from the Department of Defense (DOD), but military funds have steadily declined, relative to others, and in 1971 were down to 13 percent of the federal research funds used by universities and colleges. Funds from the AEC have also become a lesser part of the academic total, reaching 6 percent in 1971. Funds from NASA rose and fell with the overall budget of that agency and in 1971 provided 5 percent of federal funds for academic research. In contrast with these declining percentages, the NSF and the Department of Health, Education and Welfare (HEW) have come to provide steadily larger proportions of the research funds for universities. The NSF provided 18 percent and HEW 44 percent of the federal total in 1971. The position of HEW is even more dominant than this figure indicates, for the NIH, in addition to providing a large amount of money for research in the biological sciences and some social sciences, has been a major source of building funds for medical school facilities. And other HEW units provided about 95 percent of the approximately $1 billion a year the federal government grants to universities and colleges for nonscience activities. It was HEW and not the DOD that was in the strongest position to influence academic research in 1971.

When classified by fields of science, there have been some fairly substantial changes in the percentage distribution of federal funds for academic research. In 1958, the engineering sciences received 20 percent of the federal expenditures for research in universities. By 1968, the engineering science proportion had declined to 14 percent. Funds for research in the physical and environmental sciences and mathematics accounted for 36 percent in 1958 and 29 percent in 1971. The largest subdivision has regularly been the life sciences, whose portion rose from 40 percent in 1958 to 46 percent in 1971. In the same span of time, funds for research in the social sciences and psychology grew from 6 percent of the total to 10 percent.

As social priorities are changing to give more emphasis to environmental and social problems, these areas will probably come to account for larger portions of the research funds, partly because of the appropriation of increased research funds to some of the newer government agencies, and partly through adjustments of the budgets of the NSF and perhaps other agencies. As yet, however, there has been much more talk about the importance of these areas than money for research on the scientific issues involved.

GEOGRAPHIC DISTRIBUTION
Tension over feared or presumed inequities in geographical distribution has existed since the very beginning of the postwar expansion of federal funds for research. Congress considered, and rejected, the possibility of requiring the NSF to allocate a designated portion of its research funds to the several states on a formula basis. Although not bound by geographic restrictions, the NSF and all the other agencies that support research have been concerned about the geographic distribution of their funds, and all for essentially the same reasons. A fairly wide geographic distribution is good policy and good politics. Student access is easier, and it is generally agreed that the total intellectual, social, and economic benefits of universities are greater if the universities are located in different cities and regions rather than concentrated in a few places. Moreover, decentralization of grant funds gains the support of more members of Congress than does centralization. Congress has always recognized, however, that any agency has good reason to put its research funds where talent and good scientific resources are to be found in order to accomplish its mission and use its research funds as effectively as possible. A frequent resolution of the geographic dilemma has been to support and use high-quality resources where they already exist and to employ part of any new or additional funds to build up new centers of excellence. Thus over the years there has been a gradual movement toward greater distribution of federal research funds, both geographically and to a larger number of universities.

By any reasonable measure, the federal agencies that support research must be given good marks on this point. Among the 24 universities listed in Table 1, there is good agreement between the number of strong and excellent graduate departments in each and the amount of federal research support it receives. The 25 universities that in 1969 received the largest amounts for research were spread over 13 states, from Massachusetts to Maryland in the East, through Missouri and Minnesota in the Midwest, to California and Washington on the Pacific Coast. If the distribution of research funds is compared with the number of Ph.D. degrees awarded, there is usually close agreement either by region or by individual states — except for Massachusetts. Massachusetts universities award about 6 percent of the Ph.D.'s in science and engineering each year, but that state has such a concentration of research facilities and scientific talent that it receives considerably more than 6 percent of federal funds for academic research. In 1969, its share was 11 percent. Except for Massachusetts, the agreement is generally close. In 1969, California received 13 percent of the research funds and awarded 12 percent of the doctorates; in New York the percentages were 12 and 11; in Illinois, 6 and 7; in Texas, 4 and 4; in North Carolina, 3 and 2. These small differences are typical. The conclusion must be that federal research funds have been well distributed among the nation's universities in terms of their location, size, and quality.

There has also been considerable effort to increase the geographic spread of research and graduate education. In 1965, President Johnson wrote to the heads of all departments and agencies of the federal government to state the general policy, "Research supported to further agency missions should be administered not only with a view to producing specific results, but also with a view to strengthening academic institutions and increasing the number of institutions capable of performing research of high quality" (*Strengthening Academic Capability* . . . , September 13, 1965).

One of the programs that was specifically intended to accomplish this objective was the science development grant program of the NSF. Its announcement in 1964 stated that the major objective was "to increase the number of institutions of recognized excellence in research and education in the sciences." To accomplish this objective, the announcement stated that grants would be made "to institutions judged to have the greatest possibility of moving upward to a higher level of scientific quality and to have sound plans for maintaining this quality."[4] All colleges and universities were eligible to apply, but those that already enjoyed the most prestige were discouraged, and so were those that lacked a good base on which to try to build improvements. The early grants, of several million dollars each, indicate the kind of university the NSF was trying to help improve: Western Reserve and Case Institute

---

[4] Howard E. Page, director of the program, gives an account of its objectives and early years in Orlans (1968).

of Technology in Cleveland, Washington University in St. Louis, the University of Oregon, Rice University, the University of Arizona, the University of Southern California, the Polytechnic Institute of Brooklyn, Louisiana State University, the University of Colorado, the University of Rochester, the University of Virginia, and the University of Florida. By 1971, when the Office of Management and Budget cut off funds for science development grants, the NSF had made such awards to 35 universities, in amounts totaling $162 million. The universities, for their part, had provided somewhat more money for the same purposes and had undertaken to maintain the higher, and more costly, level of activities after expiration of the NSF grant. To further diversify academic research competence, the NSF supplemented this university program with two other series of developmental grants: one for individual departments within universities, and one for colleges. By the time the science development program was terminated in 1971, approximately $200 million had been used to upgrade 260 science departments.

While the NSF was undertaking its science development program, the DOD started a different program with a similar objective. Under the name Project Themis, the DOD invited proposals for substantial multiyear grants from institutions that had not been major recipients of project grants but that had or showed good promise of being able to acquire a fair level of research competence. While the NSF program was oriented around scientific areas or disciplines, Project Themis was oriented around research topics. Because military funds were being used, the research topics had to have some potential relevance to military interests, but the relationship did not have to be immediate; the work was not classified, the universities were encouraged to select research topics in which they had an interest, and one of the objectives was to increase and diversify the nation's research competence. Despite its desirable features, Project Themis soon became a target of critics of military support of university research. DOD motives were questioned, and the whole idea became a victim of efforts to divorce academic research from military support.

Nevertheless, Project Themis, the NSF science development programs, and the steady efforts of NASA, NIH, and other agencies to broaden and diversify the centers of research competence among the nation's universities succeeded. In 1958, half of all the money in university and college budgets classified for research was spent in fewer than 20 universities. In 1968, 30 universities spent half of the separately budgeted research funds. In 1958, 100 universities spent 95 percent of all the research and development funds used in universities; in 1968, the top 100 universities accounted for 86 percent of all the university expenditures for research and development.

CURRENT SCIENTIFIC CAPACITY   Partly as a result of growth in population and greater interest in higher education and partly as a result of measures taken by the federal government to increase the number of students earning the doctorate, the capacity of the nation's universities for research and graduate education has increased enormously in the past 25 years. In the middle 1950s, after the universities had recovered from the crowded period following World War II, American universities were awarding about 9,000 Ph.D.'s a year. In 1971 there were 32,000, and the number is still growing rapidly.

In January 1969, the NSF (1970c) made a detailed study of the faculty, funds, and other characteristics of academic science from which one can get an overall view of the size and capacity of the 220 doctorate-granting universities (there are a few more now that grant the doctorate). As of 1969, the 220 universities that awarded doctorates employed a science faculty of 146,000 (the actual number was larger, but equaled a full-time staff of 146,000). Their time was distributed 51 percent to teaching, 33 percent to research, and 16 percent to administration and other activities. They had the help of 45,000 technicians and of enough graduate students to equal 38,000 full-time research and teaching assistants. They were responsible for $5.5 billion for research and education in the sciences, including three-fourths of the research funds that federal agencies granted to all 2,200 American colleges and universities. In 1969, they supervised the dissertations of 17,000 recipients of the Ph.D. in the natural and social sciences and guided the studies and research of additional graduate students who earned 60,000 Ph.D.'s in the sciences in the three succeeding years.

In addition to the departments and schools within these universities, individual universities or consortia of universities were responsible for 36 research centers that were fully funded by the AEC, DOD, NASA, HEW, and NSF. These research centers employed 11,500 scientists and 900 graduate students and, in 1968, spent $507 million for research and $137 million for capital expenditures.

These figures demonstrate the size to which the American university scientific community has grown. The quality varies, up to and including some of the most highly regarded universities and research centers in the world. Overall, as measured by prizes, honors, contributions to the world's scientific literature, or any other criterion of accomplishment, the American university is a world leader. The universities and associated research centers are responsible for 60 percent of the basic research conducted in the United States and for 10 to 15 percent of the applied research. In 1968, they used $2.5 billion directly budgeted for research plus additional funds included in undifferentiated accounts for educational and supporting purposes. Of the directly budgeted total, the federal government provided $2 billion (about $1.5 billion to the universities and $0.5 billion to the research centers administered by universities).

That was the situation at the beginning of 1969 when a major conflict became obvious. On the one hand, the whole system was geared to growth. The separately funded research centers were growing fairly slowly, at a rate of about 3 percent a year, but total funds for university scientific activities were growing by 13 percent a year, and the number of Ph.D. degrees granted by 12 percent a year. In collision with these growth rates, which had been fostered and built up over the years, the growth of nonfederal funds had slowed down and the growth of federal funds for research had stopped altogether.

A reduction of growth rate was inevitable. Better planning would have made the change less abrupt and would have eased some of the necessary adjustments. But research funds could not climb indefinitely as they had from 1954 to 1966 when annual increases in federal funds for basic research went up 15 percent, 20 percent, or even more a year. From 1959 through 1964 the annual increase was never less than 25 percent. Of course the rate had to slow down. In 1963, William D. Carey, executive assistant director of the Bureau of the Budget, warned the participants at the Seventeenth Annual Conference on the Administration of Research that the period of rapid increase was soon coming to an end. "[A] reaction is at last setting in," he said. "It is apparent in the scientific community. . . . It is apparent also in the Executive Branch of the Federal Government, where the budgetary pinch is becoming acute. And it is perhaps most spectacularly apparent in the Congress, where a mounting wail of frustration and uneasiness is being reflected in a rash of proposals to bring science and technology to heel." As things turned out, large increases did continue for a little longer, and Carey's warning was forgotten. Nevertheless, a slower rate of growth was inevitable. When it came, however, it was too abrupt, and its effects were compounded by other changes in the general social and political climate which affected the universities as much as or more than they did the rest of society.

CHANGING PRIORITIES The damage done by pollution and pesticides dramatized by Rachel Carson of the U.S. Fish and Wildlife Service, the causes and consequences of smog studied by A. J. Haagen-Smit of the California Institute of Technology, the dangers of misuse of the land pointed out by Paul Sears of Yale University, and other early warnings by other pioneer students of man's effects on his environment gained increasing attention over the years until, late in the 1960s, the environment became a topic for political speeches and a cause for national attention. Concurrently, poverty, urban decay, and other social ills came into public focus, and technology and its ally science were said to be at least partly responsible for these problems as they were for pollution, ugliness, and threats to health. The sometimes naïve earlier-day faith in science was badly shaken, but public and official attitudes were not so much antiscience as they were anti-science-as-usual.

Society always frames problems in terms of purposes or objectives. Slums need healing; the environment needs protection or improvement. These and kindred problems are phrased in terms of objectives, but so were space missions, national defense, the eradication of disease, and the improvement of agriculture. Scientists are accustomed to restating problems in their own terms, breaking them up into segments they know how to handle, and rejecting the parts for which they lack knowledge or techniques. Nevertheless, the situation in recent years is different in two significant ways. First, many of these problems cannot be divided up and worked on in the customary academic manner. The scientific aspects are only a minor part of some, and all seem to call for simultaneous and integrated analysis from several different points of attack: legal, social, medical, economic, engineering, and ethical, as well as scientific. Few academic scientists are accustomed to this kind of multidisciplinary work, and the universities are not very good at it. Second, there is more impatience. The argument runs that scientists and engineers have solved other problems; they helped get the world into its present mess; they had better stop fooling around with their own little scientific concerns and get to work on important problems or we'll all go down together. Some scientists agree (Platt, 1969, pp. 1115–1121).

MILITARY SUPPORT OF UNIVERSITY RESEARCH

One result, and also a cause, of the changing climate surrounding university research was growing apprehension over university relations with the DOD. Campus confrontations were the most newsworthy expression of this change in attitude, as buildings housing research supported by military agencies were picketed, occupied, and sometimes destroyed. But dissident students were not the only persons dissatisfied with the military-university relations. Many scientists preferred other sponsorship. Dissatisfaction was also growing on Capitol Hill.

In August 1969, Senator Fulbright introduced the following amendment to the bill authorizing military procurement for 1970: "None of the funds authorized to be appropriated by this act may be used to carry out any research project or study unless such project or study has a direct and apparent relationship to a specific military function or operation" (Sec. 203, P.L. 91-121). Despite authorship by Senator Fulbright, it was Senator Mansfield's name that quickly became attached to this provision, for it was he, the Majority Leader, who spoke most vigorously in support of the principle involved and who quizzed the DOD most relentlessly to see that both the spirit and letter were followed (Nichols, 1971).

The direct and immediate effects of the Mansfield amendment were smaller than were expected. Defense officials reviewed individually some 15,000 research projects and terminated 404 for not meeting the new requirements. Later on, when Congress asked the Government Accounting Office (GAO) to review DOD research projects, some of the original decisions were reversed. But that was not surprising. There had been disagreement within the DOD over some of the decisions, for the nearer a research project is to the basic end of the research spectrum the more difficult it is to decide to what practical use it may be relevant, or whether it will have any practical use at all.

Indirect effects were more important. If the Mansfield amendment did not directly help, it certainly did nothing to reduce the pressure on universities to get rid of the defense-sponsored research centers for which they had been responsible. Some universities withdrew from the consortium that managed the Institute for Defense Analysis. Others dropped research organizations they had formed at DOD request. Some of these ties were severed with little if any loss either to the universities or the DOD, for although nominally managed by universities, the research centers were not integral parts of their parent institutions, and the military services had not benefited much from the university connection. In other cases, where the laboratory was more truly a part of its parent university, the military services stood to lose more.

Going beyond the separately staffed and financed research institutes and laboratories, university scientists who held project grants from the military services also came under attack. Such projects in 1971 accounted for about 13 percent of the federal funds granted to universities for research. Most of the work was unclassified, and about two-thirds of it was basic research. It all, however, became subject to attack because of widely held beliefs that universities should not be dependent upon military funds and that it was morally wrong for them to be engaged in research that might lead to further destruction. But these beliefs were countered by arguments that even though military strength may be an unhappy necessity, it was nevertheless a necessity to which scientists should make their contribution, and that the involvement of univerversity scientists is a protection to society against unchecked military control. Disarmament, the peaceful resolution of international disputes, and the interests of society as a whole, the argument goes, have much to gain from the existence of a group of competent, and often outspoken and critical, scientists who are intimately acquainted with the characteristics and potentialities of those weapons, counterweapons, and strategic plans that are under consideration or development, for these weapons and plans are more likely to be looked at critically and skeptically by university scientists than by members of the military services or the industrial contractors who produce military weapons.

University relations with the military services have posed moral issues more sharply than have university relations with any of the other agencies of the federal government, but some of the issues involved go beyond the DOD. These issues, most acutely in connection with military involvement, but more generally in connection with other governmental agencies, were one of the problems troubling university planning at the beginning of the 1970s. These issues were also becoming of greater interest to Congress.

GOVERNMENT ORGANIZATION FOR SCIENCE

Never in recent time has there been unanimity in answer to the question of how the federal government should organize its scientific interests and activities. All along, however, it has been generally agreed that each government agency should be responsible for such research as was required to accomplish its primary objectives. Consequently, there has been little dispute with the policy that each agency should contract for, or should conduct, the applied research and development needed for its assigned objectives. For basic research, the de facto policy has been for all or most agencies that had scientific interests to support some basic research. Congress of course knew what was going on and gave at least tacit approval. Early in the 1950s, the point came up for explicit consideration at the presidential level. President Eisenhower issued Executive Order 10521, which assigned to the NSF the responsibility for supporting "general purpose" basic research and endorsed the de facto policy by authorizing each agency with an operating mission to support basic research in the areas of science that undergirded its technical responsibilities.[5] There was a double reason for this policy. It was intended to help government agencies keep in touch with the scientific community so that they might more quickly learn of new ideas and developments, maintain close liaison with the major source of basic scientific progress, and thus be better able to accomplish their own objectives. It also provided broader support for basic research. A multiplicity of sources of support is less vulnerable than a single agency would be to sudden changes in appropriations and is also less vulnerable to whatever bias and shortsightedness might develop within a single agency.

For some years multiplicity was generally satisfactory and accepted. The NSF concentrated on basic research, chiefly but not exclusively in universities. The NIH supported research on problems of health and disease, and also basic research in the sciences underlying health problems. Similarly, the DOD, AEC, USDA, and other agencies pursued their missions and supported basic research in fields of science that were fundamental to their interests. The agencies and research scientists liked this practice, but

---

[5] In addition to defining the responsibilities of the NSF and other agencies for the support of basic research, Executive Order 10521 instructed the director of the NSF, in cooperation with the U.S. Commissioner of Education, to study the effects of governmental grant and contract policies on universities, to ensure the realization of governmental objectives "while safeguarding the strength and independence of the nation's institutions of learning."

as the total amount of money grew larger and larger, more and more congressmen began to fear that it encouraged duplication, overlap, and inefficiency. Proposals for consolidating a number of scientific programs into a single Department of Science were introduced (although never brought to vote), and by the end of the 1960s, the House Subcommittee on Science, Research, and Development recommended creation of the National Institutes of Research and Advanced Studies which would consolidate the NSF, parts of the NIH, and several other agencies or programs into a large new organization that would handle approximately 60 percent of all the federal funds for basic research (U.S. House of Representatives, 1970*b*).

Congress has not acted on this proposal, but other organizational rearrangements have been made, either through congressional vote or by exercise of executive authority: the National Oceanic and Atmospheric Administration and the Council on Environmental Quality were established; the Environmental Protection Act was passed; and the NSF was given authority to support applied as well as basic research.

It was within this general atmosphere of searching for new organizational patterns and of doubt about the ability of existing organizations to manage and support scientific activities efficiently and productively that the Mansfield amendment was introduced. Thus it was not so much the fate of a few hundred projects financed by the DOD that concerned both scientists and federal agencies but the implications of the congressional action for the more fundamental policy that was involved.

The Mansfield amendment legally applied only to the DOD, but other agencies got the message. All over Washington, agencies began to examine grant proposals more closely to determine relevance to agency missions. Because it is basic research for which such relevance is most difficult to demonstrate, the effect of the amendment was greater on university-government relations than on industry-government relations, which appeared to be Senator Mansfield's intent. If, as the amendment suggested, it was becoming congressional policy to require mission-oriented agencies to make sure that each research project they supported bore an apparent relation to one of their operational programs or objectives, two consequences were likely to follow. First, there would be less support for basic research, unless, of course, Congress made a fully compensatory increase in the budget of the

NSF, something Congress has not yet been willing to do. And second, relations between many government agencies and the universities would be weakened.

What will happen is still unclear. Congress approved the Mansfield amendment in 1969 but did not renew it in 1970. A similar provision has not been imposed on other agencies. Nevertheless, the 1969 action may have signaled the end of a long period of congressional acquiescence to using a small fraction of military funds for the general support of research.

For almost two centuries, as far back as the early surveys and the first astronomical observatories, scientists sought and welcomed support from many sources. The federal government adopted this policy after World War II, and the judgment of experience endorses its value. As Nichols summarized: "It has the virtue of being compatible with the environment of freedom, decentralization, and independent competition within which first-class research and rapid development thrive. Moreover, pluralism gives the country, through its government, a broad scientific basis for stimulating, understanding, and exploiting innovations to serve national goals" (Nichols, 1971, p. 31).

Government agencies and university scientists will try to preserve the policy of multiplicity. It gives government agencies access to the intellectual resources they need, and it gives university scientists some options in sources of support. It may be that the intent and the potential effects of the Mansfield amendment have been overemphasized. Congress has not pushed the matter as seemed likely in 1969, and Senator Mansfield has withdrawn somewhat from his earlier opposition to military support of at least some university research and has also stated that the whole matter of government policy for science needs reexamination (ibid., p. 30). Perhaps the amendment has been overemphasized, but the reasons for its adoption, and the underlying uneasiness about duplication and overlap, have not been satisfactorily answered. One problem for scientists at the beginning of the 1970s was their need to formulate a better rationale for the support of basic research and for the advantages of many different sources of support. The faith that sustained increasing appropriations until well into the 1960s was wearing thin.

SEARCH FOR PURITY It is fair to describe many of the government-university relations that have developed over the past quarter of a century as arrangements of expedience or convenience. On each side there has been freedom to seek and arrange the relations and services wanted or needed. Under these conditions many decisions were made on an ad hoc basis, and many arrangements were made piecemeal. On both sides there has been policy justification. Government agencies were expected to use universities and other nongovernment institutions to accomplish their research objectives, and while there has been some coordination among the agencies, they have not been required to integrate their plans or to pay much attention to the permanent welfare of the universities as whole institutions. At the university end, there has been some coordination within individual universities, but little enough either within or among them, and scientists normally work on a highly individualistic basis.

It is also fair to characterize a number of actions and reactions both on campus and elsewhere as expressions of a wish for simplistic purity. On the campus it is stated that it is morally wrong for faculty members to engage in military research; therefore military sponsorship should be banned. Science and technology are responsible for pesticides, pollution, and urban decay; therefore scientists should turn their talents to the amelioration of these conditions. Congress considers it wrong for the DOD to support research not directly related to military objectives; the solution is to prohibit the use of DOD funds for any research project that cannot be shown to be related to some military program or objective. Multiplicity of support leads to waste and duplication, so consolidate several agencies into one. From the public comes another reaction: universities are hotbeds of radical students and professors, so society should clamp down and make them behave.

Research is peripheral to some of these matters, and central to others. All, however, and also practices, disagreements, and confrontations regarding discrimination, university rules, the draft, and American involvement in Southeast Asia, help make up the campus climate in which research and education go on and in which policies for their guidance are or are not formulated.

There is a related kind of search for purity that is of the utmost importance for the future of the university. A century ago, scientists were attempting to transform the old college into a true university, an institution in which faculty and students with scholarly interests could search for new truths instead of dwelling on what was already known. Ironically, now that the university has become such a successful research institution, faculty members are criticized for devoting too much time to research and not enough to telling undergraduates what is already known. Many students would like to turn the university back into a school. The time may have come to separate the undergraduate college from the graduate university. But this, too, is part of the controversy over institutional objectives that helps to make up the climate in which decisions for the future must be made, now that the long period of rapid financial expansion has ended, and Congress and the executive branch are asking whether past practices should be continued and are raising more questions about fundamental policy for scientific research.

8. A University's Research Rationale

The university badly needs a rationale for its research activities, one that is both politically persuasive and intellectually honest (Kaysen, 1969, p. 59). One frequent justification is that basic research lays the foundation for later practical applications. Historically the claim has often been true, and no doubt practical applications will emerge from some of the basic research now being conducted. But if the research is truly basic, no one knows what the applications will be, when they will emerge, or who will benefit. Thus, some of the esoteric topics under investigation lead at worst to ridicule and at best to the unanswerable question, "But what is the good of it?" The cases in which a direct ancestry can be traced from commercial wealth back to basic research—for example, the development of hybrid corn—have been cited so often that they have lost much of their political influence. And even if a direct practical outcome does follow, that is not the real motivation for much basic research.

A very different justification is offered in the claim that man is an explorer, that science is the new frontier, and that research is ennobling. Robert Oppenheimer (1959, p. 3) paired the two reasons in asking:

Why, then, do we seek new knowledge, and ask for the help of others in enabling us to acquire it? To this question there is not one answer, there are two. They are disturbingly unrelated.... One answer is that new knowledge is useful; the other answer is that the getting of it is ennobling. Indeed it is ennobling, as anyone who has spent his life, or an honest part of it, in studying nature can attest. Science today, the study of nature and of man as part of nature, is continuous, despite all that makes it unique in scope, brilliance, and virtuosity, with the long tradition of attempting to comprehend our situation in the world in which we live.

Sometimes a third justification is given: science builds our modern monuments. Giant telescopes, huge accelerators, or missions to the moon are modern equivalents of Egyptian pyramids or medieval cathedrals. They test and prove our technological virtuosity and provide an arena for constructive instead of destructive international competition.

But why, the critic insists, should society spend so much money to enable a few self-selected scientists to enjoy Oppenheimer's ennobling experience, or, when there are so many other claims on public funds, why waste money on useless monuments? There is no easy and politically persuasive answer to the critic's question, and so one usually falls back on the claim that new knowledge will be useful.

If the arguments in support of more research are not altogether convincing, neither are the objections. There is widespread and firm faith that research is worth pursuing, that it is right to provide the scientist with the tools of his trade, that his findings help all men to get a clearer view of themselves and their universe, and that, often enough to pay the bills and give society a good return in addition, those findings also prove practically useful.[1] This faith is not held by scientists alone. It is still shared, as it was in earlier days, by some philanthropists, legislators, and taxpayers, but not by all. And now, as if to reinforce the unpersuaded, the voices of antirationalism seem to be more frequent and more strident than they have been in recent decades.

These uncertainties and disagreements will influence budgets and priorities. They will affect decisions about sponsorship and responsibility. But all this will be within a high level of research

---

[1] The cases in which it is possible to compute the monetary benefits from basic research and to compare those benefits with the costs are rare; they seem to be limited to research in agriculture (Schultz, 1968, pp. 327–347). Nevertheless, it is often clear that basic research, when combined with the results of other basic research often conducted at different times and places, and usually supplemented with applied research specifically directed toward the development of a new product or process, has made significant and valuable contributions toward a practical outcome. The situation is too complex to justify the assignment of dollar values to each of the several streams of research that have been usefully combined. But it is clear that each has made important contributions. Several well-analyzed case histories are described in a report to the NSF (Illinois Institute of Technology Research Institute, 1968). The innovations traced through to their origins are magnetic ferrites, the videotape recorder, the oral contraceptive pill, the electron miscroscope, and the method of matrix isolation.

activity. Scientific, governmental, industrial, and social demands for research will continue, and funds will be available for much work. Where, within this high level, should a university fit? What kinds of research activities, or sponsorship, or support, should it seek? Or avoid? A university needs a rationale for its research activities. And this is no easy time to formulate one. University presidents would testify that the American university is struggling through one of the most difficult periods in its history. Financial problems are becoming so great that reduction of faculty size, research activities, services to students and community, and maintenance of buildings and grounds are becoming commonplace (Cheit, 1971). Confrontations over international and national issues and over campus rules and customs make news headlines and presidential headaches. Students, faculty members, alumni, state legislators, taxpayers, and news analysts are critical of something the university is doing, or failing to do, or doing in the wrong way.[2]

Despite the pressures of current troubles, even because of them, planning and policy guidance are essential. And planning at the university level is necessary because there is more planning at the national level. There is a general governmental trend toward making more of its decisions on the basis of adopted policies and programs and fewer on the basis of individual projects or difficulties. The National Science Board has begun the practice of writing an annual report on the state of some major aspects of science. Congressional committees are asking executive agencies for longer-range forecasts of their financial needs and for supporting projections of their programmatic plans. The emphasis on environmental improvement and the resulting interest in establishing procedures for making searching assessments of the secondary and tertiary as well as the primary effects of proposed new technological developments are further indications that there will be more planning on a long-range basis. To these more immediate reasons must be added the university's enduring obligations to students whose lives and well-being are involved.

At both national and university levels, one of the elements of planning involves periodic reconsideration of why the university

[2] Kerr (1970) summarizes the concerns of college and university presidents under seven headings in decreasing order of frequency: money, faculty relations, control of the institution, student relations, new directions for programs, aims and purposes, and personal considerations. See also Hodgkinson (1971).

needs to engage in research and why society needs to have the university conduct research. Of the several reasons that can be stated from either point of view, three concern functions on which societal interests and university interests are in agreement, even though not always in harmony: to educate students, to maintain and enhance the scientific capabilities of the faculty, and to undergird the university's role as an informed and objective social critic.

Education of students This is the most generally recognized and least-challenged reason for conducting a substantial amount of research in universities. Commerce, labor, the professions, and the government itself all become increasingly dependent on expert knowledge and professional skill. The nation needs a continuing flow of bacteriologists, economists, chemists, and specialists in what seems to be an ever-widening variety of specialties; the nation also needs generalists to serve in positions of leadership. An apprenticeship in research is an essential part of the education of those students who will become scientists or scholars and of many of those who will enter the applied science professions.

Faculty competence Faculty members need research facilities not only to educate students but so that they themselves may continue to learn and improve. Without adequate research opportunities, the best faculty members would leave, and the rest would deteriorate. From the standpoint of the university, the need is self-evident; to add to knowledge is the primary reason for being a scientist or scholar. Research is a large part of the difference between a university and a school of lower level.

These two reasons—the education of students and the maintenance and enhancement of faculty competence—determine the minimum essential level of university research. The minimum may not be the optimum, but the minimum is clear: it is that amount of research that a university needs to give research training of high quality to those students who will follow careers in science, together with what is needed to recruit, retain, and improve a science faculty of high competence.

The university as critic Society is ever at the mercy of the demagogue, the charlatan, the slick advertiser, or the unprincipled self-seeker. For its own protection, society needs the antidote of objectivity, the clear-headed analysis of trends and alternatives, and sometimes the unmasking of false claims. Many of society's most useful social critics have worked outside the university, but academic halls have been the favorite home of others. And the university, first in Europe and later in the United States, has had an honored role in society because even when an academician's views have been unpopular, they have generally been considered more objective than the views of politicians, businessmen, labor leaders, or other advocates of special interests.

The role of critic was not originally a scientific role, and it is by no means wholly one now. A keen sense of values, judgment, awareness of social problems, a broad and clear perspective—these traits are as likely to be found in a philosopher or historian as in a scientist. Yet as science and technology have come to pervade more and more aspects of human life, the need for objective scientific critics has increased, and so, for the same reason, has the need for critics of science. As Abraham Flexner observed 40 years ago, "The more vigorously science is prosecuted, the more acute the need that society be held accountable for the purposes to which larger knowledge and experience are turned. Philosophers and critics, therefore, gain in importance as science makes life more complex—more rational in some ways, more irrational in others" (Flexner, 1930, p. 21).

If faculty members are to be useful social critics, obviously they must be well informed. In some cases, but not all, active involvement in relevant research is an essential, or at least a highly desirable, means of acquiring the necessary knowledge. Some of the research needed for this function also satisfies the requirements stated above for student education and faculty improvement, but there is no guarantee that the amount and kind of research conducted for those reasons will also fill the critic's needs. What is required to fill these needs is a matter on which it will sometimes be impossible to reach calm agreement, for emotions sometimes run high. Probably the best current example, and a good illustration of the kind of conflict of values that can become involved, is found in discussions of the participation of university scientists in military research. Those university scientists who have been engaged in military research have become the targets of much recent criticism, which has sometimes been generalized to apply to any university research supported by the DOD, regardless of its nature, and to any use of university scientists as off-campus consultants on military matters.

Yet before academic scientists are forced to disengage themselves completely from all military affairs, even the most ardent antimilitarists should ask themselves whose views and judgments they wish to have considered in military matters. Do they wish all responsibility to be left to those who are inside the military-industrial complex and to external critics who more often than not are poorly informed on technical details? Congressmen and news analysts serve as external critics, but few have the detailed and specialized knowledge that is required to form independent judgments on the technical aspects of weapons development and capabilities. Thus a question is posed for society: Does society need to have informed and independent critics of weapons and their characteristics and potentialities, or are its interests adequately served if technical information comes only from within the military services and the industries that build weapons? The record of congressional hearings shows that the most penetrating and best-informed analyses of plans for the development or use of new weapons have often come from university scientists with firsthand experience in military research. If society wants this kind of criticism available, some scientists from outside the military services and from outside the industry that produces military equipment must obtain the necessary technical knowledge, and that is most likely to be done through active involvement.[3]

UNIVERSITY OPTIONS

How much and what kind of research beyond the minimum needed for educational purposes and the maintenance of faculty competence should be conducted in a particular university is a matter for decision at the university level and for negotiation with the funding agencies. The better-qualified universities, and the more aggressive ones, will normally want to do more than the minimum. And there is much more than the minimum to be done, for scien-

---

[3] Critics of classified research in universities are right. Classification creates special problems for a university and under normal circumstances is out of place on a campus, for classification of research violates the principle that methods and results should be freely open for discussion and criticism. But the more radical critics are wrong, from the standpoint of their own values, in attacking the faculty members who have served as consultants to government or industry. They have not "sold out," as the critics seem to think. Rather it is the most successful scholars who are most likely to be called upon to serve as consultants to government and industry and who are usually most supportive of minority movements and most critical of government policy in Vietnam. See Lipset (1970, p. 111).

tists, industry, government agencies, foundations, and other representatives of society all have problems that call for investigation.

At one extreme lies the situation in which some external organization has a quite specific problem to solve and expects to use the information for its own private or proprietary purposes. By common consent, this is the kind of work which is least appropriate for a university. At the opposite end of the spectrum lies the most basic and fundamental kind of research, research which contributes to scientific knowledge and for which practical usefulness is uncertain in form and location. This is the kind of research for which the university has accepted an especial responsibility.

Between these two extremes is a wide range of problems for which decisions usually have to be made on a case-by-case basis. One consideration is the simple matter of efficiency; a particular university may have the best facilities or the best-qualified staff for a particular study, and the faculty members may be interested in conducting the research. Another situation is that in which the further investigation of interesting scientific questions requires equipment of such very great cost that only the federal government can provide the necessary funds, and it must balance the merits of that proposed investigation against other claims for always limited funds. Still another category is the research that is needed to help achieve some national purpose—in medical research, transportation, space, or any other program for which an agency of government requires research and wishes to follow the usual policy of contracting with an external agency for the necessary work.

An additional reason for a university to conduct research is public duty. The university may be well qualified, and even though the faculty members involved would prefer to work on other problems, they, like other good citizens, feel an obligation to do what they can to contribute to society. Self-interest is also a motive, and although self-interest may perhaps be considered the least praiseworthy of all the reasons for conducting research under university auspices, neither scientists nor university presidents can afford to neglect practical considerations. At land-grant colleges, the entire faculty was long under substantial obligation to the agricultural scientists because it was they who conducted research and provided services that the public wanted. Their work enhanced the public reputation of the whole university and helped secure appropriations for the work of all their colleagues.

In all these situations, and for these various reasons, the amount and kind of university research—always above the essential minimum—are often subject to negotiation. The university is usually not the only possible agency; industrial laboratories and independent research institutes are also available. Where a particular research program is conducted depends upon facilities, the qualifications and interests of the scientists involved, and, in the last analysis, the political and policy decisions of the persons responsible for initiating a research proposal and of their counterparts who are responsible for awarding a research grant or contract.

In most cases the distinction between basic and applied research is unimportant in deciding about university involvement. It creates an artificial barrier within science, and to contend that one kind of research belongs in the university and the other does not restricts university flexibility. Research is appropriate for the university if it is educationally useful, if it contributes significantly to knowledge and to faculty competence, and if it is of excellent quality (Kidd, 1959, pp. 32–33). The label is unimportant.

Nevertheless, employment trends now point to the desirability of giving students greater acquaintance with some of the interesting problems in the area of applied research. The industrial and business sectors have already become the largest employers of persons with Ph.D.'s in the physical sciences, and in nearly all fields of science, business and industrial requirements will increase more rapidly over the next two decades than will academic requirements.

MULTI-DISCIPLINARY RESEARCH

In the zone between the kind of research that is rarely appropriate for a university and the kind that is always appropriate, the most difficult policy questions are likely to center around the university's responsibility for multidisciplinary research on large problems of great social importance. Pollution, population control, drug abuse, waste disposal, crime, health care, and improvement of the social and physical environment all call for integrated efforts of lawyers, economists, sociologists, physicians, psychologists, engineers, biologists, chemists, systems analysts, and perhaps other kinds of specialists. Friends and critics are urging universities to give more attention to these pressing social problems. The National Science Board (1969a) has recommended multidisciplinary programs to give graduate students opportunities to engage in research on the needs and problems of society. John R. Platt (1969, pp. 1115–1121) has gone so far as to propose that the large-scale mobilization of scientists may be the only effective way to deal with the multiple crises now facing the world.

In opposition, however, there is one sound reason for not developing large multidisciplinary research programs within regular university faculties: universities simply have not been very good at this kind of research. If many people from different disciplines are to work effectively together, their individual work must be coordinated, planned, and assigned within a hierarchical organization that is foreign to the university's tradition of individualism.

The departmental structure that has fostered the development of individual scientific disciplines has also, and by its very strength, created difficulties for multidisciplinary work. Cooperation is impeded by such procedural, and sometimes petty, barriers as the problem of allocating costs and credits to the budgets of the several departments involved. More importantly, cooperation is impeded by departmental or disciplinary allegiance. After a faculty member has gained tenure and seniority he is free to work on what he pleases. A young beginner knows that his scientific reputation and professional advancement depend primarily on gaining the respect of senior men in his own discipline. The approval of workers in other fields may not be a handicap, but neither is it of much help. It is easy to be impatient with such barriers, but they exist, and because they exist the university is not as well adapted to multidisciplinary research as are special-purpose institutes.

NASA made a deliberate effort in the 1960s to encourage a number of universities to foster multidisciplinary cooperation (Task Force . . . , 1968; Webb, 1967, pp. 53–61, & 1970). Of course NASA wanted university help on its own research program, but beyond that NASA, and particularly James Webb, the administrator, thought the space effort gave interested universities an opportunity to gain experience in using their wide and varied resources in an integrated fashion—experience they would find valuable in learning how to work on other large problems of great national importance.

To help achieve these objectives, NASA developed a program of sustaining university grants to supplement grants for specific projects and programs. Grants were made for the study of the management and coordination of research and development activities, analysis of the socioeconomic effects of large technological programs, and the study of NASA's own management techniques and their possible application to other endeavors. In addition, a number of universities that were conducting substantial amounts of research for NASA were provided with funds for the construction of new buildings that would permit much of that research to be brought together under one roof. Finally, because changes in attitudes, working habits, and university arrangements were also necessary if the whole effort was to succeed, one of the conditions for the building-construction grants was a memorandum of understanding in which the university agreed to use its best efforts to encourage multidisciplinary work on its own campus and to seek better means of coordinating some of its own research with related work being conducted in industry or government.[4]

In designing experiments, building equipment flown on unmanned space missions, analyzing samples brought back from the moon, and in other specialized ways, universities contributed notably to the NASA program. At the same time, NASA grants helped the universities to increase their competence and to acquire new facilities. In contrast, the effort to induce significant increases in multidisciplinary interests and programs was of little value to NASA and had little effect on universities. Discussions with faculty members and administrative officers on several campuses which signed memorandums of understanding indicated that they did not make serious efforts to comply with the agreements they had signed. As the value structures of the university and of the specialized disciplines would lead one to expect, the strength of interest in multidisciplinary work and in planning for the university as an institution was associated with a person's rank. Presidents and other central administrative officers were most interested; junior faculty members were least interested. A considerable number of faculty members simply did not take the memorandum of understanding seriously; they disdained it as something some Washington bureaucrat had decided to write into the grant for the new building they wanted, but not as anything that need cause them to alter their ways of working. Often enough the funds and building were used cooperatively by scientists in closely related fields; such combinations as physicists and electrical engineers, chemists and geophysicists, or geneticists and physiologists were found working productively together, just as they had done before NASA was established. But the universities did not effectively develop the

---

[4] British observers consider the linkage closer in the United States. See *Industry, Science, and Universities* (1970).

kind of broad, multidisciplinary research experience and competence that NASA tried to encourage.

In the continuing debate on how to conduct research on large multidisciplinary problems, there are now two diverging trends. One proposes to assign all or nearly all such work to specially created institutes. The other insists that the university must learn how to work effectively on some of these problems. The first trend is exemplified by many recommendations for the creation of new institutes or the use of existing ones to work on social and environmental problems. Looking into the future, and considering the kinds of research institutions that are likely to be most useful in the twenty-first century, Alvin Weinberg (1967, p. 110) has contrasted the research styles of the university and the separate research institute in this way:

In the individualistic, competitive university environment, genius flourishes; but things go slowly because each genius works by himself with his own small group of students and assistants. In the less individualistic, cooperative institute environment, genius probably does not flourish as well, but things go very fast because so many different talents can be brought to bear on a given problem. It is a place in which, however, a single very able man can exert much more power and influence than he can in the university environment.

Speed and organization are important, but beyond these differences there is a substantial distinction between the kind of science that usually flourishes in universities and the kind needed for work on society's pressing problems. As a scientific discipline advances under the guidance of its own internal logic and the direction of scientists whose primary interests are in pure science, it almost inevitably becomes more remote from practicality. In a research institute or in industry most of the work is organized about problems; thus, the scientists have a different motivation, and their criteria of what constitutes successful work differ from the measures of success of a scientist working in a university department. This distinction between basic and applied research is sharper in mathematics, physics, and other branches of science in which there is a well-developed body of rigorous quantitative theory than it is in the social sciences and those parts of biology that lack a rigorous theoretical base. One result is that it is in these latter fields that one is most likely to find colleagues with pure and applied interests working happily together in the same department, while it is in mathematics that there seems most often to be a separation between the purists in departments of mathematics and the applied mathematicians who are pushed off into lower-caste departments such as computer sciences.

Thus there is a division within the university as well as between the university and independent research institutes, and the division is sharpest in the most rigorous and highly developed fields of science. As knowledge of solid-state physics advances, much of the work is moved from the department of physics to the college of engineering or to an institute on materials research. As knowledge of atomic and nuclear processes grows, nuclear engineering takes over responsibility. The more an academic department learns about its field, the more it is inclined to delegate the useful applications elsewhere.

Knowing these trends, and projecting them into the future, Weinberg (1971, p. 314) concluded that no existing institutions are adequate to handle the complex, multidisciplinary problems on which society is urgently asking for help:

The existing institutions are not quite adequate for this task. The industrial laboratories fall short because these global problems have little to do with the market place. The universities fall short because they are fragmented and disciplinary. It therefore seems to me that society will have to invent new institutions that can apply science to the broad socio-technological problems of the future. Just as the scientific university sprang up as the dominant landmark of pure science in the present century, so the national socio-technological institution could emerge as the dominant home of socially applicable science in the next century.

Altogether there is a strong case against the universities. They have not been very good at multidisciplinary research. They did not take advantage of the help offered by NASA. The scientifically purest parts of the university move to new problems and leave the practical application of past successes to others. If these characteristics are permanent, if the universities will not be able to conduct useful studies of social and environmental problems, the proper policy for university and scientific leaders would seem to be to help create excellent independent research institutes. To justify this stance they will have the correlative task of convincing society that the role of the university and the role of these institutes are quite different and that both institutions need support and can work more effectively if each is encouraged to concentrate on its own area of responsibility.

This is one conclusion, but some people find it unacceptable. They do not want the university written off as being unable to cope with current problems. The distinction, they say, between pure science and applied sciences is overdrawn; many scientists enjoy working in both areas and find a mixture intellectually stimulating. Excellently trained young scientists are available and eager for work on socially relevant research, and it is a duty of the university to conduct such research.

Franklin Long (1971, p. 961) has asserted:

But the most important reason why the universities must become involved in interdisciplinary research—and the central reason why society must *insist* on their participation—is their obligation to youth. Coming generations must be taught about society's problems and about the best ways to solve them. College students must learn a genuinely interdisciplinary approach; this can only happen when their professors have personal knowledge of and commitment to interdisciplinary research and when there are programs wherein students can learn by doing—in short, when an interdisciplinary approach permeates the university.

Pressure the universities if you will; castigate their occasionally overly narrow behavior; insist on changed structures and reward mechanisms. But for earth's sake, don't count them out.

Some universities are trying to respond, and their responses have taken a variety of organizational patterns. The Joint Institute for Laboratory Astrophysics was established by the University of Colorado and the National Bureau of Standards following extensive planning to try to foresee all the difficulties of an organization partly staffed by tenured faculty members and partly by government employees, financed partly by a university and partly by a government agency, working on a range of basic and applied problems, and offering opportunities for government employees to teach university classes and graduate students to do their dissertation research under the supervision of Bureau of Standards personnel.[5]

Encouraged by its successful collaboration with the National

---

[5] See Branscomb (1969). A discussion of the problems, uses, and advantages of joint government-university laboratories and the reasons for their success are given in Tillinghast (1970, pp. 206–217).

Bureau of Standards, the University of Colorado has entered into a similar agreement with the National Oceanic and Atmospheric Administration for a jointly sponsored laboratory to work on environmental problems. Lewis Branscomb, who was primarily responsible for the creation of the Joint Institute for Laboratory Astrophysics, believes that essentially the same organizational pattern could be effective in linking university and government work on transportation, urban problems, or other social areas if the university involved is conducting good basic research in the area, and if the government agency has both operating and research responsibilities and has real research competence within its own staff.[6]

A quite different organizational structure is illustrated by the Environmental Studies Institute of the University of Illinois. This institute was formed as a new university unit with its own faculty, staff, budget, and facilities. To augment its permanent core staff, the institute has authority to arrange joint appointments, part-time appointments, and temporary transfers of faculty members from other parts of the university and to work cooperatively with state agencies. The institute selected as its first specific problem an interdisciplinary effort to develop a detailed mathematical model of the transport of lead from its sources in the earth's crust through the many intertwined pathways by which it moves through industry, plants, animals, human beings, air, water, and soil and to determine what happens to lead and what happens because of its presence as it proceeds along these transport routes (Ewing, 1970; Ad Hoc Committee . . . , 1970).

A still different structure is represented by the Academy for Contemporary Problems, jointly sponsored by Ohio State University and the Battelle Memorial Institute. In this case a university and an independent consulting firm have agreed to finance for 10 years an organization that will conduct studies of selected social problems and at the same time use that work as a basis for studying how to conduct such studies, how best to secure cooperative efforts, how to transfer knowledge from one field to another, and how a research institute can be effectively linked with the public it is attempting to serve.

A fourth and more radically different organizational possibility was proposed in a planning paper Erich Jantsch wrote for M.I.T. Jantsch (1969) proposed a sweeping reorganization to integrate

---

[6] Personal communication from Lewis M. Branscomb, December 1970.

the university's education, research, and service functions in a fashion designed to blur the distinctions between faculty and students and to equip the whole institution to work together in planning the future, preparing students to work on major problems, and advancing knowledge necessary to deal with those problems. Specifically, he proposed a matrix type of organization involving the continuous interaction and movement of students and faculty among three types of departments or laboratories: departments of the basic disciplines; departments of the applied technologies; and laboratories in which the appropriate disciplines and technologies would work together in designing systems to deal with major sociotechnological problems.

These examples by no means exhaust the list of multidisciplinary programs in universities. They illustrate a range of organizational patterns, each of which was given form only after careful analysis of the substantive problems to be dealt with and the organizational problems of dealing with them effectively.

Other universities have tried other organizational arrangements, some of which, it must be admitted, are multidisciplinary in name only: a new name has been added to an organization chart, but the people go on working as before. Even these changes, however, demonstrate a belief that universities should devote more effort to the problems on which society places high priority.

Public decisions as to where such research is to be conducted and university decisions as to how they should be involved are both matters of major policy. Environmental and social problems are of increasing public interest. So far, there is more talk than money, but appropriations will increase under the pressure of the overwhelmingly evident need for social and environmental improvement. The concept of technology assessment is one illustration of the kind of work that is to be done. In the field of social legislation more advance analyses and experimentation and more use of pilot projects are needed. The Head Start program was begun without carefully controlled pretests or pilot projects. In fact, Congress was reluctant to approve funds for the evaluation of social programs. More recently, Congress has sometimes insisted that new social legislation be tried out experimentally and that the experiments be thoroughly evaluated before the program is put into widespread use.

From the standpoint of public policy it will be proper and efficient to have much of the work done by industry and independent institutes. And at least in the short run, this arrangement is likely to be the most productive one. But a longer-range view argues for some major university involvement. The university includes the whole range of talents that are required for multidisciplinary work of high quality. It includes some faculty members who are eager to pool their talents in joint efforts. And it includes many students who would welcome the experience of working in such settings. To gain intimate contact with vital public issues and to develop an essential kind of research experience for some students, those universities which have the qualifications and the necessary flexibility should carefully weigh the costs and benefits of breaking down the existing barriers and developing substantial programs of multidisciplinary research.

Not every university need take this course; diversity of research styles is desirable. The whole university should not be converted to a new work mode; analytical, discipline-oriented research will continue to provide the main channel toward advancement of basic scientific knowledge. Not all social problems need become topics of major university research; the university must be selective because research has little to offer on some problems. Finally, and never to be forgotten, intellectual freedom, high standards of quality, and attention to educational objectives should be as insistently demanded in these new programs as in more traditional research.

After all these qualifications are stated, there still remains a university obligation: to society, to students, and to interested faculty members. To meet the obligation and accept the opportunity offered will produce strains and difficulties. If large, multidisciplinary programs are to match the quality expected in more traditional types of university research, the new efforts must have facilities, funds, strong leadership, and freedom to select and reward their own staffs. Establishing such an organization is therefore a matter of major institutional policy. The decision is not one to make at the departmental or individual level; this decision calls for the best policy-making wisdom the faculty and the administration can muster. Deans, presidents, and trustees must agree, but they cannot make such a new system work. Only the faculty can make research productive, just as the faculty can prevent any change from becoming effective. The major decision must therefore be worked out by the faculty in that cumbersome and often undisciplined arena called faculty politics. If out of such debate there does come a concerted move into this new kind of research, if departmental barriers are breached and multidisciplinary work successfully encouraged, a permanently important change in the character of the university will have been made.

This decision, like decisions on the minimum research requirements for the attainment of educational objectives and the enhancement of faculty capabilities and decisions on the nature and amount of research that seems desirable above the minimum, need not and should not be the same in all universities. A diversity of styles is desirable, and university specialization is becoming increasingly necessary.

9. Future Policy

In each year since 1967, federal government agencies have granted approximately $3.5 billion to American colleges and universities. Each year's total included $1.5 billion for scientific research, close to $1 billion for other scientific purposes, and $1 billion or more for other educational activities.

Annual amounts of this magnitude would seem to call for a rational, carefully thought out policy to serve as a guide in planning future programs and expenditures. It is fashionable to say that there is no such policy, and it is true that the government has no coordinated annual budget for research and other scientific activities and no long-range plan for federal support of science or of higher education. New programs are added to meet an emergency and are sometimes dropped or curtailed with equal abruptness. Budgets are prepared on an annual basis and are usually not settled until several months after the fiscal year has started. Michael Reagan (1968, pp. 33–36) summed up the situation in giving a 1968 article the derisive title, "$17 Billion in Search of a Policy."

Yet if there is not A Science Policy, there are some science policies. There will probably be more; and there is considerable room for negotiation and debate over their nature, scope, and details, for Congress and the academic world have some different objectives, and both are ambivalent about having policies for science become too formal and specific. Certainly the absence of a national science policy is not an oversight. In addition to all the recommendations that have been made by individual scientists, political scientists, and educational leaders, there has been a succession of requests and recommendations from within the federal government. The NSF has never gotten around to carrying out its original congressional instruction "to develop and encourage the pursuit of a national policy for the promotion of basic research and education in the sciences" (National Science Foundation Act of 1950). After the Office of Science and Technology was established, it was given some of the policy-making responsibility earlier assigned to the NSF, and it, too, declined to promulgate a national policy for science. In 1964, the National Academy of Sciences reviewed the science-university-government relationship in response to a congressional request and in its review included recommendations by a number of individual authors, but it did not agree on policy proposals (National Academy of Sciences, 1964). At congressional request, the National Science Board does now make an annual report on some aspect of the state of science in the United States. Its first report, in 1969, included a number of policy recommendations for graduate education in the sciences. A year later, Eliot Richardson, the newly appointed secretary of Health, Education and Welfare, called for the development of a federal policy toward higher education (American Council on Education, 1970). From the congressional side, the group that is most concerned with science matters — the House Subcommittee on Science, Research, and Development — has been making pleas for a national science policy and in 1970 recommended that the President appoint a special task force to prepare a statement of national science policy that could be considered by Congress during the 1972 legislative session (U.S. House of Representatives, 1970a).

In disregarding this recommendation, on which Congress as a whole took no action, the President followed the precedent of the NSF, the Office of Science and Technology, and the NAS. Perhaps the fact that neither the federal government nor the universities have made much progress in developing a national science policy means that both prefer to continue to operate without one. Some congressmen and congressional committees have pressed for the development of a national science policy, but many congressmen have been reluctant to see one formalized. The Constitution includes no direct provision for the support of research or higher education,[1] and congressmen learned a very long time ago that when constitutional questions were introduced into discussions of science or education the debate could be prolonged. The bequest of James

---

[1] No provision, that is, other than the patent and copyright provision: "To promote the progress of science and useful arts, by securing for limited times to authors and inventors the exclusive right to their respective writings and discoveries" (Art. 1, sec. 8).

Smithson became known in 1829, but not until 1846 did Congress establish the Smithsonian Institution.

To avoid lengthy and troublesome debates, Congress has frequently skirted the constitutional issue. It has been easier to treat each problem individually and pragmatically, by acting as if the problem were temporary or unique. When the first Russian satellite shocked the nation, emergency measures seemed to be called for, and although many congressmen knew that in reality they were initiating a substantial and long-term increase in federal support for higher education, passage of the bill they adopted was made easier by calling it the National Defense Education Act (NDEA).

Reluctance to formulate a policy will continue. The existence of a formally stated and codified policy would restrict congressional options; scientists and university presidents could then wave the document in the air whenever they were disappointed with appropriations and complain, "But you promised. . . ." In short, the question of policy is partly a question of power, and Congress is not eager to reduce its own power.

For much the same reason, some scientists and some university presidents would prefer not to have a detailed, formal policy. Their individual freedom of action would be reduced if they were obligated to comply with the plans and policies that could be agreed upon by universities acting collectively or by scientists acting as a group. They, too, would lose power.

As for research scientists, many fear that "policy" means "control" or "directives." Basic research cannot be programmed in advance or have its new ideas and findings directed from a bureaucratic center. Knowing the surprises, the spontaneity, and the need to follow the logic of the science itself in making fundamental advances, scientists tend to resist any effort to establish priorities or make any plans other than for expansion.

The concept of a national policy for science is too pretentious, too much like a treaty between the federal government and the universities. (Who, by the way, would sign such a treaty on behalf of the universities?) Although a policy in this comprehensive sense is improbable, there is a reasonable likelihood that government plans will be more explicitly formulated and that there will be more long-range planning than in the past. Because every major governmental decision affects a complex social system in a variety of ways, there is pressure to do more planning on an overall basis in terms of specific policies and less in terms of individual programs and immediate claims or problems (Moynihan, 1970). Thus it is quite possible that, in one way or another, within a few years, the federal government will formulate not *a* science policy but a number of science policies more clearly and explicitly than has been done in the past. The chances that this will happen are good enough to make it prudent for scientists and universities to try to decide what they think those policies should be. Whatever the form, or timing, or details, policies in this more specific sense—call them working rules—will be based on ideas and recommendations from a variety of sources. Three sets of values have to be involved: those of the public, as represented by the federal government and perhaps other institutions; those of the universities and, in a less immediate but nevertheless real sense, the rest of higher education; and those of the scientists, the people who will do the work. (It is not unlikely, nor need it be disturbing, that there will be some clashes among these three sets of values.) It is necessary to understand what the values and the value conflicts are so that appropriate compromises can be worked out.[2]

In broad outline, society and the government need from scientists and the universities assurance that publicly important work will be done effectively, confidence that the universities will continue to be strong and adaptable institutions responsibly able to manage their own affairs, and a workable understanding that the universities will be, in some proper sense, publicly accountable for the public funds entrusted to them. The universities, in turn, need sufficient independence from federal control so that they can be responsible for their own policies and internal development. And to aid them in their own planning, they need longer-range projections of national objectives, reasonable assurance of fiscal continuity, and greater authority to decide how some reasonable portion of their federal support can be most productively used.

There are obvious interrelationships among these needs. For example, if the universities are to remain independent of external control and are to be given greater freedom to decide how a portion of their federal support will be used, the public, in return, has a right to insist upon responsible internal management of the universities and on a public account of what they have accomplished.

---

[2] Wilson (1971, pp. 171–196) presents a well-documented discussion about some of the government-university policy problems.

The debates that will be involved in agreeing upon details and working rules within this broad set of national and university needs will be more incisive and reflect better judgment if science, the universities, and the government are clearly informed about what they need from each other in order to make their cooperation as fruitful and effective as possible.

CONSTRAINTS AND TRENDS

In considering government-university-science relations, it is obviously desirable to plan for what would be most generally beneficial, but planning must start from where we are now. Government bureaucracies resist rapid change. So do university faculties. So does the nature of scientific thought and practice. Future relations linking science, the universities, and the federal government are already partially determined by what they have been in the past. Because the inertia of established procedures and values sets limits on future relations, some of the dimensions of future policy can already be stated with reasonable confidence.

Use of the private sector The federal policy of using universities, industry, and other agencies in the private sector for research and other services that are not required to be performed within government agencies is so well established and has worked so satisfactorily that it is not likely to be changed in the foreseeable future.

Procurement of research The federal government may in the future assume greater responsibility for maintaining the strength and welfare of colleges and universities as institutions. But even if this happens, the major part of the funds for research will still be granted on a project basis, for purposes determined by federal agencies, and usually in response to proposals submitted by interested scientists.

Public and private universities Use of both public and private universities will continue. The facilities available, the qualifications of faculty and students, and the merit of the proposals submitted will continue to determine the amount of research funds a university receives from federal agencies.

Use of multiple sources of support Reorganization and new combinations of federal agencies are likely to occur from time to time, but agencies with scientific interests will not be gathered together into a single superagency. Universities, therefore, will continue to deal with several federal sources of financial support.

Establishment of special institutes As new interests develop and as priorities change, recommendations (and reasons) will continue for the establishment of special-purpose institutes to deal with the new problems. For some kinds of research, these institutes, or industry, will be preferred over the universities.

Progress over a broad front Robert Gilpin (1970, pp. 441–448) has classified the nations of the world into three groups according to their national strategies for science and technology. The U.S.S.R., the United States, and, earlier, the United Kingdom adopted the strategy of trying to achieve excellence and even leadership across the broadest possible front of scientific and technological advance. Other countries, such as Sweden, Switzerland, and the Netherlands, specialized in areas of particular interest to their own economic conditions and plans. Still others, of which Japan has been the outstanding example, have given modest support to many areas of science while depending heavily upon the importation of technology under license from other countries. Although some parts of "big" science—for example, atmospheric studies—are of a nature that requires international cooperation and other parts—high energy physics, for example—are so expensive that international cost sharing is becoming increasingly necessary, the United States will continue to seek excellence across a broad front. But whether or not it should, or can afford to, seek leadership in all fields will be asked more frequently as costs continue to rise and as other countries continue to gain scientific strength.

In addition to these established policies, there are four clearly evident trends that help to determine what future policy must be:

1 *Slower growth of research funds* Congressional appropriations to the NSF, NIH, and other federal agencies that support research will increase, but less rapidly than they did from 1953 to 1967.

2 *Slower growth of universities* Undergraduate enrollment in colleges and universities will continue to increase until about 1982. Then a decline can be expected, for there will be a period of several years when the number of people in the 18- to 22-year-old age group will be smaller than in the 1970s. Graduate enrollment will be subject to counteracting pressures. The annual number of college graduates qualified to continue to the master's

or doctorate levels will continue to increase until about 1985. However, there will be efforts to decrease the rate of expansion of graduate schools because the number of doctorates being awarded already equals or exceeds the effective demand in several fields.[3]

3 *Utilization of Ph.D.'s* In the past, half or more of new Ph.D. holders were appointed to the faculties of universities and four-year colleges. In the sciences and engineering, the next largest group has been engaged in research and development in industry or government. The occupational distribution is now changing. Slower growth of undergraduate enrollment means that fewer new Ph.D.'s will be required for academic positions than were required during the long period of rapid expansion. Because research and development funds for industry are not expected to increase as rapidly as they did during the 1953–1967 period of emphasis on the military, aviation, space, and related high-technology areas, industrial research positions will increase less rapidly. Thus in comparison with the past, a smaller percentage of new Ph.D.'s will be employed in universities and in research, and a correspondingly larger percentage will enter other kinds of work (NSF, 1971c). Some graduate students can continue to be trained in the image of their major professors, but for others a less specialized education with less emphasis on research skills will be more appropriate and will be available.

4 *Interinstitutional competition* There will be much competition for federal funds that support research and other scientific activities. Since 1966 deficits have been appearing in the operating budgets of a growing number of universities, both public and private (Cheit, 1971), yet enrollment pressure will force some of the universities to continue to expand. Approximately 150 four-year colleges have announced that during the 1970s they expect to begin offering graduate programs leading to the Ph.D. (Mayhew, 1970). Nonprofit institutes and industry will continue to seek funds for research and development. Research institutes that used to work exclusively for the DOD have been encouraged to diversify and seek part of their support from other sources. Research funds will probably not increase in the next few years as rapidly as will the number of scientists. For all these reasons, competition for research funds is likely to be intense.

THE GOVERNMENT-UNIVERSITY RELATIONSHIP

The persistence of these policies and trends establishes some characteristics of the government-university relationship but leaves substantial maneuvering room for agreement on improvements.

[3] Projections of future numbers of Ph.D. degrees, the utilization of doctorates, and the problem of reducing the rate of increase in numbers of Ph.D.'s are discussed in Cartter (1971, pp. 132–140), NSF (1971c), and Wolfle & Kidd (1971, pp. 784–793).

The most general change called for is one of style and scope. National policy for the support and conduct of scientific activities can no longer be formulated without considering universities as whole institutions. Such a large fraction of the research that is supported by federal funds is carried out in universities, and science is such a large part of any major university that is no longer tolerable to try to formulate policy for science without giving full consideration to the long-term health of the institution that is its principal home. And it is no longer realistic to try to formulate such policy without recognizing that in some respects the big prestigious universities have become quasi-governmental agencies (Waldo, 1970, pp. 106–113).

In 1969, federal funds for scientific and other purposes were granted to 2,249 institutions of higher education, including junior colleges, four-year colleges, universities, and other more specialized institutions. One hundred universities received 69 percent of the total, and the same one hundred universities received 80 percent of the federal funds for scientific activities. The federal allocation system has sometimes been criticized for concentrating so much money in so few institutions. Concentration, however, must be judged in terms of some reasonable base line. The 100 institutions that received 80 percent of the funds for science were the large, high-quality, scientifically productive universities that awarded 86 percent of the Ph.D. degrees in science and engineering.

In terms of judged quality of their graduate departments, the federal funds were less concentrated than were the scientific departments of highest quality. Of all the 2,249 institutions of higher education that received some federal funds in 1969, about 10 percent offer the Ph.D. degree in one or more fields. These 225 to 250 institutions (the number changes every year) can be called universities. The 24 excellent universities listed in Table 1 constitute only 10 percent of all the universities, but they include 75 percent of all the graduate departments considered distinguished or strong. The graduate faculties of highest quality, as judged by their peers, are indeed highly concentrated in the largest and strongest universities: 10 percent of the universities include 75 percent of the distinguished and strong graduate departments; 20 percent of the universities include 96 percent of such departments; 30 percent of the universities include every distinguished and strong graduate department in the country. The other 70 percent include not a single such department (Roose & Anderson, 1970).

Of course these statements do not mean that only in the top-ranking universities are students well educated. Some of the finest colleges offer no work beyond the bachelor's or master's level. There are good junior colleges. On many campuses that do not have national reputations, there are excellent teachers and good matches between a student's needs and the opportunities offered him.

Nevertheless, the high-quality universities with large scientific and scholarly resources have such a distinctive and special role in the whole scheme of higher education that policies for their support have to be considered on a national basis and have to be treated differently from policies for the support of higher education as a whole. Junior colleges, like elementary and secondary schools, are local institutions. Most colleges draw their students from nearby. Universities draw from a wider geographic range, especially at the graduate level, and the higher the quality of the university the more it attracts students from all over the country or the world. The high-quality universities are national, rather than regional or local, institutions. Their responsibilities are increasingly national; their support is increasingly national.

In a study of the migration of men and women who received Ph.D. degrees between 1957 and 1960, the Commission on Human Resources found that 52 percent earned the doctorate in a region of the country other than that in which they had had their high school education. (For this analysis, the United States was divided into seven geographic regions.) After receiving the doctorate, 57 percent accepted employment in a geographic region other than the one in which they had earned the degree. Students who took their doctorates in university departments of the highest quality were even more mobile: 56 percent left their home regions to attend universities in other regions of the country, and 61 percent moved from the region in which they had earned the doctorate to a different region for their first post-Ph.D. positions (Folger, Astin, & Bayer, 1970, p. 224).

Viewed from the national or governmental standpoint, the university was the chosen instrument to accomplish the national commitment to achieve excellence across a broad scientific front. It is the site of much of the research that is conducted to achieve the objectives of governmental agencies. Universities administer national laboratories planned and financed entirely by government agencies. In addition to their research activities, universities educate and certify most of the people who will later occupy positions of responsibility throughout society and government; they manage international educational programs on behalf of the United States; and they provide midcareer education for officers of the government.

That the universities are much more than job shops to be called upon when needed for particular research projects—that their continued strength is intimately bound up with the welfare of the nation as a whole—has been recognized in numerous presidential statements and other governmental documents. Yet the government-university relationship continues to be handled primarily in a piecemeal fashion. It is time for a change of style, for policies that assume a continuing instead of a temporary relationship, and for greater governmental concern for the permanent well-being of the university as an institution. This change of style would involve an alteration of the means by which federal agencies support university activities and alterations within and among universities to give them greater institutional strength and responsibility in dealing with government agencies so that they may better serve national purposes while retaining independence of government control. As for the changes on the government side, there are three that would help universities plan more constructively and conduct their scientific activities more productively: universities should have fuller and earlier information on national scientific needs and resources, more stable funding than they have had in recent years, and discretionary use of some reasonable portion of their federal support.

PROJECTIONS OF SCIENTIFIC NEEDS AND RESOURCES

It is sometimes charged that American scientists and engineers are not meeting their responsibilities with respect to high-priority goals of social and environmental improvement. Here, only the research aspect of that charge can be considered. Harvey Brooks has replied that scientists and engineers are being asked to shoot at a moving target. They can learn to do that if the target has a predictable trajectory, but not if it follows an erratic course. Research is a time-consuming activity; if research scientists are to make useful contributions to future problems, they must have reasonable warning of what those problems are to be and sufficient time to conduct the necessary research. When given such time, the record demonstrates, they can make effective contributions to the attainment of national goals. Brooks (1970, pp. 225–226) cites the record of the past decade:

It is less than ten years ago that President Kennedy announced . . . that the nation should land a man on the moon and return him safely to earth within the decade. Now we have achieved that goal. . . . It was less than ten years ago that the "missile gap" was an object of almost universal concern and apprehension. The nation geared up to close this gap in a remarkably short time and achieved a "stable deterrent. . . ." Less than ten years ago we saw lagging economic growth as a major source of social dislocation, and we set bold objectives of accelerated growth to absorb a rapidly expanding and underutilized labor force. With the technology of modern macro-economics, and backed by a national consensus, we achieved a halving of the unemployment rate despite an annual addition to the working population at twice the rate of the previous decade. . . . From the launching of Sputnik through the early 60's, the whole thrust of national educational policy was toward the advancement of the achievement of the most academically talented segments of our population. . . . The goals of such programs were largely achieved.

In these cases, goals were set. The unavoidable time lag was recognized, and money and motivation were provided. Scientists, engineers, economists, and educators went to work, and the goals were achieved. Some of the goals are now being criticized, but the point is that goals must be determined early if research is to make useful contributions.

The House Subcommittee on Science, Research, and Development (U.S. House . . . , 1970a, p. 21) has recognized this fact in recommending that the Office of Management and Budget publish annually a five-year projection of scientific and technological trends, probable national needs for scientific resources, expected levels of federal support in various areas, and the relations of these projections to social and other factors that may affect the trends.

This is an operational proposal. It is not an exhortation that goals be set — every President and every Congress does that already — but rather a plea that the Office of Management and Budget extend and make public projections and information that it must have for its own operations but now keeps secret.

There is no doubt that scientists and universities would find such projections useful in their planning. There is also no doubt that the Office of Management and Budget would lose some flexibility if plans for five years ahead were always publicly known. But there is a strong probability that the nation would gain in the effectiveness, relevance, and efficiency of the research it supports.

A good part of the research work that goes on in universities is not specifically aimed at solving practical problems or at meeting national goals. Nor should it be. The basic researcher who has mapped out his own 10-year program of research might pay no attention to changing national goals or to projections of support level for their attainment. But many faculty members are not so self-directed and would be influenced in choosing their own research problems by information concerning national plans and priorities. Moreover, many faculty members prefer to have students work on problems that the students themselves have chosen or find interesting. Knowledge of national research objectives would influence the direction of some university research and could do so without distorting or harming science. Substantial contributions to basic science have appeared in the course of problem-oriented work. The maser and the laser first appeared in laboratories that were working on problems of electronic communication. Interest in transistors and other new electronic devices stimulated fundamental research in solid-state physics, partly to gain knowledge needed to go forward with practical applications but partly also because the new devices suggested research questions that had not been thought of before (Brooks, 1966). In a recent analysis of 62 important social science developments of the twentieth century, Deutsch, Platt, and Senghass (1971, pp. 450–459) found that about three-fourths had come out of efforts to deal with practical demands or conflicts rather than with purely theoretical concerns.

In a university's planning of its educational programs, attention to national goals can also be helpful. What kind of specialists, in what numbers, will be needed in the future? This question is always important in setting educational budgets and planning curricular changes, especially in professional and graduate schools. Leonard Lecht (1966, 1969) has projected the dollar costs and the manpower requirements to meet national goals in each of 16 areas, as those goals have been expressed in presidential statements, congressional actions, and policy papers. The gross national product (GNP) will not be large enough and there will not be enough workers in the foreseeable future to meet all the goals in all 16 areas. Choices will have to be made, but if those choices are made and announced, universities will have a better basis for planning their work.

Goals change, of course, and some that once seemed attractive no longer do. In fact, each of the goals of the early 1960s now has more critics than it did a decade ago. We reached the moon, but the feeling of success is diluted by the charge that the resources spent on that effort might better have been devoted to other objectives. We closed the "missile gap," but military strength is less widely supported than it once was. Interest in improving educational opportunities for the ablest students has been largely superseded by efforts to improve educational opportunities for those who have been most deprived. Whether one agrees with these charges or not, from the standpoint of planning and organizing national effort, the point is still valid that only if plans are known well in advance can research be expected to make major contributions toward the attainment of national goals. It is no accident that scientists and engineers have made greater contributions toward the attainment of the clearly stated and consistently supported military and space goals than they have toward the attainment of social objectives that have been neither clearly formulated nor steadily pursued. If there is a lesson to be learned from the changing attitudes toward the goals of the early 1960s, it is that more comprehensive consideration must be given to the original formulation of national objectives.

Whatever the goals and government plans may be, scientists and universities will be better able to contribute to their formulation, to make such contributions as they can toward their achievement, and to plan their own programs if the necessary information is made public as fully and on as long a time basis as possible. The recommendation of the House Subcommittee on Science, Research, and Development (U.S. House . . . , 1970a, p. 21) should therefore be adopted: "The Office of Management and Budget should make 5-year projections of scientific and technological trends, probable national needs for scientific resources during such times, plus indications of probable levels of Federal support for meeting the needs."

Such projections can be made in applied areas, and plans and allocations for applied research can properly continue to depend on the social, medical, military, or other objectives to which the applied research is intended to contribute. Within each field of basic science — or better, each subfield — there is often a fair consensus as to which research problems are most interesting or likely to be most rewarding. But judgments among fields of basic research are another matter. Is physical chemistry more important or more likely to be rewarding than embryology? Or less? Even here, some wise judgments can be made, as the experience of the Rockefeller Foundation demonstrated nearly 40 years ago in selecting experimental biology for special emphasis; and several scientists, most notably Alvin Weinberg (1963, pp. 159–171), have proposed criteria for scientific choice among research fields.

When there was enough money available, the problem of priorities among fields of basic research was not troublesome; proposals could be supported in all fields. Now that there is not enough money to go around, each field can enter its claims, those claims can be debated, and allocations can then be made as the budget makers think best. This essentially political process has its critics, but neither scientists, university administrators, nor government officials have agreed upon any better method.[4] What can be hoped for is better agreement on the criteria of choice and more incisive statements and criticisms of the claims and potentialities of the several fields — with enough multiplicity of sources of support so that choices and comparisons can be made from more than one point of view.

STABLE FUNDING

From 1953 to 1971, educational expenditures of American colleges and universities increased at an average rate of 12 percent a year. The increase resulted partly from inflation and higher costs and partly from the rapid increase in the number of students. From 1953 on, federal grants to colleges and universities also increased, but at not nearly as steady a rate. From 1965, the first year for which complete data are available, through 1967, federal support to universities and colleges increased at an average rate of 24 percent a year. Since 1967, while college and university expenses have continued upward at the rate of 13 percent a year, the federal contributions suddenly stopped growing and have remained slightly above or below the 1967 level (NSF, 1970*a;* 1970*d;* 1971*b*).

From 1953 through 1966, government grants supported a steadily increasing portion of college and university research activities, reaching 60 percent of the total in 1966. After 1966, research funds increased for two years and then dropped or remained constant for three (NSF, 1970*d*). The federal budget for 1972 contained an increase for academic science, but whether or not that increase marked the resumption of an upward trend or was a one-year phenomenon made possible by a presidential decision that the whole federal budget for 1972 would be unbalanced is something that universities were left to guess about.

This instability and uncertainty, following a long period of fairly regular growth and coming at a time when costs and numbers of students were continuing to rise, caused serious difficulties for universities (NSF, 1970*c*) and led to many demands for a more stable funding policy.

---

[4] Orlans (1968) and Shils (1968) present good discussions about the problem of establishing or using criteria for choosing among research areas.

Before the 1960s were half over it was clear that federal funds for research and development could not go on increasing at the high rate that had prevailed since 1950. Expressed as a percentage of all federal government expenditures, research and development funds accounted for 2.5 percent of the 1950 total and for 12.6 percent of the 1965 total. In dollars, the amount climbed from $1 billion to $15 billion in these years. Obviously, such a growth rate could not be permanently sustained, and the rate of increase for academic science would have to slow down along with the total.

Nevertheless, both in and out of government it was recognized that funds for academic science should continue to increase—albeit at a slower rate—and that a predictable and regular rate would be highly desirable. The budget that President Johnson sent to Congress in January 1965 (for fiscal year 1966) was based on this policy and was accompanied by a statement that funds for academic research should increase at a fairly steady annual rate. Because funds for academic research in the budgets of NASA and other mission-oriented agencies would rise or fall as their overall missions changed in nature and priority, the statement also provided that the NSF should serve as a balancing agency and that its budget should be adjusted to keep the total for academic science rising at a steady rate. Elmer B. Staats (1968, p. 220), Deputy Director of the Bureau of the Budget, explained that "in the 1966 budget, we agreed to aim for a 15 percent growth in basic research funds going to the universities. We came out of Congress with some 17 percent."

The attempt to hold to a 15 percent annual increase lasted exactly one year. The 1966 budget met the target growth rate, and in 1967 and 1968 there were increases of 12 percent each year. But that was the end of any semblance of steady growth. The 1969, 1970, and 1971 amounts for academic science were each slightly smaller than the year before. In current dollars, the 1971 figure was 2 percent below 1968. If one takes account of inflation, the 1971 amount had only 85 percent of the purchasing power of the 1968 figure (Milton, 1971)..

Graduate enrollment and university needs will continue to rise, and inflation will no doubt continue. To take account of these factors and to permit more orderly planning than has been possible in the last few years, several proposals have been made for determining a predictable rate of increase of federal funds for academic science.

All these proposals start with the assumption that we have about completed the substantial reallocation of national resources that began shortly after World War II in order to accomplish the national commitment to attain a high level of scientific and technological excellence. In 1950, less than one-half of 1 percent of the GNP was spent on research and development. Each year from 1961 through 1968, between 2.8 and 3.0 percent of a much larger GNP was so used. In the same period, the fraction accounted for by research in universities and colleges approximately doubled, to reach 10 percent of all money spent on research and development.

The several proposals assume that the period of rapid growth is over, that the amount in some recent year was about right as a base for determining future growth, and that predictable future growth can be achieved by calculating funds for academic research as a function of some other index or economic variable. The Carnegie Commission on Higher Education has recommended that federal funds for research in colleges and universities increase at the same rate as the GNP. In order to smooth out fluctuations, the Commission suggested using the average rate of increase of the GNP over a five-year period as the basis for determining each year's increase in the amount for academic research (Carnegie Commission. 1970). This average is projected by the Bureau of Labor Statistics to be 4.3 percent a year, in constant dollars (U.S. Department of Labor, 1970).

Lee DuBridge, taking 1968 as an acceptable base year, has proposed that research funds, in constant dollars, granted to universities and colleges by the federal government be increased by 1 percent each year. The amounts that have actually been granted since the $1.5 billion of 1968 have all fallen short of this modest goal.[5]

Eugene Fubini recommends a rate between the rate of increase in the number of graduate students and the rate of increase of the GNP. The number of graduate students (reduced to a full-time equivalent basis) has been increasing about 7 percent a year, and the GNP, he assumed, would increase about 5.5 percent a year in constant dollars. Fubini suggested 6.5 percent a year as an appropriate intermediate rate.

[5] The proposals of DuBridge, Fubini, and Price are discussed and compared in an analysis by Carl M. York, technical assistant to the director of the Office of Science and Technology. York also considers a number of related problems of federal support for academic science. See York (1971, pp. 643-648). For the original presentation of Price's proposal, see Price (1971, pp. 85-94). For another analysis of the principles upon which a formula approach might be adopted, see Brooks (1971a, pp. 364-374).

Derek Price's proposal differs from the others in that it includes all federal funds for academic science—research funds, as do the others, and also funds for other scientific purposes. In 1969, grants from the federal government for all scientific purposes in colleges and universities amounted to $2.35 billion, a figure which equaled 0.256 percent of the year's GNP. Price has recommended that this percentage be increased in pace with the increase in the nation's scientific manpower, which is growing at about 6 percent a year. Six percent of 0.256 percent is 0.015. Thus the percentage of the GNP used for academic science should be raised by 0.015 percentage points each year. Under this formula, the percentages of GNP would be 0.271 in 1970. 0.286 in 1971, 0.301 in 1972, etc.

In summary, in terms of constant 1968 or 1969 dollars, the four proposals are:

Carnegie Commission	Same rate as GNP
DuBridge	1 percent a year
Fubini	Between rate of GNP increase and rate of increase of graduate students, or 6.5 percent a year
Price	Percentage of real GNP (starting at 0.256 percent in 1969) increased by 0.015 percentage points a year

To translate them into current dollars, any of these proposals should be adjusted to take account of inflation at about 5 percent a year or whatever the future rate turns out to be.

Alvin Weinberg (1970) has made a different kind of proposal, one intended to provide a predictable and rising minimum amount for academic research, but not intended to include all funds for that purpose. In addition to whatever amounts Congress appropriates to the NIH and other mission-oriented agencies, Weinberg recommended that 0.1 percent of the GNP each year be assigned to the NSF for the support of research. This sum would be considered a general overhead on the cost of the whole scientific-educational-technological enterprise and could be used to provide for balance among the fields of science, to explore new research areas, and to take up the slack left by the mission-oriented agencies.

Scientists would obviously find the DuBridge formula the least satisfactory of the four, but all formulas would have the advantage of providing regular and predictable increases. None of the formulas could or should be used indefinitely. The purpose of adopting any formula would be to provide predictability over a reasonable span of years. Before the end of that span, it would be necessary to reconsider the formula and decide whether it should be modified or continued for the next span.

There is a further principle that can be helpful in determining the appropriate rate of increase: federal support of academic research should increase at least as rapidly as does other support. All but a trivial fraction of academic research is freely publishable; the results are available to anyone. Because the information gained and the potential commercial or other uses are available to the whole nation, and beyond, it is appropriate that the costs be equally widespread. Historically, because of the nature of the American educational system, that has not been the case. But since World War II, the federal portion rose more rapidly than the nonfederal portion to reach a level of 60 percent of the total in the years from 1966 to 1968. Since 1968, the federal government has been lagging behind other supporters of academic research, and the NSF has projected that the federal portion would increase at a slightly lower rate than the nonfederal portion in the decade of the 1970s.

From the standpoint of economics, there is reason to claim that federal funds for research and development (in total, not for academic research alone) should increase more rapidly than industrial investment in research and development, which since 1962 has been increasing at a compound rate of 8 percent a year in constant dollars and is projected to continue at about the same rate (NSF, 1969; Bueche, 1970). The total value of applied research and development is always greater than the value to the agency that pays the bills. Some of the results may be proprietary and some may be protected by patents, but not all can be. There is some spin-off, some direct stimulation of other developments, some benefits that accrue to others besides the agency or company that did the work. If industry, working on a profit basis, is assumed to invest in research and development an amount it finds profitable, it must also be assumed that the industrial companies conducting the research and development realize only part of the benefit and therefore understate the total benefit. Consequently, the government can expect the nation as a whole to profit from a higher level of investment in research and development than industry finds economically profitable.

In view of the inescapable increase in university enrollment over the next decade and the fact that other sources of university support will have to increase at least as rapidly as the GNP, it seems reasonable to recommend that federal support of academic research increase at no less a rate than the increase in the GNP. It also seems reasonable to recommend that the increase be regular and predictable, with the understanding that before the end of a stated period, say five years, the matter will be reviewed and a decision made for the next five-year period.

To put this policy into effect, the NSF budget should be adjusted annually to take account of changes in the priorities and budgets of other federal agencies that support academic science. As these agencies' missions, priorities, and needs change, the NSF can serve as a balancing agency, in providing federal funds for research in universities and colleges.

INSTITUTIONAL SUPPORT

Federal support of scientific research and graduate education in universities is only part of the problem of research support, and only part of the problem of financing higher education. Three caveats are therefore in order. The federal government will continue to use industry, independent institutes, and its own facilities to achieve many of its research and development objectives. Educational levels other than the graduate university need financial support, and the forms of support appropriate to their needs are not necessarily the same as those appropriate for the graduate university. And the university should continue to derive support from sources other than the federal government. The heavy emphasis on research at the graduate level may even make it desirable to separate the graduate university from the undergraduate college so that each may be better planned and financed in terms of its own needs and characteristics.[6] Regardless of whether the two are physically sep-

---

[6] Recommendations that graduate and undergraduate work be separated have been made by a number of people. Of particular relevance here because the discussion is specifically in terms of justifications for public support of academic research is Kaysen (1969). Tyler (1969, pp. 305–320) thinks that despite college and university opposition to such a separation, it will come about as a consequence of two pressures: demands for greater efficiency and for greater accountability on the part of universities, and pressures from students and parents for more faculty time and attention than undergraduates are likely to get in a graduate university. Wolff (1969) recommends that professional schools be taken out of the university entirely and would be glad to see undergraduate and graduate work separated, for, in his judgment, confusion between the aims and principles of the two is a major cause of current educational difficulties. Lipset (1970) pleads for understanding that a university must be a very different kind of institution than a school. Universities can have undergraduate as well as graduate students, but should have none who are not interested in scholarship. There can be thousands of colleges, but there are few universities, and they should be protected from being required to take on the attributes of a school.

arated, their financial needs are different, and the difference calls for different forms of federal support.

In addition to the support the graduate university receives from endowment income, state appropriations, tuition, gifts, and other sources, three types of federal support are desirable:

1   First is the grant to an individual or small group to support a specific research project, activity, or development that is defined and agreed upon in advance. One distinguishing characteristic of this kind of grant is that a government agency decides what work is to be done. The agency may initiate the research plans and then seek an institution to conduct the work, or it may select from among proposals submitted to it, but in either case the government agency decides on individual project plans. Under several rather different circumstances, it is clearly appropriate to support research on this basis. Project grants or contracts are used to support applied research and development on problems defined by government agencies. A project grant is the appropriate instrument to use for a research study at an institution where there is little research but where someone has a good idea and the ability to carry it out. Project grants are well designed to make certain that much of the available research money goes to the scientists with the best ideas and the greatest competence. And project grants are the only politically feasible means of financing the construction of specialized and expensive new scientific facilities. In some cases the political and economic factors, or the regional jealousies, may even be of such an order as to take the final decision out of the hands of the supporting agency and move it up to a higher level of government. President Eisenhower personally made the decision to go ahead with construction of the Stanford Linear Accelerator.[7] Project grants are so well liked by research scientists and have served so effectively in giving government agencies access to scientific talent that they will undoubtedly continue to constitute the preferred means of financing a large part of the research that is supported by federal funds.

Nevertheless, the project system has deficiencies. Young and unknown scientists are widely believed to have more difficulty in securing grants than are established investigators. The project grant does not normally provide funds for initial explorations to determine whether an idea is worth describing in a formal proposal. If during the course of his research a scientist decides that it would be more productive to follow a new track not envisaged when he wrote the proposal, he may be inhibited by the

---

[7] For a brief account of White House coordination of plans for the 2-mile-long Stanford Linear Accelerator and President Eisenhower's personal involvement, see Robinson (1968, pp. 167–170). For President Eisenhower's announcement of plans to go forward with the new accelerator, see Eisenhower (1959, pp. 140–141).

restrictions of the original grant, and there will be a time delay if he decides to ask the supporting agency to approve a change in plans. In either event a decision on a scientific point is likely to be taken out of his hands. In the early days, a few research grants increased a university's budget only slightly, and if the grant did not cover all the direct and indirect costs, as often was the case, the university could make up the difference, for the research was work that members of the faculty wanted to do. Later on, as the whole grant system grew to include more different programs, more grants, more universities, and more money, it also acquired, not surprisingly, more rules, more rigidity, more red tape, and more auditors. Failure of the federal agencies to pay all the indirect costs, the requirement of some agencies that the university participate in cost-sharing arrangements, the fact that federal funds were restricted to selected portions of a university's responsibilities, the poor match that sometimes existed between government interests and the university's ideas of what constituted its own proper balance—all these problems became increasingly critical as project funds came to account for a large fraction of a university's budget.

2   The second type of grant that is needed is called an institutional grant because it is intended for the benefit of the institution rather than for a particular project. This proposal is not new. The NSF and NIH have made institutional grants for a decade. Therefore, the principle involved has already been established: it is desirable to delegate to the individual university responsibility for deciding how some part of its federal funds for science can best be used. In accepting this principle, the federal government went beyond the purchase of research and accepted partial responsibility for the continuing well-being of those universities at which it expects to have research conducted.

Universities receiving institutional grants have used them to redress imbalances resulting from the large amounts of project funds, to purchase equipment that would be broadly useful but that could not be justified in the budget of any individual project, to help young scientists get started, to help explore new ideas, or for other scientific purposes that the university considers important. Because the difficulties created by project grants, like their advantages, increase with size, the size of an institutional grant is based on a formula that takes account of the amount received competitively as project grants.

What it desirable now is that a larger percentage of the federal funds granted to universities in support of science be in the form of institutional grants. It follows that a smaller percentage would be in the form of project grants. From 1964 to 1966 The Brookings Institution sponsored a continuing seminar that brought together officers of the Bureau of the Budget, the NSF, and other federal agencies, university scientists and administrators, and other persons involved in the analysis of science policy. The seminar dealt with national science policy and the universities and included several discussions about the merits and uses of institutional and project grants. It was generally agreed that increased use of institutional grants would be advantageous to science and the universities and that from the standpoint of the government the change would be administratively advantageous (Orlans, 1968, pp. 40–45). There may also be a significant economic advantage in the greater use of institutional grants. Money available for only one purpose can be spent only for that purpose, and the university, having no control, has no means to require austerity. Money for which the university is responsible is likely to be spent more prudently, for what is left is available for other needs. Many research administrators believe that a given amount of money all locked up in a number of individually planned and administered research projects achieves no more scientific advance than would, say, 80 percent as much money that could be spent more freely and flexibly by a responsible university.[8]

The Carnegie Commission has recommended that "a grant amounting to 10 percent of the total research grants received annually by an institution be made to that institution to be used at its discretion" (Carnegie Commission, 1970, p. 26). Ten percent of the total is a satisfactory move up from present practice and can serve as a general guideline, but there are a number of technical details to be settled that can be left to the responsible federal agencies in consultation with university representatives. The change to be achieved is to give each institution that has received competitive project grants, or project grants above some minimum, responsibility for deciding how some reasonable portion of its federal support can most constructively be used. Ten percent is a reasonable level for the time being, although a higher percentage will probably become desirable later.

3   The third form of grant that is needed can be called a university development grant. These grants would be highly selective, of substantial size, for periods of several years, and intended to achieve broadly defined objectives that had been agreed upon in advance between the university and the NSF, the appropriate agency to manage such a program. These would be special

---

[8] Two statements to this effect are Price (1968, p. 32) and Brooks (1971b, p. 328). Some confirmatory evidence was secured in Project Hindsight, a study conducted by Arthur D. Little Company for the Department of Defense. The investigators made analyses of new ideas or new developments that resulted in significant improvements in military weapons capabilities. Most of the significant new ideas had not been foreseen when the research grants or contracts were written, but instead emerged during the course of the work. To avoid the months of delay that would have been required to secure a new grant or contract, the company or university financed the extra work itself, borrowed money from another contract, or used discretionary funds that were available in a few cases. These examples are all in the military sphere, and most of them occurred in applied research conducted by industry, but there is no reason to suspect that research for the Department of Defense differs in this respect from research in other fields of interest. The Project Hindsight report is summarized in Sherwin & Isenson (1967, pp. 1571–1577).

grants, intended to meet the special needs of universities of high quality. These universities will continue to receive substantial amounts of money for research projects and will continue to receive annual institutional grants of the present small size, or somewhat larger ones if something like the preceding recommendation is put into effect. Moreover, it is likely that they may receive additional funds from a national program of general support to higher education. Just when Congress may adopt some form of general aid to higher education is uncertain, but there has already been much work in congressional committees, and legislation of this kind would be widely popular, for many large and small colleges all over the country would be helped with their financial problems.

Project funds are specific to individual projects. The present institutional grants provide an amount of money that is comparatively large for a small institution but comparatively small for a big one. Any program of general support to higher education will be based on a formula that takes account of enrollment, number of graduates, number of students receiving federal scholarships or other forms of assistance, or some combination of these or other objective factors, for only a method based on an objective formula would be politically acceptable. Consequently, any formula approach will be of relatively less value to universities of high quality than to smaller and weaker institutions; no formula that could be adopted would take full account of the higher costs involved in graduate education and research.

Although all three of these forms of financial assistance have their place, none meets some of the special problems of the universities that provide graduate work of high quality to large numbers of students. Moreover, during the 1970s those universities will experience the difficulties of transition from accelerating growth to decelerating growth. Undergraduate colleges will have to expand to meet the needs of a student body that will grow larger until about 1982. At the graduate level, however, universities should curb expansion. Since 1900, the number of Ph.D. degrees awarded has increased at an average rate of approximately 7 percent a year. There have been fluctuations of this rate, most markedly during and following World Wars I and II, but the fluctuations were compensatory until about 1960. After 1960, the growth rate jumped to 12 percent a year. This increase above the long-term trend was in part the effect of fellowship and traineeship programs and other deliberate attempts to encourage more students to earn doctor's degrees. To bring future numbers of Ph.D.'s into line with the number of positions requiring the doctorate projected to be available during the 1970s and 1980s calls for reducing the growth rate to a lower level, perhaps back to the long-term rate of 7 percent a year.

During the time that this curtailment is necessary, the number of college graduates eligible for admission to graduate schools will continue to mount. Moreover, institutional aspirations continue to rise; some universities are attempting to increase their graduate enrollment. And, as pointed out above, 150 additional colleges are hoping to begin awarding the doctorate before 1980.

If we wanted to be callous, we could simply allow these pressures for rapid growth to collide with the need to slow down the growth rate. One effect would be that competition would force some of the weaker institutions out of the graduate level. This has already happened: of 157 institutions that began to offer the master's degree over the period 1956–57 to 1965–66, 41 percent quit, and of 65 that tried to offer doctoral work, 31 percent quit (National Science Board, 1969b). Financial difficulties during the 1970s are likely to thwart the hopes of a number of the 150 colleges that aspire to offer work for the doctorate.

However, shaking out the weaker efforts to offer graduate work would not be the only consequence. Some of the most excellent universities in the country are attempting to reduce the number of their graduate students, while some that are upwardly mobile but much less well qualified are attempting to increase theirs. Formula grants based directly or indirectly on enrollment would encourage the latter to continue on such a course.

From the societal standpoint, the competition that served so well in the early years of university development and that has in recent decades been a powerful factor in achieving a high level of scientific competence in the leading universities may not be the best policy for the next phase of university development. What each university and would-be university considers good for its own future does not add up to what is good for universities as a whole, or good for the nation. The time has come to exercise controls on the birth and growth of new universities.

In a period of decelerating growth it is necessary to substitute some form of national decision making for the old habits of individual decision making and free competition. Universities acting independently cannot achieve the necessary controls. Only a national agency responsible for substantial institutional grants for the maintenance and development of universities of high quality could support new or expanded universities or departments where they are needed and discourage them where they are not. Such an agency could make these decisions in terms of overall priorities and in terms of the maintenance of an adequate total capacity of high quality, effectively distributed over the country.

Thus university development grants could be used as an effective means of influencing university growth and direction. To accomplish this general objective, grants could be used to help sustain universities of high quality, the 50 or more universities that are of greatest national significance;[9] to improve universities in parts of the country that are now inadequately represented in the distribution of academic excellence; to encourage diversity and specialization among universities; or to foster new styles of university work, such as the large multidisciplinary research programs discussed in Chapter 8. Whatever the specific objectives, a guiding criterion would be development and maintenance of graduate education and research of high quality, for unlike programs of general support of higher education, this program would have to be selective in order to accomplish its purpose.[10]

AUTONOMY AND CONTROL

The recommendations presented in the preceding section for federal support of university research and graduate education have all been made before. All have been endorsed by spokesmen for science, education, and government. They are in keeping with recommendations of the National Science Board (1969a). Ironically, as the United States worries about a technology gap in which Japan and some of the European countries are challenging or outpacing American achievements, the recommendations are much the same

---

[9] Cartter (1971, pp. 132–140) calls these "National Universities" and suggests that if it proves to be politically too difficult to select 75 to 100 universities that would be widely thought of as "the best" because of the receipt of such grants, then 50 to 75 departments in each major field should be given similar, though lesser, support. One can make a case for using either the university or the department as the unit to be selected for such grants; nevertheless, the arguments are strong in favor of making the university accountable for the use of its grants and to do that requires giving the university the responsibility to manage its own affairs.

[10] In Great Britain, major support to all universities is handled through the University Grants Committee, which operates on a five-year cycle. The committee reviews plans and requests from each university, requests a single appropriation from the Treasury, and then divides the appropriation granted by the Treasury among the universities as it thinks best. This method could not be used in the United States because of the variety of types of control and sources of support of American universities. But the five-year span and the amount of discretion given to Britain's University Grants Committee could well be copied in establishing the administrative machinery for the proposed university development grants program.

as Joseph Ben-David's (1968, p. 78) to European universities when he was asked in 1965 how they could match the scientific achievements of American universities.

Why do we not have more consistent policies? What is wrong with government-university-science relations? No one is in charge. On the government side, formal responsibility for science policy seems to rest somewhere between the Office of Science and Technology and the National Science Board, but with the Office of Management and Budget making many of the important decisions on a year-to-year basis. The NSF, the Office of Education, and the other agencies that use the universities all have their interests, but no agency has responsibility.

On the university side, no one has ever been in charge. Universities have competed with each other and copied each other. From time to time they come together in the AAU or other organizations. Their representatives have worked effectively with government representatives on some issues. But in the main, each university acts independently, and within each, the tradition of individualism is widely honored.

The result is that everybody has tried to use the universities. Scientists used them to advance science over the opposition of faculty colleagues who resented the intrusion of research and graduate education. The nation used them to improve agricultural education and research over the opposition of many congressmen, one President, and a considerable number of academic purists. Since World War II, universities have been used to help achieve the scientific and technological objectives of federal agencies over the opposition of critics who charge that the university has lost all integrity, that it is for hire by anyone with cash in his pocket. In recent years political activists have used universities for their purposes, and they, too, have encountered strong opposition.

Universities are so much used because of their capabilities. In the process, the integrity of the institution has been jeopardized, not from deliberate capture by government agencies that want to control the university, but from gradual erosion that runs its course while everyone involved proclaims his loyalty to the principles of academic freedom, university independence, and the absence of government control.

In the case of science, universities are under the combined pressure of scientists, who are guided primarily by their interest in the advancement of science, and the federal government, which wishes to accomplish its objectives of strengthening science and technology.

The close cooperation between federal agencies that support science and the scientists who advise those agencies at all levels, from program planning to decisions on the funding of individual research proposals, has often left the universities with little maneuvering room in their efforts to control their own development or to influence national science policies. Universities have accepted research grants that did not fit well, that committed them to provide space and money which their own priorities should have directed elsewhere. Growth has often been greatest where money was most easily available, not where the institution's educational needs were most pressing. More than individual projects and temporary dislocations are involved here: the direction of development, faculty balance, the relative emphasis on different fields and kinds of work, and the logic of the university's own development are all involved, and all are substantially influenced by decisions concerning specific projects, funded by different agencies, to accomplish different purposes, and, to a considerable extent, made by faculty members individually or in small groups.

Yet the university cannot place all the blame on federal agencies or their fractious scientific allies on campus. How free a university can be of control by external sources of funds is a function of the clarity of its own goals and its internal agreement on means to achieve those goals. One observer has stated the matter in this way:[11]

> The Federal agencies and Federal money will tend to set policy for an institution more or less in direct proportion to the absence of a strong policy by the institution itself. In many respects undesirable consequences assumed to flow from Federal aid actually flow from the intellectual flabbiness of the schools in dealing with Federal funds. It takes some experience, I suppose, to use money effectively when the absence of money has been such a convenient excuse for the absence of policy on many issues. I suspect that many schools . . . follow the lead of Federal agencies not because the Federal agencies "control" them, but because the schools have no clear policies of their own.

The federal government, state governments, industry, politicians, advocates of a variety of social programs and actions, and special factions within the university all see the university as a possible ally, a useful tool, or an aid in the achievement of their objectives. There is no lack of potential users. What the university needs is a stronger hand in determining how it will be used, to what ends,

---

[11] See letter to the author in Babbidge & Rosenzweig (1962, pp. 163–164).

and the conditions under which it will accept support. Eric Ashby (1967a, p. 8), in an article speculating on whether or not the nineteenth-century idea of the university can survive, summarized the problem:

> Today universities everywhere face a common peril: the peril of success. Formerly they were detached organisms, assimilating and growing in accordance with their own internal laws. Now they have become absolutely essential to the economy and the very survival of nations. Under the patronage of princes or bishops they were cultivated as garden flowers of no more significance to the state's economy than the court musician. Under the patronage of modern governments they are cultivated as intensive crops, heavily manured, and expected to give a high yield essential for the nourishment of the state.

The uses of universities described above will continue. Yet, by common consent, university autonomy is a value to be retained and defended. Defended, yes, but also qualified and limited, for the university is a public agency. If it is to have the continued support of society and be given the kinds of federal support recommended above, it must be responsive to public needs, which means that freedom must be earned by responsibility.

RESPONSIBILITY AND ACCOUNTABILITY If universities were suddenly given much of their federal support in the forms recommended above, many would find themselves poorly equipped to handle the responsibility. Much decision making within the university has purposefully been decentralized, and there are issues on which faculty votes should be decisive. But these are not the procedures to use in making quality comparisons among the university's educational and research units, executive decisions concerning the university as a whole, or decisions concerning other matters. A university needs a strong faculty if it is to continue as an institution of high intellectual quality. But it also needs a strong central government if it is to act promptly and responsibly in managing its funds and planning its future. The problem this latter need poses for the faculty is essentially a political one of using democratic means to resolve conflicts over institutional goals and objectives and then of expecting the president and his staff to handle institutional grants, maintain control of university balance and direction of development, negotiate with government agencies over matters of policy, control the rate of expansion of graduate programs, and be responsible for other major actions in which the university as a whole is involved.

More than management is involved in this division of responsibility. The federal government, divided into separate agencies, tends to use the university on a piecemeal basis, and none of its agencies has responsibility for the continuing welfare of the university as an institution or for universities as a group. And it is precisely here that the universities themselves are usually weak. Thus the universities often react, rather than plan, and are swayed by government actions whether those actions are based on policies the government has adopted or are ad hoc responses to current pressures or budgetary changes. Again, there is the problem of democratic decisions on goals and of executive responsibility for keeping the institution on course. The university's own future calls for filling what Edward Shils has called "the hole in the center" (Shils, 1970, pp. 1–7), the lack of a strong steering mechanism.

Moreover, because of the intellectual importance of the university, the public can rightfully insist upon responsible governance and public accountability. The more powerful the work of the university becomes, in the sense that those who make political, economic, social, or technological decisions are influenced by the results of university research and scholarly analysis, the more the public needs assurance that the university and its faculty members are acting objectively and responsibly. And here again, the need is evident for clarity of institutional objectives and responsible management in their achievement.

With responsibility goes accountability. Discussions of accountability too often get stalled on the requirements and the irritations of the seemingly endless process of auditing the financial records of grants and contracts. Of course universities must keep accurate accounts and make full reports of their stewardship of public funds. But proper financial records are not enough and neither is the individual scientist's accountability to his peers. The amount of attention devoted to fiscal accountability might well be less if greater attention were given to what David Robinson calls program accountability in an essay on the several ways in which recipients of federal grants may be held accountable for their work.[12]

The continuing university-government relationship and the legitimate interests of society call for comprehensive and informative accounting by the university of its activities and achievements, the

---

[12] See Robinson (1971). This entire volume, the report and papers of a British-American conference, is concerned with the problems of independence and accountability in situations in which a government uses industry, universities, or other agencies in what has traditionally been called the private sector to accomplish public purposes.

balance and emphasis among them, and the effectiveness with which it serves as an institution of higher learning and research and as an objective critic and analyst of the public concerns with which it deals. One way to get better program accountability would be to give universities an incentive for preparing full and informative analyses of their work. If each recipient of a substantial institutional grant—the third type of grant discussed above—issued a public report on its activities and accomplishments at, say, five-year intervals, it would have to examine its own progress with care. A university would have plenty of incentive to do a good job, for its report would be carefully studied before another such grant was made and would be a major basis for deciding what the amount of that grant would be.

Above the level of the individual university, there is need for more agreement among universities. Some of the agreements would be to divide responsibility for different programs and activities. Other agreements could be to act in concert, for example, on the general terms upon which funds from federal sources can be accepted. Local and regional consortia and statewide coordinating boards are moves in this direction. Beyond these, it would seem desirable for some organization such as the AAU to accept responsibility as the collective voice of universities in dealing with major matters of policy that affect both universities and the federal government.

All federal government agencies must follow some standards and rules set by Congress or the Office of Management and Budget. Thus, despite their differences, government agencies may speak with a united voice in some of their relations with universities. On matters of general policy, universities should have comparable unity and strength. For this they need both the spirit and the machinery of coordination. To maintain the independence of the university as an institution may require each individual university to invest some of its independence in the collectivity. Eric Ashby (1967a, p. 16) has warned:

Universities in each country must seek collective security. The days are over when each university can expect to be a fully autonomous corporation, autarchic as a medieval dukedom. In tomorrow's world there will be no security in the fragmented autonomy of scores of independent institutions. Universities, combined in this collective autonomy, could become the "intellectual estate" of the nation, indeed still financially dependent on governments, but collectively strong enough to set the conditions under which they fulfill their function in society.

Jacques Barzun (1968) has given a different reason for joint planning. Because universities compete within a single pattern of now well-defined goals, he fears that none will dare make really major changes unless supported by a common agreement. Universities may have to relinquish part of their individual independence so that together they can protect the independence of the university as an institution and can assure the public that they are acting responsibly.

There is a choice to be made. Government support is essential, and the movement within government is toward more planning, more coordination, and more control of expenditures. Faculty members may let government establish the rules for the government-university relationship or may set aside their habits of individualism to give universities individually and collectively a stronger voice in establishing those rules.

Universities do not command the financial resources or the political strength that are found in government, but they do have the intellectual resources required to solve the problems of their own governance, accountability, and cooperation and to participate fully in establishing working rules of the government-university relationship. Working together, government and universities — with scientists included among the representatives of both parties — can work out a more satisfactory set of guiding policies for the interdependent relations among science, universities, and the federal government than have operated in the past.

Yet, spectacular changes in university governance — either individually or collectively — are not to be expected. The habits of competition and individualism are too deeply entrenched, and although science itself is a cumulative discipline, the politics of science is not.

A century has passed since Yale awarded the country's first Ph.D., Abraham Lincoln signed Justin Morrill's Land-Grant Act, Harvard started its graduate department, and Johns Hopkins provided a new and permanently successful inspiration to the colleges that aspired to become universities. Change came very rapidly in the last quarter of the nineteenth century. From 1875 to 1900 the university was established; research and graduate education grew; and the university clearly became the primary home of science.

Since World War II, the universities have experienced another quarter-century of rapid change. The national decision to seek the highest possible level of competence across a broad scientific and technological front and the decision to accomplish this objective by granting federal funds to nongovernmental institutions have multiplied academic science vastly and have aided in the achievement of unprecedented university growth. Scientists have poured so many new truths on the apex of Joseph Henry's pyramid of science that most of its volume would be wholly new to the scientists of a century ago. And the federal government has poured so many dollars into research and graduate education that university budgets would be unrecognizable to Daniel Coit Gilman and his contemporaries.

Yet beneath the growth of science and the changes in the universities, three features that were familiar in the past are still operative and promise to be influential in the future. First is the absence of any master plan. Major developments have often resulted from cumulative decisions made gradually by many participants. Much of the scientific work that has been done and many of the characteristics of the universities in which research has been conducted have been the joint products of the scientists' continuing search for patrons and the nation's continuing need for scientific work. In its use of science and in its support of science, the federal government has responded to the perceived needs of the time and has changed its course when old needs were met or new ones took priority. It is not at all clear that either science or the national interest has been less well served by this pragmatic approach than they would have been by the adoption of a long-term and overall plan. Any plan that could have been adopted prior to World War II would have been more limited in scope than were the activities which actually developed, for Congress has often been willing to go farther in fact than it would have been willing to endorse in principle.

The second feature is competition. Here, too, both continuity and change can be expected. Competition has helped to build science and to build universities, but it has channeled too many institutions of higher education into the same mold. Now that graduate education has reached its present size, it has become necessary to foster greater diversity of educational institutions and programs so that research, the graduate university, and other educational institutions can all better fulfill their purposes. Within several different educational realms, competition can continue to be a stimulant to individual initiative in science and to the development of new research programs and university activities.

The third continuing feature is the existence of much cooperation between government agencies and private institutions. The cooperation that started with the Western surveys, the analysis of the causes of explosions of steam boilers, and other early joint ventures was extended in the latter part of the nineteenth century to include agricultural education and research and more recently has been further extended in still different directions, ranging in scope from such specific examples as the Joint Institute for Laboratory Astrophysics to the generality of the policy of using nongovernmental institutions to achieve public purposes. Research in the foreseeable future promises to continue to be primarily a joint responsibility of public agencies and private institutions.

Pragmatism, competition, joint responsibility—all will continue, but within larger boundaries than in the past, for the public need for many and continuing scientific services is recognized, and there is emerging acceptance of a national obligation to help maintain and strengthen the institutions upon which the nation relies for scientific work. The national welfare requires research and universities, and they in turn need national support. And that is why the working rules that guide their relations need as thoughtful formulation and as widespread understanding as we can give them.

References

Ad Hoc Committee on Environmental Science Programs: *Report of the Committee on Long-Range Planning,* vol. 2, no. 1, The Long-Range Planning Committee, University of Illinois at Urbana-Champaign, October 1970.

American Association for the Advancement of Science: *Proceedings,* vol. 1, 1848.

American Council on Education: *Higher Education and National Affairs,* vol. 19, no. 40, Nov. 13, 1970.

Ashby, Eric: "The Future of the Nineteenth Century Idea of a University," *Minerva,* vol. 6, no. 1, pp. 3–17, Autumn 1967*a*.

Ashby, Eric: "Anatomy of the Academic Life," *Educational Record,* vol. 48, no. 1, pp. 45–50, Winter 1967*b*.

Babbidge, Homer D., Jr., and Robert M. Rosenzweig: *The Federal Interest in Higher Education,* McGraw-Hill Book Company, New York, 1962.

Bache, Alexander D.: "Address upon Retiring as President," *Proceedings,* vol. 6, pp. xli–lx, American Association for the Advancement of Science, 1851.

Barnard, Frederick A. P.: "On Improvements Practicable in American Colleges," *American Journal of Education,* vol. 1, no. 2, pp. 174–185, January 1856; vol. 1, no. 3, pp. 269–284, March 1856.

Barzun, Jacques: *The American University,* Harper & Row, Publishers, Incorporated, New York, 1968.

Beaver, Donald deB.: "The American Scientific Community, 1800–1860: A Statistical-Historical Study," unpublished doctoral dissertation, Yale University, 1966.

Ben-David, Joseph: "Scientific Productivity and Academic Organization in Nineteenth-Century Medicine," *American Sociological Review,* vol. 25, no. 6, pp. 828–843, December 1960.

Ben-David, Joseph: *Fundamental Research and the Universities,* Organization for Economic Cooperation and Development, Paris, 1968.

Ben-David, Joseph: "The Universities and the Growth of Science in Germany and the United States," *Minerva,* vol. 7, no. 1, pp. 1-35, Autumn-Winter 1968-69.

Bowden, Lord, et al.: *Science and the University,* The Macmillan Co. of Canada, Limited, Toronto, 1967.

Branscomb, Lewis M.: "Joint Institute for Laboratory Astrophysics," *Symposium on Education and Federal Laboratory-University Relationships,* Oct. 29-31, 1968, Federal Council for Science and Technology and the American Council on Education, U.S. Government Printing Office, Washington, D.C., 1969.

Brooks, Harvey: "Basic Science and Agency Mission," in F. Joachim Weyl (ed.), *Research in the Service of National Purposes,* Office of Naval Research, Washington, D.C., 1966.

Brooks, Harvey: "Commentary on Paper by Mr. Corson," in James C. Charlesworth (ed.), *Harmonizing Technological Development and Social Policy in America,* Monograph 11, American Academy of Political and Social Science, Philadelphia, 1970.

Brooks, Harvey: "Models for Science Planning," *Public Administration Review,* vol. 31, no. 3, pp. 364-374, May-June 1971*a*.

Brooks, Harvey: "Thoughts on Graduate Education," *The Graduate Journal,* vol. 8, no. 2, p. 328, 1971*b*.

Brown, David G., and Jay L. Tontz: *The Mobility of Academic Scientists, A Report to the National Science Foundation,* April 1966. (Unpublished.)

Bueche, A. M.: *Issues in the Changing Relationships between Industry and Academic Science,* General Electric Corporate Research and Development, Schenectady, N.Y., Aug. 18, 1970. (Lithoprinted.)

Burtt, E. A.: "The Value Presuppositions of Science," *Bulletin of the Atomic Scientists,* vol. 13, no. 3, pp. 99-106, March 1957.

Bush, Vannevar, et al.: *Science, The Endless Frontier: A Report to the President,* U.S. Government Printing Office, Washington, D.C., 1945.

Carey, William D.: Address at the Seventeenth Annual Conference on the Administration of Research, October 1963.

Carnegie Commission on Higher Education: *Quality and Equality: Revised Recommendations, New Levels of Federal Responsibility for Higher Education,* McGraw-Hill Book Company, New York, 1970.

Cartter, Allan M.: "Scientific Manpower for 1970-1985," *Science,* vol. 172, pp. 132-140, Apr. 9, 1971.

Chase, Harry W.: "Making a University Faculty," *Journal of Proceedings and Addresses,* vol. 26, pp. 65–68, Association of American Universities, Nov. 1, 1924.

Cheit, Earl F.: *The New Depression in Higher Education,* McGraw-Hill Book Company, New York, 1971.

Clarke, Frank W.: "Laboratory Endowment," *Popular Science Monthly,* vol. 10, pp. 729–736, April 1877.

Committee on Academic Freedom and Academic Tenure: "Committee Report," *AAUP Bulletin,* vol. 1, part 1, 1915.

Cordasco, Francesco: *Daniel Coit Gilman and the Protean Ph.D.,* E. J. Brill, NV, Leiden, Netherlands, 1960.

Curti, Merle, and Vernon Carstensen: *The University of Wisconsin, A History, 1848–1925,* 2 vols., The University of Wisconsin Press, Madison, 1949.

Dana, James D.: "Science and Scientific Schools," *American Journal of Education,* vol. 2, pp. 349–374, December 1856.

Danhof, Clarence H.: *Government Contracting and Technological Change,* The Brookings Institution, Washington, D.C., 1968.

Daniels, George H.: *American Science in the Age of Jackson,* Columbia University Press, New York, 1968.

Davis, Bertram H.: "From the General Secretary," *AAUP Bulletin,* vol. 56, no. 4, p. 357, December 1970.

Deutsch, Karl W., John Platt, and Dieter Senghass: "Conditions Favoring Major Advances in Social Science," *Science,* vol. 171, pp. 450–459, Feb. 5, 1971.

Dimitroff, George J., and James G. Baker: *Telescopes and Accessories,* Blackiston, Philadelphia, 1945.

Dupree, A. Hunter: *Science in the Federal Government,* The Belknap Press, Harvard University Press, Cambridge, Mass., 1957.

Dupree, A. Hunter: *Asa Gray, 1810–1888,* The Belknap Press, Harvard University Press, Cambridge, Mass., 1959.

Eisenhower, Dwight D.: "Science: Handmaiden of Freedom," in Dael Wolfle (ed.), *Symposium on Basic Research,* American Association for the Advancement of Science, Washington, D.C., 1959.

Eliot, Charles W.: "Academic Freedom," *Science,* vol. 26, pp. 1–12, July 5, 1907.

Everett, Edward: in *American Journal of Education,* vol. 1, January 1856.

Ewing, Ben D.: *Interdisciplinary Academic Research Programs in Environmental Improvement,* paper presented at a meeting of the Scientific Research Society of America, Chicago, Dec. 29, 1970.

Executive Order 10521, Office of the President, The White House, Mar. 17, 1954.

Fleming, Thomas: *The Man from Monticello: An Intimate Life of Thomas Jefferson,* William Morrow & Company, Inc., New York, 1969.

Flexner, Abraham: *Universities: American, English, German,* Oxford University Press, New York, 1930.

Florer, John H.: "Major Issues in the Congressional Debate of the Morrill Act of 1862," *History of Education Quarterly,* vol. 8, no. 4, pp. 459–478, Winter 1968.

Folger, John K., Helen S. Astin, and Alan E. Bayer: *Human Resources and Higher Education,* Russell Sage Foundation, New York, 1970.

Franklin, Fabian: *The Life of Daniel Coit Gilman,* Dodd, Mead & Company, Inc., New York, 1910.

Fulton, John (ed.): *Memoirs of Frederick A. P. Barnard,* Columbia University Press, New York, 1896.

Gates, Charles M.: *The First Century of the University of Washington, 1861–1961.* University of Washington Press, Seattle, 1961.

Gerard, Ralph W.: "Problems in the Institutionalization of Higher Education: An Analysis Based on Historical Materials," *Behavioral Science,* vol. 2, no. 2. pp. 134–146, 1957.

Gilman, Daniel C.: "Scientific Schools in Europe," *American Journal of Education,* vol. 1, no. 3, pp. 315–328, March 1856.

Gilpin, Robert: "Technological Strategies and National Purpose," *Science,* vol. 169, pp. 441–448, July 31, 1970.

Gould, Benjamin A.: "Address of the President," *Proceedings,* vol. 18, pp. 1–37, American Association for the Advancement of Science, 1869.

Gould, Laurence: "Basic Research and the Liberal Arts College," in Dael Wolfle (ed.), *Symposium on Basic Research,* American Association for the Advancement of Science, Washington, D.C., 1959.

Hall, Callie, and Clarence J. West: "Distribution of Graduate Fellowships and Scholarships between the Arts and the Sciences," *School and Society,* vol. 15, pp. 424–428, Apr. 15, 1922.

Handlin, Oscar, and Mary F. Handlin: *The American College and American Culture,* McGraw-Hill Book Company, New York, 1970.

Harper, William Rainey: *The Trends in Higher Education,* The University of Chicago Press, Chicago, 1905.

Haskins, Caryl P. (ed.): *The Search for Understanding,* The M.I.T. Press, Cambridge, Mass., 1967.

Hawkins, Hugh: "Three University Presidents Testify," *American Quarterly,* vol. 11, no. 2, pp. 99–119, 1959.

Hay, Carolyn D.: "A History of Science Writing in the United States," unpublished master's thesis, Northwestern University, 1970.

Henry, Joseph: "Organization of the Smithsonian Institution," *Proceedings,* vol. 1, pp. 82–90, American Association for the Advancement of Science, 1848.

Hodgkinson, Harold L.: *Institutions in Transition,* McGraw-Hill Book Company, New York, 1971.

Hofstadter, Richard, and C. DeWitt Hardy: *The Development and Scope of Higher Education in the United States,* Columbia University Press, New York, 1952.

Hofstadter, Richard, and Wilson Smith: *American Higher Education: A Documentary History,* The University of Chicago Press, Chicago, 1961.

Holland, W. J.: letter to the editor, *Science,* Oct. 17, 1902, p. 601.

Holmfeld, John D.: "From Amateurs to Professionals in American Science: The Controversy over the Proceedings of an 1853 Scientific Meeting," *Proceedings of the American Philosophical Society,* vol. 114, no. 1, pp. 22–36, 1970.

Illinois Institute of Technology Research Institute: *TRACES, Technology in Retrospect and Critical Events in Science, A Report Prepared for the National Science Foundation,* December 1968.

Industry, Science, and Universities, The Report of a Working Party on Universities and Industrial Research to the Universities and Industry Joint Committee, Confederation of British Industry, London, July 1970.

James, Edmund J.: "The Origin of the Land-Grant Act of 1862 (The So-called Morrill Act) and Some Account of Its Author, Jonathan B. Turner," *University of Illinois Bulletin,* vol. 8, no. 10, Nov. 7, 1910.

Jantsch, Erich: *Integrative Planning for the "Joint Systems" of Society and Technology—The Emerging Role of the University,* Massachusetts Institute of Technology, Cambridge, Mass., 1969. (Lithoprinted.)

Jencks, Christopher, and David Riesman: *The Academic Revolution,* Doubleday & Company, Inc., Garden City, New York, 1968.

Jewkes, John, David Sawes, and Richard Stillerman: *The Source of Invention,* Macmillan & Co., Ltd., London, 1958.

Kaysen, Carl: *The Higher Learning, the Universities, and the Public,* Princeton University Press, Princeton, N.J., 1969.

Kennon, W. L.: "A Century of Astronomy," *Ole Miss Alumni Review,* vol. 1, October 1947.

Kennon, W. L., and Sanford C. Gladden: "Historical Apparatus at the University of Mississippi," *The American Physics Teacher,* Feb. 6, 1938, pp. 1–7.

Kerr, Clark: "Presidential Discontent," in David C. Nichols (ed.), *Perspectives on Campus Tensions: Papers Prepared for the Special Commission on Campus Tensions,* American Council on Education, Washington, D.C., 1970.

Kidd, Charles V.: *American Universities and Federal Research,* The Belknap Press, Harvard University Press, Cambridge, Mass., 1959.

Lawrence, Abbott: in *American Journal of Education,* vol. 1, 1856.

Lecht, Leonard A.: *Goals, Priorities, and Dollars,* The Free Press, New York, 1966.

Lecht, Leonard A.: *Manpower Needs for National Goals in the 1970's,* Frederick A. Praeger, Inc., New York, 1969.

Lederman, Leonard L., and Margaret L. Windus: *An Analysis of the Allocation of Federal Budget Resources as an Indication of National Goals and Priorities,* Report No. BMI-NLVP-TR-69-1 to the National Aeronautics and Space Administration, Battelle Memorial Institute, Columbus, Ohio, Feb. 10, 1969.

Lipset, Seymour M.: "The Politics of Academia," in David C. Nichols (ed.), *Perspectives on Campus Tensions: Papers Prepared for the Special Committee on Campus Tensions,* American Council on Education, Washington, D.C., 1970.

Long, Franklin A.: "Interdisciplinary Problem-Oriented Research in the University," *Science,* vol. 171, p. 961, Mar. 12, 1971.

Madsen, David: *The National University, Enduring Dream of the U.S.A.,* Wayne State University Press, Detroit, 1966.

Marx, Guido H.: "Some Trends in Higher Education," *Science,* vol. 29, pp. 759–787, May 14, 1909.

Mayhew, Lewis B.: *Graduate and Professional Education, 1980: A Survey of Institutional Plans,* McGraw-Hill Book Company, New York, 1970.

Miller, Howard S.: *Dollars for Research,* University of Washington Press, Seattle, 1970.

Milton, Helen S.: *Cost of Research Index, 1920–1970,* Research Analysis Corporation, McLean, Va., 1971.

Morton, J. E.: *On the Evolution of Manpower Statistics,* W. E. Upjohn Institute for Employment Research, Kalamazoo, Mich., 1969.

Moynihan, Daniel P.: "Counsellor's Statement," *Toward Balanced Growth: Quantity with Quality,* first report of the President's National Goals Staff, U.S. Government Printing Office, Washington, D.C., July 4, 1970.

Munsterberg, Hugo: letter to the editor, *Science,* vol. 16, Oct. 3, 1902.

Nash, Gerald B.: "The Conflict between Pure and Applied Science in Nineteenth-Century Public Policy: The California State Geological Survey, 1860-1874," *Isis,* vol. 54, part 2, no. 176, pp. 217-228, June 1963.

National Academy of Sciences: *Federal Support of Basic Research in Institutions of Higher Learning,* Washington, D.C., 1964.

National Science Board: *Toward a Public Policy for Graduate Education,* NSB 69-1, National Science Foundation, Washington, D.C., 1969a.

National Science Board: *Graduate Education: Parameters for Public Policy,* U.S. Government Printing Office, Washington, D.C., 1969b.

National Science Foundation: *Science and Engineering Doctorate Supply and Utilization, 1968-80,* NSF 69-37, 1969.

National Science Foundation: *Federal Support to Universities and Colleges, Fiscal Year 1969,* NSF 70-26, 1970a.

National Science Foundation: *Federal Support to Universities, Colleges, and Selected Nonprofit Institutions, Fiscal Year 1969,* NSF 70-27, 1970b.

National Science Foundation: *Impact of Changes in Federal Science Funding Patterns on Academic Institutions,* NSF 70-48, 1970c.

National Science Foundation: *National Patterns of R&D Resources, 1953-71,* NSF 70-46, 1970d.

National Science Foundation: *Resources for Scientific Activities at Universities and Colleges, 1969,* NSF 70-16, 1970e.

National Science Foundation: *Federal Funds for Academic Science,* NSF 71-7, 1971a.

National Science Foundation: *Federal Support to Universities and Colleges, Fiscal Year 1970,* NSF 71-16, 1971b.

National Science Foundation: *1969 and 1980. Science and Engineering Doctorate Supply and Utilization,* NSF 71-20, 1971c.

National Science Foundation: *Federal Funds for Research, Development, and Other Scientific Activities,* published annually.

National Science Foundation Act of 1950, P.L. 507, 81st Cong., 1950.

Newman, John H.: *On the Scope and Nature of University Education,* J. M. Dent & Sons, Ltd., Publishers, London, 1915.

Nichols, Rodney W.: "Mission-Oriented R&D," *Science,* vol. 172, pp. 29-37, Apr. 2, 1971.

Oppenheimer, Robert: "The Need for New Knowledge," in Dael Wolfle (ed.), *Symposium on Basic Research,* American Association for the Advancement of Science, Washington, D.C., 1959.

Orlans, Harold (ed.): *Science Policy and the University,* The Brookings Institution, Washington, D.C., 1968.

Page, Howard E.: "The Science Development Program," in Harold Orlans (ed.), *Science Policy and the University,* The Brookings Institution, Washington, D.C., 1968.

Pake, George W.: "Whither United States Universities?" *Science,* vol. 172, pp. 908–916, May 28, 1971.

Peirce, Benjamin: "Opening Address," *Proceedings,* vol. 7, pp. xvii–xx, American Association for the Advancement of Science, 1853.

Pendray, G. Edward: *Men, Mirrors, and Stars,* Funk and Wagnalls, New York, 1935.

Platt, John: "What We Must Do," *Science,* vol. 166, pp. 1115–1121, Nov. 28, 1969.

Price, Derek J. deSolla: "Principles for Projecting Funding of Academic Science in the 1970's," *Science Studies,* vol. 1, pp. 85–94, 1971.

Price, Don K.: "Federal Money and University Research," in Harold Orlans (ed.), *Science Policy and the University,* The Brookings Institution, Washington, D.C., 1968.

Reagan, Michael D.: "$17 Billion in Search of a Policy," *Bulletin of the Atomic Scientists,* vol. 24, no. 4, pp. 33–36, April 1968.

Reingold, Nathan: *Science in Nineteenth Century America. A Documentary History,* Hill and Wang, Inc., New York, 1964.

Reingold, Nathan: "Alexander Dallas Bache: Science and Technology in the American Idiom," *Technology and Culture,* vol. 11, pp. 163–177, April 1970.

Rhees, William J. (ed.): *The Smithsonian Institution: Documents Relative to its Origin and History,* The Smithsonian Institution, Washington, D.C., 1879.

Ripley, S. Dillon: "Opening Remarks," *Symposium on Education and Federal Laboratory-University Relationships,* Oct. 29–31, 1968, Federal Council for Science and Technology and the American Council on Education, U.S. Government Printing Office, Washington, D.C. 1969.

Robinson, David Z.: "Resource Allocation in High Energy Physics," in Harold Orlans (ed.), *Science Policy and the University,* The Brookings Institution, Washington, D.C., 1968.

Robinson, David Z.: "Government Contracting for Academic Research: Accountability in the American Experience," in Bruce L. R. Smith and D. C. Hague (eds.), *The Dilemma of Accountability in Modern Government: Independence Versus Control,* St. Martin's Press, Inc., New York, 1971.

Roose, Kenneth D., and Charles J. Anderson: *A Rating of Graduate Programs,* American Council on Education, Washington, D.C., 1970.

Rowland, Henry A.: "A Plea for Pure Science," *Proceedings,* vol. 32, pp. 105–126, American Association for the Advancement of Science, 1883.

Ryan, W. Carson: *Studies in Early Graduate Education: The Johns Hopkins, Clark University, The University of Chicago,* Bulletin No. 30, Carnegie Foundation for the Advancement of Teaching, 1939.

Schultz, Theodore W.: "Resources for Higher Education: An Economist's View," *Journal of Political Economy,* vol. 76, no. 3, pp. 327–347, May–June 1968.

Science, vol. 1, Aug. 17, 1883.

Science, vol. 6, Oct. 16, 1885.

Science, vol. 16, Oct. 3, 1902.

Scientific American, vol. 225, no. 2, August 1971.

Section 203, P.L. 91-121, 1969.

Sherwin, C. W., and R. S. Isenson: "Project Hindsight," *Science,* vol. 156, pp. 1571–1577, June 23, 1967.

Shils, Edward (ed.): *Criteria for Scientific Development: Public Policy and National Goals,* The M.I.T. Press, Cambridge, Mass., 1968.

Shils, Edward: "The Hole in the Centre: University Government in the United States," *Minerva,* vol. 8, no. 1, pp. 1–7, January 1970.

Silliman, Benjamin: "Introductory Remarks," *American Journal of Science,* vol. 1, p. 8, 1819.

Silliman, Benjamin: Address before the Association of American Geologists and Naturalists, Boston, Apr. 24, 1842, in *American Journal of Science,* vol. 43, pp. 217–250, July–September 1842.

Sinclair, Bruce: *Early Research at the Franklin Institute: The Investigation into the Causes of Steam Boiler Explosions, 1830–37,* The Franklin Institute of the State of Pennsylvania, Philadelphia, 1966.

Staats, Elmer B.: "Making the Science Budget for 1967," in Harold Orlans (ed.), *Science Policy and the University,* The Brookings Institution, Washington, D.C., 1968.

Storr, Richard J.: *The Beginnings of Graduate Education in America,* The University of Chicago Press, Chicago, 1953.

Strengthening Academic Capability for Science throughout the Nation, memorandum from the President to the heads of departments and agencies, The White House, Sept. 13, 1965.

Tappan, Henry P.: "Progress of Educational Development in Europe," *American Journal of Education,* vol. 1, no. 3, pp. 247–268, March 1856.

Task Force to Assess NASA University Programs: *A Study of NASA University Programs,* NASA SP-185, National Aeronautics and Space Administration, Washington, D.C., 1968.

Tillinghast, Carlton W.: "Joint Government-University Laboratories in the United States," *Smithsonian Year 1969,* The Smithsonian Institution, Washington, D.C., 1970.

Trelease, William: "Botanical Opportunities," *Science,* vol. 4, pp. 367–382, Sept. 18, 1896.

True, Alfred C.: *A History of Agricultural Experimentation and Research in the United States, 1607–1925,* U.S. Department of Agriculture, Miscellaneous Publication No. 251, July 1937.

Tyler, Ralph W.: "The Changing Structure of American Institutions of Higher Education," *The Economics and Financing of Higher Education in the United States,* Joint Economic Committee, 91st Cong., 1st Sess., 1969.

U.S. Department of Labor: *Patterns of U.S. Economic Growth,* Bureau of Labor Statistics, BLS Bulletin 1672, 1970.

U.S. House of Representatives, Committee on Science and Astronautics: *Government, Science, and International Policy,* 90th Cong. 1st Sess., 1967.

U.S. House of Representatives, Subcommittee on Science, Research, and Development: *Toward a Science Policy for the United States,* 91st Cong., 2d Sess., Oct. 15, 1970*a*.

U.S. House of Representatives, Subcommittee on Science, Research, and Development: *The National Institutes of Research and Advanced Studies.* 91st Cong., 2d Sess., 1970*b*.

Veysey, Laurence R.: *The Emergence of the American University,* The University of Chicago Press, Chicago, 1965.

Walcott, Charles D.: "Relations of the National Government to Higher Education and Research," *Science,* vol. 13, pp. 1001–1015, June 28, 1901.

Waldo, Dwight: "The University in Relation to the Government-Political," *Public Administration Review,* vol. 30, pp. 106–113, March–April 1970.

Walsh, John: "Their Decision-Making Process Bothers Some of the British," *Science,* vol. 155, p. 1655, Mar. 31, 1967.

Weaver, Warren: *Scene of Change,* Charles Scribner's Sons, New York, 1970.

Webb, James E.: "The Role of the University in Research," *The University and the Body Politic, Proceedings from a Major Conference Commemorating the Sesquicentennial of the University of Michigan,* July 12–14, 1967.

Webb, James E.: "Commentary on a paper by Dr. Hagerty and Discussion," in James E. Charlesworth (ed.), *Harmonizing Technological Developments and Social Policy in America,* Monograph 11, American Academy of Political and Social Science, Philadelphia, 1970.

Weinberg, Alvin M.: "Criteria for Scientific Choice," *Minerva,* vol. 1, no. 2, pp. 159–171, April 1963.

Weinberg, Alvin M.: *Reflections on Big Science,* The M.I.T. Press, Cambridge, Mass., 1967.

Weinberg, Alvin M.: Address to American Political Science Association, Los Angeles, Sept. 11, 1970.

Weinberg, Alvin M.: "The Scientific University and the Socio-Technological Institute in the 21st Century," *The Graduate Journal,* vol. 8, no. 2, pp. 311–316, 1971.

White, Andrew D.: *Autobiography,* vols. 1 and 2, Century Company, New York, 1907.

Wilson, John T.: "A Dilemma of American Science and Higher Educational Policy: The Support of Universities," *Minerva,* vol. 9, no. 2, pp. 171–196, April 1971.

Wolff, Robert P.: *The Idea of the University,* Beacon Press, Boston, 1969.

Wolfle, Dael: "The Inter-Society Committee for a National Science Foundation: Report for 1947," *Science,* vol. 106, pp. 529–533, Dec. 5, 1947.

Wolfle, Dael: *America's Resources of Specialized Talent,* The Macmillan Company, New York, 1954.

Wolfle, Dael (ed.): *Symposium on Basic Research,* American Association for the Advancement of Science, Washington, D.C., 1959.

Wolfle, Dael, and Charles V. Kidd: "The Future Market for Ph.D.'s," *Science,* vol. 173, pp. 784–793, Aug. 27, 1971.

York, Carl M.: "Steps Toward a National Policy for Academic Science," *Science,* vol. 172, pp. 643–648, May 14, 1971.

Index

Academic freedom, 44, 78, 91, 92, 95, 98, 174–176
Academic power, 91–97
Academy for Contemporary Problems, 144
Academy of Natural Sciences, 60
Adams, President John, 1
Adams, President John Quincy, 1, 17, 20, 24
Agassiz, Louis, 7, 10, 13, 24, 29, 38, 39, 41, 57, 58
Agriculture, U.S. Department of, 21, 53–55, 125
Amateurism in science, 6–9
American Academy of Arts and Sciences, 15, 60
American Association for the Advancement of Education, 41, 44, 58, 61
American Association for the Advancement of Science, 8–10, 20, 25, 26, 30, 56–58, 60, 61, 66, 67, 71, 72
American Association of University Professors, 91–92
American Council on Education, 97, 102
American Journal of Education, 47
American Journal of Science, 9, 48, 49, 57, 70
American Philosophical Society, 15, 32*n.,* 60
Anderson, Charles J., 102, 156
Angell, James B., 45–47
Arizona, University of, 119
Armsby, James, 25
Ashby, Eric, 92, 175, 178
Association of American Colleges, 97
Association of American Geologists, 20

Association of American Universities, 63, 97, 103, 105, 174
Astin, Helen S., 157
Astronomical observatories, 22–32
Atomic Energy Commission, U.S., 90, 110, 116, 120, 125
Avogadro, Amedeo, 14

Babbidge, Homer D., Jr., 175
Babbitt, Irving, 44
Babcock, Stephen M., 55
Bache, Alexander D., 10–11, 21, 25, 29, 41, 45, 56–60, 66, 73–75
Bache, Richard, 10
Bacon, Francis, 6
Baird, Spencer F., 18
Baker, James G., 28*n.*
Barnard, Frederick A. P., 25–28, 41, 43, 44, 88
Barnard College, 25
Barzun, Jacques, 179
Battelle Memorial Institute, 144
Bayer, Alan E., 157
Beaver, Donald deB., 6, 59
Beck, Charles, 36, 37, 40
Bell, David E., 111
Bell Telephone Laboratories, 78
Ben-David, Joseph, 69, 73, 80, 82, 97, 100, 108, 173
Blackett, Patrick M. S., 82
Bonaparte, Charles, 8
Bonaparte, Napoleon, 8
Boston Society of Natural History, 60
Botanical Society of America, 16

195

Bowden, Lord, 5
Branscomb, Lewis M., 143*n.*, 144
British Association for the Advancement of Science, 9
British universities, 3, 98
Brookings Institution, 169
Brooks, Harvey, 157–158, 160, 164*n.*, 170*n.*
Brown, David G., 94
Brown University, 42*n.*, 103, 104
Buchanan, President James, 51
Budget, U.S. Bureau of the, 110–111, 121, 159, 161, 163, 169, 174, 178
Bueche, A. M., 166
Burgess, John W., 88
Burtt, E. A., 9
Bush, Vannevar, 11, 107

California, University of:
   at Berkeley, 47, 48, 73*n.*, 99, 101, 103, 108, 111
   at Los Angeles, 103
California Academy of Sciences, 28–30
California Institute of Technology, 93, 103–105, 108, 122
California State Geological Survey, 74–75
Cambridge University, 5, 93, 98
Carey, William D., 121–122
Carnegie, Andrew, 2, 45, 61, 68–69
Carnegie Commission on Higher Education, 164, 165, 170
Carnegie Institution of Washington, 61, 62, 69, 70*n.*
Carson, Rachel, 122
Carstensen, Vernon, 55
Cartter, Allan M., 155*n.*, 173*n.*
Case Institute of Technology, 118–119
Catholic University of America, 105
Cattell, James McKeen, 91–92
Chamberlin, Thomas C., 88
Chase, Harry W., 95
Cheit, Earl F., 133, 155
Chicago, University of, 2, 3, 30, 36*n.*, 50–51, 62–63, 73, 77–79, 87, 88, 92, 98, 99, 101, 103, 108
Cincinnati College, 23
Cincinnati Observatory, 23–25, 77

Clark, Alvan, 27–29, 66
Clark, Alvan Graham, 28, 30
Clark, Jonas, 49
Clark University, 3, 33, 36*n.*, 49–50, 62, 77, 87, 105
Clarke, Frank W., 16, 18, 19
Cleveland, President Grover, 60
Coast Survey, 10, 11, 18, 21, 25, 29, 57, 60, 72–76
Cold Spring Harbor Biological Laboratory, 93
Colleges:
   as prospective home of science, 33–43
   support of science by, 18, 19, 22
Colorado, University of, 119, 143, 144
Columbia University, 25, 42, 43, 63, 73*n.*, 87, 88, 99, 103, 108
Commission on Fish and Fisheries, U.S., 21
Commission on Human Resources, 157
Commissioner of Education, 125*n.*
Competition:
   among government agencies, 95
   international, 52, 66–67, 81
   in science, 23–32, 65–70, 81–83
   among universities, 96–101, 155, 172, 179, 180
Congress, 61, 81, 121, 125, 126, 133, 136, 163, 165, 171, 178
   Mansfield amendment, 123–124, 126–129
   opposition to science, 16–20, 55
   science policies, 110, 117, 145, 150, 151, 159, 161, 180
Contracting for research, 81, 82, 109–112, 153
Cordasco, Francesco, 77, 89*n.*
Cornell, Ezra, 2, 60, 62, 92, 93
Cornell University, 42, 46, 62, 73*n.*, 77, 86, 88, 92, 93*n.*, 98, 103
Coulter, John M., 88, 92
Council on Environmental Quality, 126
Curti, Merle, 55

Dallas, Alexander James, 10
Dallas, George M., 10
Dana, James D., 7, 24, 40, 41, 47–49, 57, 59

Danhof, Clarence H., 81n., 109n., 110, 111
Daniels, George H., 5, 7–9, 12, 54
Dantzig, Tobias, 35n.
Darwin, Charles, 14, 66, 67, 85, 86
Davidson, George, 29
Davis, Bertram H., 92
Defense, U.S. Department of, 110, 116, 119, 120, 123–126, 128, 135, 155, 170n.
Deutsch, Karl W., 160
Dewey, John, 49, 89, 92
Dimitroff, George J., 28n.
DuBridge, Lee, 164, 165
Dudley, Blandina, 25
Dudley Observatory in Albany, New York, 24–26, 57, 58, 77
Duke University, 103
Dupree, A. Hunter, 17, 19–22, 57–59, 66, 67, 85n.
Dwight, Timothy, 5

Education, U.S. Office of, 89n., 104n., 174
Einstein, Albert, 86
Eisenhower, President Dwight D., 110, 125, 168
Eliot, Charles W., 2, 35, 39, 45–47, 87, 94
Elwyn, Alfred L., 10
Enrollment, college and university, 33, 154, 171
Environmental Protection Act, 126
Everett, Edward, 37–40, 58
Ewing, Ben D., 144

Faculty size, 33, 120
Faraday, Michael, 10, 13, 14, 67, 71
Federal government support of science, 19–22, 94, 96, 103–105, 109–121, 149, 154–156, 162–173
Fellowships, graduate, 48, 73n., 90
Field, Marshall, 50
Fleming, Thomas, 17n.
Flexner, Abraham, 135
Florer, John H., 51, 52
Florida, University of, 119
Folger, John K., 157
Foundations, private, 93–94, 96

Franklin, Benjamin, 10, 54n.
Franklin, Fabian, 47, 56, 69, 77, 87, 100
Franklin Institute, 11, 16
French Academy of Sciences, 8
Fubini, Eugene, 164, 165
Fulbright, J. William, 123
Fulton, John, 25, 27

Gates, Charles M., 98–99
General Electric Company, 18
Geological Survey, U.S., 21, 109
Gerard, Ralph W., 95
German universities, 3, 35, 36, 42n., 45, 61, 69, 73, 97, 98, 101
Gibbs, Josiah Willard, 40, 63
Gibbs, Wolcott, 57, 87
Gillis, James, 20, 28
Gilman, Daniel C., 2, 40, 45–50, 56, 60, 61, 69, 77, 78, 87, 92, 99, 100, 180
Gilpin, Robert, 154
Gladden, Sanford C., 27
Goldsborough, L. M., 20
Gould, A. A., 7
Gould, Benjamin Apthorp, 11, 25, 57, 66, 71
Gould, Laurence, 19n.
Government Accounting Office, U.S., 123
Government organization for science, 125–127
Government planning, 151, 179
Graduate education:
    early attempts, 36–45
    pioneer graduate universities, 45–51
    purposes of, 44
    rate of growth, 153–154
Gray, Asa, 10, 19, 22, 59–60, 67
Gray, Francis C., 57
Greeley, Horace, 52, 54n.
Green Bank (West Virginia) Observatory, 111
Guyot, Arnold Henry, 47

Haagen-Smit, A. J., 122
Hale, George Ellery, 30, 31
Hall, Callie, 73n.
Hall, G. Stanley, 33, 49–50, 77, 87

Hall, James, 10
Hamilton, Alexander, 17n.
Handlin, Mary F., 34, 36n.
Handlin, Oscar, 34, 36n.
Hardy, C. DeWitt, 87
Harper, William Rainey, 2, 19, 30, 50, 62, 77, 78, 87, 98
Harvard Observatory, 24–25, 30
Harvard University, 2, 24, 35–40, 45, 46, 50, 57, 59, 63, 73n., 74, 86–88, 98, 99, 101, 103, 108, 179
Haskins, Caryl P., 69
Hatch Act of 1887, 53, 54
Hawkins, Hugh, 45, 47
Hay, Carolyn D., 54n.
Head Start program, 145
Health, Education and Welfare, U.S. Department of, 116, 120, 150
Henry, Joseph, 10, 13, 14, 18, 22, 25, 29, 34, 57–59, 67, 71, 180
Hodgkinson, Harold L., 133n.
Hofstadter, Richard, 87
Holland, W. J., 12n.
Holmfeld, John D., 67
Hooker, Joseph, 67
Hopkins, Albert, 23
Hopkins, Johns, 2, 45, 62, 87, 93
Hopkins, Mark, 23
Horsford, Eben, 10, 38, 39, 53, 57, 87n.
Howe, Timothy, 51
Hull, Charles J., 50
Hutchinson, Charles, 30
Huxley, Thomas H., 86

Illinois, University of, 73n., 103, 144
  Chicago Circle Branch, 101
Illinois citizens' petition, 52–53
Illinois Institute of Technology, 132n.
Indiana University, 88, 103
Institute for Defense Analysis, 124
Inventions, major modern, 80–81
Isenson, R. S., 170n.

James, Edmund J., 52
James, William, 48
Jantsch, Erich, 144–145

Jefferson, President Thomas, 1, 17, 20, 36, 98
Jencks, Christopher, 101
Jewkes, John, 80
Johns Hopkins University, 2, 3, 6, 33, 36n., 40, 45–50, 60, 62, 63, 73, 76, 77, 79, 86–89, 92, 98–100, 103, 104, 108, 179
Johnson, President Lyndon B., 118, 163
Johnson, Walter R., 10, 16–18, 76
Joint Institute for Laboratory Astrophysics, 143–144, 181
Jones, William L., 38
Julius, H. W., 81

Kaysen, Carl, 131, 167n.
Kennedy, President John F., 111, 158
Kennon, W. L., 27, 28
Kent, Sydney A., 50
Kerr, Clark, 100, 133n.
Kidd, Charles V., 138, 155n.
Kitt Peak Observatory, 111

Labor Statistics, U.S. Bureau of, 164
Lake Forest University, 88
Land-Grant Act, 47, 51–56, 61, 86, 179
Land-grant colleges, 51–56, 77, 92, 97
Langley, Samuel, 35
Lanier, Sidney, 48
Lawrence, Abbott, 2, 37–39
Lawrence Scientific School, 37–40, 43, 53, 57, 58, 77, 86, 87n., 92, 99
Lecht, Leonard A., 160
LeConte, Joseph, 38
Lederman, Leonard L., 113
Leidy, Joseph, 7
Lewis and Clark expedition, 17, 20
Library of Congress, 21
Lick, James, 29–30, 58
Lick Observatory, 29, 30
Liebig, Justus von, 14, 39, 53
Lincoln, President Abraham, 52, 179
Lipset, Seymour M., 136n., 167n.
Little, Arthur D., Company, 170n.
Long, Franklin A., 143
Louisiana State University, 119
Lovering, Joseph, 24
Lowell, James Russell, 48

McCosh, James, 45, 86, 88
Madison, President James, 17n.
Madsen, David, 68n.
Major, Robert, 81
Management and Budget, U.S. Office of, 159, 161, 174, 178
  (*See also* Budget, U.S. Bureau of the)
Mansfield Amendment, 123–124, 126–129
Marx, Guido H., 105
Massachusetts Institute of Technology, 87n., 99, 103, 104, 108, 144–145
Master's degree, honorary, 35
Maxwell, James Clerk, 48
Mayhew, Lewis B., 101, 155
Michigan, University of, 41, 42, 50, 59, 61, 73n., 98, 101, 103
Military support of research, 116, 119, 123–124, 128
Miller, Howard S., 14, 23, 30, 31, 38, 40, 71
Milton, Helen S., 163
Minnesota, University of, 103
Mississippi, University of, 26–28, 30, 43, 88
Missouri, University of, at Kansas City, 101
Mitchel, Ormsby MacKnight, 23–25
Mobility of scientists, 7, 94–95, 157
Morrill, Justin, 51–56, 86, 179
Morton, J. E., 35n.
Mount Palomar, 23, 31
Mount Wilson, 30, 31
Moynihan, Daniel P., 152
Münsterberg, Hugo, 70n.

Nash, Gerald B., 74
National Academy of Sciences, 57, 58, 61, 150
National Aeronautics and Space Administration, 110, 116, 120, 139–142, 163
National Association of State Universities and Land-Grant Colleges, 97
National Center for Atmospheric Research, 111
National Defense Education Act, 90, 151
National Foundation on the Arts and Humanities, 89, 90

National goals, 158–162
National Institutes of Health, 90, 96, 108, 116, 119, 125, 126, 154, 165, 169
National Institutes of Research and Advanced Studies, 126
National Oceanic and Atmospheric Administration, 126, 144
National Radio Astronomy Observatory, 27
National Research Council, 89n.
National Science Board, 133, 138, 150, 172–174
National Science Foundation, 1, 32n., 89, 90, 96, 104n., 107, 108, 110, 112n., 114–120, 125–127, 132n., 149, 150, 154, 155, 162, 163, 165–167, 169, 171, 174
National university, 17, 58, 59, 61, 68
Naval Observatory, 20, 28
Naval Ordnance Testing Station, 111
Naval Research, U.S. Office of, 108–110
Naval Research Laboratory, 78
Needs of science, 8–9
New York State, support of agricultural and scientific societies by, 54
New York University (founded as the University of the City of New York), 36, 40
Newcomb, Simon, 48
Newman, John H., 35
Nichols, Rodney W., 127
Nobel prizes, 78, 83, 93
Northwestern University, 28, 103, 104
Norton, John P., 24, 40

Ogden, William B., 50
Ohio State University, 144
Oppenheimer, Robert, 131, 132
Oregon, University of, 119
Organization for Economic Cooperation and Development, 80
Origin of Species (Darwin), 14, 66, 85–86
Orlans, Harold, 118n., 162n., 170

Page, Howard E., 118n.
Pake, George W., 95

Pasteur Institute, 93
Patrons, search for, 2, 15-31
Peirce, Benjamin, 10, 24-25, 37-39, 41, 48, 57, 58, 66
Pendray, G. Edward, 28n.
Pennsylvania, University of, 10-11, 41, 58, 60, 73n., 103
Phillips, Edward Bromfield, 24
Ph.D. degrees:
  early recipients of, 40, 89, 99
  numbers of, 89, 101, 103-105, 120, 121, 171
  relation to research support, 118, 120
  utilization of, 155-157
Pickering, Edward C., 30, 31
Platt, John, 123, 138, 160
Playfair, Lyon, 67
Polk, Leonidas, 43
Polytechnic Institute of Brooklyn, 119
Porter, John A., 39, 40, 53
Porter, Noah, 45, 47, 62
Potter, Alonzo, 41, 58
Powell, John Wesley, 11, 21
Practical education, 34, 51-56, 92-93
President's Science Advisory Committee, 90
Price, Derek J. deSolla, 164n., 165
Price, Don K., 170n.
Princeton University, 10, 63, 88, 99, 103, 104
Project Hindsight, 170n.
Project Themis, 119
Pulkova Observatory, 27, 28
Purdue University, 103

Quincy, Josiah, 19

Reagan, Michael D., 149
Redfield, William C., 8, 10
Reingold, Nathan, 5, 6, 13, 22, 40, 48, 74
Rensselear Polytechnic Institute, 48, 93
Research:
  annual expenditures, 112-117, 120-122
  classified, 136n.
  current capacity, 120-122
  geographic distribution of funds, 96, 117-120

Research (cont.):
  growth of funds, 112-117
  industrial support of, 18, 22, 114, 115, 166
  institutes, 16-18, 66-68, 79, 98, 111, 141-143, 154, 155
  multidisciplinary, 122, 138-147
  priorities, 152-155
  reasons for conducting, 131-147
  (*See also* Science)
Rhees, William J., 16
Rice University, 119
Richardson, Elliot, 150
Riesman, David, 101
Ripley, S. Dillon, 35
Robinson, David Z., 168n., 177
Rochester, University of, 119
Rockefeller, John D., 2, 45, 50, 93
Rockefeller Foundation, 93, 161
Rockefeller Institute for Medical Research, 62
Roose, Kenneth D., 102, 156
Roosevelt, President Franklin D., 107
Rosenzweig, Robert M., 90n., 175
Rothamsted Experimental Station, 53
Rowland, Henry A., 16, 18, 22, 31, 48, 67-68, 72, 73, 79, 88
Royal Institution, 71
Royal Society, 15
Royce, Josiah, 49
Runkle, John D., 38
Ryan, W. Carson, 36n., 42, 43, 51, 77, 78, 99
Ryerson, Martin, 30

Salk, Jonas, 76
Sawes, David, 80
Schleiden, Matthias Jakob, 14
Schultz, Theodore W., 132n.
Schwann, Theodore, 14
Science:
  policy, 149-181
  professionalization, 2, 6-11
  pure versus applied, 2, 6, 11-12, 70-79, 138-147
  specialization in, 70, 86-87, 91, 101, 146

Science (cont.):
  United States compared with Europe, 14, 66–68, 79–83
  (*See also* Research)
Science, 12n., 13, 22, 67, 70n., 92, 99
Science, Department of, 21, 96, 126
Science, The Endless Frontier, 107n.
Science and Technology, U.S. Office of, 149, 150, 174
Science development grants, 118–119
Scientific American, 32n.
Scientific journals, 6, 8, 9
Scientific Lazzaroni, 57–59, 61, 68, 87n.
Scientific Research and Development, U.S. Office of, 107
Scientists:
  most productive, 6–8, 59–60
  number of active, 6, 59
  positions for, 5, 7–8, 155
Sears, Paul, 122
Senghass, Dieter, 160
Sheffield, Joseph, 2, 40
Sheffield, Josephine, 40
Sheffield Scientific School, 39–41, 43, 44, 47, 54, 56, 77, 86, 89, 92
Sherwin, Chalmers W., 170n.
Shils, Edward, 162n., 177
Silliman, Benjamin, 5, 6, 9, 12, 13, 39, 58, 59, 70, 74, 86
Silliman, Benjamin, Jr., 10
Sinclair, Bruce, 11
Smith, Wilson, 87n.
Smithson, James, 16, 18, 20, 150–151
Smithsonian Institution, 10, 18, 21, 57, 58, 66, 151
South Florida, University of, 101
Southern California, University of, 30, 119
Spencer, Herbert, 67, 86
Staats, Elmer B., 163
Standards, National Bureau of, 21, 109, 143, 144
Stanford Linear Accelerator, 168
Stanford University, 50, 62, 73n., 77, 101, 103
State surveys, 19
Steam boilers, explosions of, 11, 16
Steenbock, Harry, 55
Steinmetz, Charles, 18

Stillerman, Richard, 80
Storr, Richard J., 36n., 41, 43
Struve, Fredrich George Wilhelm von, 27
Struve, Otto, 27

Tappan, Henry P., 36, 41, 42, 44, 58, 60, 61, 68, 87
Technology assessment, 133, 145
Technology gap, 80, 173
Texas, University of, 103
Thompson, Elizabeth, 2
Throop College, 105
Tillinghast, Carlton W., 143n.
Tocqueville, Alexis de, 11
Tontz, Jay L., 94
Torrey, John, 59
Trelease, William, 16, 18, 19
True, Alfred C., 53
Turner, Jonathan B., 52n.
Tyler, Ralph W., 167n.
Tyndall, John, 13, 71, 86

Union College, 41
Universities:
  comparison with European, 98, 108, 140n.
  competition among, 96–101, 155, 172, 179, 180
  departmental organization, 97, 139, 142, 145, 146
  essentials for establishment, 43–45
  first attempts, 36–45
  fragmentation, 91–95
  future growth, 154
  institutional grants to, 167–173
  multidisciplinary research, 138–147
  as national research agencies, 107–115, 128, 157–176
  pioneer, 45–51
  practical education in, 51–56
  problems, 102, 133n.
  quality ratings, 102–105, 156
  relations with federal government, 155–181
  research rationale, 131–138
  specialization of, 147, 178
  unity, 94

University development grants, 171–173
University Grants Committee, 173n.
University of the South, 43, 88, 98

Veysey, Laurence R., 33, 36n., 44, 62–63, 86, 88
Virginia, University of, 36, 98, 119

Walcott, Charles D., 21
Waldo, Dwight, 156
Walker, Robert J., 10
Walsh, John, 81n., 82
Washington, President George, 1, 17, 68, 69
Washington, University of, 98, 103
Washington University (St. Louis), 119
Watson, Richard, 5
Weaver, Warren, 93n.
Webb, James E., 139
Weinberg, Alvin M., 141–142, 161, 165
Wells, David A., 38
West, Clarence J., 73n.
West Point Military Academy, 93
Western Reserve University, 37, 118
White, Andrew D., 42, 45–48, 60, 61, 88, 92, 93n.
Whitney, Josiah, 74–75
Wilkes expedition, 7, 20, 59
Williams College, 22, 23, 31
Wilson, John T., 152n.
Wilson, President Woodrow, 89
Windus, Margaret L., 113
Wisconsin, University of, 48, 55–56, 73n., 88, 98, 99, 101, 103
Wöhler, Friedrich, 14
Wolff, Robert P., 167n.
Wolfle, Dael, 89, 90, 155n.
Wyman, Jeffries, 59

Yale University, 2, 5, 7, 39–41, 47, 50, 59–63, 73n., 86, 88, 89, 98, 99, 101, 103, 104, 122, 179
Yerkes, Charles Tyson, 30, 31, 50
York, Carl M., 164n.

*This book was set in Vladimir by University Graphics, Inc.
It was printed on acid-free, long-life paper and bound by The
Maple Press Company. The designers were Elliot Epstein and
Edward Butler. The editors were Nancy Tressel and Cheryl Allen
for McGraw-Hill Book Company and Verne A. Stadtman, Dennis A.
Wynn, and Terry Y. Allen for the Carnegie Commission on Higher
Education. Alice Cohen supervised the production.*